Quality and Speed in Administrative Decision-Making: Tension or Balance?

Editors:
Chris Backes
Mariolina Eliantonio
Sander Jansen

Quality and Speed in Administrative Decision-Making: Tension or Balance?

intersentia

METRO

Ius Commune Europaeum

Intersentia Ltd
Sheraton House | Castle Park
Cambridge | CB3 0AX | United Kingdom
Tel.: +44 1223 370 170 | Fax: +44 1223 370 169
Email: mail@intersentia.co.uk
www.intersentia.com | www.intersentia.co.uk

Distribution for the UK and Ireland:
NBN International
Airport Business Centre, 10 Thornbury Road
Plymouth, PL6 7PP
United Kingdom
Tel.: +44 1752 202 301 | Fax: +44 1752 202 331
Email: orders@nbninternational.com

Distribution for Europe and all other countries:
Intersentia Publishing nv
Groenstraat 31
2640 Mortsel
Belgium
Tel.: +32 3 680 15 50 | Fax: 32 3 658 71 21
Email: mail@intersentia.be

Distribution for the USA and Canada:
International Specialized Book Services
920 NE 58th Ave. Suite 300
Portland, OR 97213
USA
Tel.: +1 800 944 6190 (toll free) | Fax: + 1 503 280 8832
Email: info@isbs.com

Quality and Speed in Administrative Decision-Making: Tension or Balance?

ISBN 978-1-78068-445-1
D/2016/7849/161
NUR 823

British Library Cataloguing in Publication Data. A catalogue record for this book is available from the British Library.

CONTENTS

CONTENTS

LIST OF AUTHORS

Chris Backes, Professor of Environmental Law, Utrecht University

Roberto Caranta, Professor of Administrative Law, University of Turin

Olivier Dubos, Professor of Public Law, Jean Monnet Chair, CRDEI, University of Bordeaux

Mariolina Eliantonio, Associate Professor of European Administrative Law, Maastricht University

Lena Gipperth, Professor of Environmental Law, University of Gothenburg

Sander Jansen, Associate Professor of Administrative Law, Maastricht University

Victoria Jenkins, Senior Lecturer, Swansea University

Gerhard Roller, Professor of Environmental Law, University of Applied Sciences Bingen

LIST OF ABBREVIATIONS

ABRS	*Afdeling bestuursrechtspraak van de Raad van State* (Judicial Division of the Dutch Council of State)
Actal	*Adviescollege toetsing regeldruk* (Dutch advisory council on the burden of public regulation)
Ad.L.Rev	Administrative Law Review
ADR	Alternative Dispute Resolution
AJDA	Actualité Juridique Droit Administratif
ANAC	*Autorità Nazionale Anticorruzione* (Italian National Anticorruption Authority)
Awb	*Algemene wet bestuursrecht* (Dutch General Administrative Law Act)
BDB	Bircham Dyson Bell
BGBl	Bundesgesetzblatt (German Federal Law Gazette)
BGH	*Bundesgerichtshof* (German Federal Court of Justice)
BIICL	British Institute of International and Comparative Law
BVerwG	Bundesverwaltungsgericht (German Federal Administrative Court)
CAB	*Länsstyrelse* (Swedish County Administration Board)
Cass.	*Corte di cassazione* (Italian Supreme Court of Cassation)
C. cost.	*Corte costituzionale* (Italian Constitutional Court)
CE	*Conseil d'État* (French Council of State)
CE Ass.	*Conseil d'Etat, assemblée du contentieux* (Plenary Session of the Litigation Division of the French Council of State)
CE Sect.	*Conseil d'Etat, section du contentieux* (Litigation Division of the French Council of State)
C. Env.	*Code de l'environnement* (French Environmental Code)
CFR	Charter of Fundamental Rights of the European Union
C.g.a.	*Consiglio di giustizia amministrativa per la regione siciliana* (Italian Council of Administrative Justice for the Region of Sicily)
C. just. adm.	*Code de justice administrative* (French Administrative Justice Code)
C. urb.	*Code de l'urbanisme* (French Urban Planning Code)

CGCT	*Code général des collectivités territoriales* (French Local Government Code)
Chw	*Crisis en herstelwet* (Dutch Crisis and Recovery Act)
CJEU	Court of Justice of the European Union
Cons. St.	*Consiglio di Stato* (Italian Council of State)
Cons. St., A.G.	*Consiglio di Stato, adunanza generale* (Italian Council of State, Plenary Session)
Corr. giur.	Il Corriere giuridico. Mensile di attualità, critica, opinione
Corr. mer.	Corriere del merito (Il)
CPR	Civil Procedure Rules (English)
CRA	Dutch Crisis and Recovery Act
CRDEI	*Centre de Recherches et de Documentation Européennes et Internationales* (Center of European and international research and documentation)
CRPA	*Code des relations entre le public et l'administration* (French Code on Relations between the Public and the Administration)
CRvB	*Centrale Raad van Beroep* (Dutch Administrative High Court)
CUP	Cambridge University Press
DATAR	*Délégation interministérielle à l'aménagement du territoire et à l'attractivité régionale* (French inter-ministerial delegation for territorial development)
DCO	Development Consent Order (English)
DCLG	Department for Communities and Local Government (English)
DEFRA	Department for Environment, Food and Rural Affairs (English)
DIA	*dichiarazione di inizio attività* (declaration on the commencement of activity)
Dig. disc. pubbl.	Digesto (discipline pubblicistiche)
Dig. disc. Priv., Sez. Civ	Digesto (discipline privatistiche) sez. civile
Dir. amm.	Diritto amministrativo
Dir. proc. amm.	Diritto processuale amministrativo
D.l.	*decreto legge*
D.legisl.	*decreto legislativo*
DPC	*decreto del Presidente del Consiglio dei ministri* (Italian decree of the President of the Council of Ministers)
DPR	*decreto del Presidente della Republica* (Italian decree of the President of the Republic)
DVBl	Das Deutsche Verwaltungsblatt
DÖV	Die Öffentliche Verwaltung
ECHR	The European Convention on Human Rights
ECtHR	The European Court of Human Rights
EELR	European Environmental Law Review
EIA	Environmental Impact Assessment
ELJ	European Law Journal

ELM	Environmental Law and Management
ELNI	Environmental Law Network International
EPA	*Naturvårdsverket* (Swedish Environmental Protection Agency)
ESI	Edizioni Scientifiche Italiane
Eur. Pub. L.	European Public Law
EU	European Union
EUR	Euro
EWCA	England and Wales Court of Appeal
Foro it.	Il Foro italiano
GALA	General Administrative Law Act (Dutch)
Gior. dir. amm.	Giornale di diritto amministrativo
Giur. It	Giurisprudenza italiana
Giur. mer.	Giurisprudenza di merito. Rivista bimestrale di giurisprudenza dei giudici di merito genetically modified organism genetically modified organism
GMO	genetically modified organism
Guida dir.	Guida al diritto
HMG	Her Majesty's Government
HMSO	Her Majesty's Stationery Office
ILM	International Legal Materials
Int. Pub. Adm. Rev	International Public Administration Review
IPC	Infrastructure Planning Commission (English)
ISO	International Organization for Standardizations
JB	Jurisprudentie Bestuursrecht
JCl. Administratif	JurisClasseur Administratif
JEL	Journal of Environmental Law
JORF	Journal Officiel de la République Française (Official Journal of the French Republic)
JPL	Journal of Planning Law
JPEL	Journal of Planning and Environmental Law
JR	Judicial Review
kap.	*kapitel*
l.	*legge*
LEC	Land and Environment Court (Swedish)
LPA	Local Planning Authority (English)
LS	Legal Studies
MAP	*Modernisation de l'Action Publique* (French modernization of public action)
MLR	Modern Law Review
M en R	Milieu en Recht
MvT	*Memorie van Toelichting* (Dutch explanatory document to legislation)
NABEG	*Netzausbaubeschleunigungsgesetz Übertragungsnetz*
NGO	Non-Governmental Organisation
NIMBYISM	Not in my Backyard (-ism)
NJB	Nederlands Juristenblad

NJW	Neue Juristische Wochenschrift
NPPS	National Planning Policy Statement (English)
NRW	Nordrhein-Westfalen (North-Rhine Westphalia)
NSIP	nationally significant infrastructure project
Nuove leggi civ.	*Le Nuove leggi civili commentate*
NVvP	*Nederlandse Vereniging voor Procesrecht*
NVwZ	Neue Zeitschrift für Verwaltungsrecht
NZB	*Nieuwe Zaaksbehandeling* (Dutch New Case-Management)
OJ	Official Journal of the European Union
OJLS	Oxford Journal of Legal Studies
OUP	Oxford University Press
PELJ	Potchefstroom Electronic Law Journal
PL	Public Law
PPA	Public Policy and Administration
Prop.	Proposition (Government bill)
Quad. cost.	Quaderni costituzionali
Resp. civ. Prev.	Responsabilità civile e previdenza
RFSP	Revue Française de Science Politique
RGPP	Révision générale des politiques publiques (French general review of public policies)
Riv. dir. pubbl.	Rivista di diritto pubblico
Riv. it. dir. pubbl. com.	Rivista italiana di diritto pubblico comunitario
RSPB	Royal Society for the Protection of Birds
Riv. trim. dir. pubbl.	Rivista trimestrale di diritto pubblico
SCIA	*segnalazione certificata di inizio attività* (certified declaration on the commencement of activity)
SEA	Strategic Environmental Assessment
Sez	*Sezione*
SFS	*Svensk författningssamling,* (Swedish Code of Statutes)
Skr.	*Regeringens skrivelse* (Government Communication)
SOU	*Statens offentliga utredningar* (Swedish Government Official Reports)
SRU	*Sachverständigenrat für Umweltfragen* (German Advisory Council on the Environment)
SS	Secretary of State (English)
StAB	advisory board for the Judicial Division of the Council of State (Dutch)
Stb.	Staatsblad
Stcrt.	Staatscourant
TAR	*Tribunale Amministrativo Regionale* (Italian Regional Administrative Court)
T. Amb. R	Tijdschrift voor Ambtenarenrecht
TBO	Tijdschrift voor bouwrecht en onroerend goed
TOO	Tijdschrift voor omgevingsrecht en omgevingsbeleid
Transylvania Rev. of Adm. Sciences	Transylvanian Review of Administrative Sciences

Trema	Tijdschrift voor de rechterlijke macht
Trib.	*Tribunale*
UES	Umeå Economic Studies
UK	United Kingdom
UNTS	United Nations Treaty Series
Urb app.	Urbanistica e appalti
Utrecht L. Rev.	Utrecht Law Review
VROM-Raad	Dutch Council for Environment and Infrastructure
VwVfG	*Verwaltungsverfahrensgesetz* (German Administrative Procedure Act)
VwGO	*Verwaltungsgerichtsordnung* (German Administrative Court Procedure Act)
Wabo	*Wet algemene bepalingen omgevingsrecht* (Dutch General Act on Environmental Law)
West. Eur. Polit.	Western European Politics
Wmb	*Wet milieubeheer* (Dutch Environmental Management Act)
WODC	*Wetenschappelijk Onderzoek en Documentatie Centrum*
WWF	World Wildlife Fund
ZRP	Zeitschrift für Rechtspolitik
ZUR	Zeitschrift für Umweltrecht

Chris Backes
Mariolina Eliantonio
Sander Jansen

INTRODUCTION

The economic crisis that afflicted Europe in 2008 has been considered a major hindrance to investments and development in many EU countries. While in 2016 the situation is not as dire as a few years back, the effects are still very much present in today's EU economy. In various European countries (such as France, Italy, or the Netherlands), lawmakers have adopted legislation in order to deal with the consequences of the crisis. These laws contain provisions that are aimed at speeding up administrative decision-making and judicial proceedings and which therefore have an impact on various provisions of general administrative law. Along with the aim of facing the economic crisis, measures to speed up decision-making and judicial proceedings have also been taken to make administrative law more up-to-date and enable it to meet the needs of current society.

However, the need for speedier decision-making and judicial proceedings and the consequent acceleration mechanisms may clash with the need to preserve the quality of these proceedings. On the one hand, swift procedures can be considered as one aspect of quality of decision-making. On the other hand, other aspects of quality, like public participation and thoroughly weighing all relevant aspects and interests, may come under pressure when speed of decision-making is the only focus of reforms. The question is thus where the balance between these two competing interests ought to be placed, and to what extent proceedings can be sped up without prejudice to their quality. Even better, perhaps there are ideas that both foster speed and a higher quality of decision-making at the same time. Furthermore, speeding up decision-making and judicial proceeding may run contrary to certain constitutional fundamental principles and values, such as the rule of law, the right of access to court and the right of defence. Last but not least, as legal systems do not operate in a legal vacuum, it important that acceleration reforms do not violate European and international standards.

This book presents six national perspectives on those issues, together with a comparative overview comparing and contrasting the national contributions on the need to find a balance between, on the one hand, the need to have faster administrative decisions and court rulings, and, on the other, the necessity to preserve and enhance the quality of administrative and judicial decisions.

The six legal systems have been selected because of multiple factors. First of all, they represent a mix of different legal traditions: Romanic, Germanic, and common law, reflecting different views of the role of administrative law and administrative justice. The aim of this selection is to see whether different approaches to administrative law have induced differences in acceleration reforms. Secondly, the countries represented in this study have different economic strength and size, and have been impacted differently by the economic crisis. The selection thus allows a comparative examination of whether the magnitude and intensity of acceleration measures is linked to the economic conditions of a country.

The contributors have discussed, each in as far as it is considered relevant for his or her legal system, the acceleration measures which have been taken in the last years, both with regard to administrative decision-making and to court proceedings, and the impact these measures have had on the quality of administrative decisions. The measures discussed in the various contributions range from the creation of a one-stop shop, the curtailing of the participatory positions of stakeholders, the restriction of the standing rules applicable before administrative courts or the dispute settlement powers attributed to administrative courts. Where relevant, the contributions discuss the role played by European and international standards in the debate and whether European and international law have served as a limit to acceleration reforms. Furthermore, in some countries a more general discussion about enhancing the quality of decision-making can be identified. We hope, through this book, to have provided a useful source of inspiration for policy-makers with 'acceleration ambitions' and some thoughts about the necessity of a broader discussion about the means to improve quality of decision-making.

The research and its comparative analysis have shown that, while speeding up decision-making and court proceedings has been high on all national agendas, quality has not been treated with the same interest and it often cannot even be said with certainty whether acceleration reforms had any (positive or negative) impact on the quality of decisions. This might be the case because it is more difficult to measure quality of decision-making compared to measuring its duration. However, recently in some of the countries examined, the focus begins to change from speed to (some) aspects of quality. We therefore hope to stir the debate on a more comprehensive conceptualization of quality of decision-making.

The book reflects the law as it stands in June 2016.

Gerhard Roller

QUALITY AND SPEED IN ADMINISTRATIVE DECISION-MAKING: A GERMAN CASE STUDY[1]

1. Introduction

Measures have been taken to speed up administrative decision-making procedures in Germany since the early 1990s. The drive for the efforts to do so came from the need to (1) rapidly improve the infrastructure of the new German federal states (*Länder*) after reunification, and (2) to remove what the government and industrial lobby groups considered to be obstructions to economic investment. In the same time period a vague notion of minimizing 'bureaucracy' flooded the political debate in the EU and within a number of Member States. This has led to ongoing activities such as the passing of deregulation rules which aim to abolish laws regarded as an unnecessary burden for the economy. There is some criticism of this overloaded 'anti-bureaucracy' movement.[2]

At the beginning the application of some of these deregulation laws was restricted regionally to the new *Länder* and temporally. But eventually there was an expansion in scope to include all of Germany and they were made permanent.

The peak of the deregulation movement had been reached in 2011. After that an opposite current commenced, aimed at improving the legal instruments that enable participation of citizens, especially in planning procedures for infrastructure. Intensive local protest movements like 'Stuttgart 21' against railway and urban development and local opposition against measures in the context of the sustainable energy transition (*Energiewende*) triggered legislative action and debates.

This contribution deals with the ambiguous relationship between the speed of administrative procedures and the quality of administrative decision-making (section 2) and analyses the measures that are taken to speed up procedures (sections 3 and 4). Two categories of measures can be distinguished here.

1 This contribution has been already published in *ELNI Review* 2014 (2), p. 51. It has been slightly updated for this publication and is originally based on the contribution presented at the Conference organized by the Faculty of Law at Maastricht University in 2010.

2 Knospe 2010, p. 43. For the background to the German debate, see the country report in: Backes *et al.* 2010, p. 121.

The first category includes measures of a general scope: these are not specific to a certain sector (such as environmental law) but concern administrative procedures as such (section 3). In this category two types of rules need to be differentiated and placed in subcategories: the rules governing the administrative procedure before an administrative act is adopted by the competent authority are laid down in the German Administrative Procedure Act (*Verwaltungsverfahrensgesetz*)[3] and the rules governing the judicial review of these decisions before the courts are laid down in the German Administrative Court Procedure Act (*Verwaltungsgerichtsordnung*).[4]

In the second category are measures that have been taken to speed up infrastructure and licensing procedures in particular (section 4). They can generally be described as procedures under the German Federal Emission Control Act, which applies to industrial plants (section 4.2) and procedures where a specific planning permit (*Planfeststellung*) is required (section 4.3). This is the case for all types of infrastructure projects such as airports, roads, landfills and so on.

The contribution will come to a close by moving on to look at a complete shift from the 'deregulation' paradigm in 2011 (section 5), and finally, will address the impact on the quality of the decisions in terms of environmental protection and citizens' rights (section 6).

2. Quality of Decision-Making in Relation to the Speed of the Decision-Making Procedure

There is no simple, unanimous answer to the question of finding the right balance between the temporal framework of an administrative procedure to uphold the quality of administrative decision-making (and the same holds true for court procedures). Under German law, the competent authority is obliged to carry out the procedure efficiently. The justification for this is twofold. Firstly, the administration generally has to perform its activities in the most effective way (principle of public economy and budget discipline) and, secondly, in cases where fundamental rights are involved (such as property, freedom or health), the right to receive a response from the authority in due time is part of those rights.[5] As a result, the time period of the procedure has to be considered a quality criterion of sound administrative procedures. Undue delays in the decision-making process may even entail government liability.[6]

With regard to court procedures the question of speed becomes even more crucial. Article 6(1) of the European Convention of Human Rights (ECHR) provides that court procedures have to be terminated 'within a reasonable time'. The

3 Verwaltungsverfahrensgesetz in der Fassung der Bekanntmachung vom 23. Januar 2003 (BGB1. I S. 102), zuletzt geändert durch Artikel 1 des Gesetzes vom 20. November 2015 (BGBl. I S. 2010).

4 Verwaltungsgerichtsordnung in der Fassung der Bekanntmachung vom 19. März 1991 (BGBl. I S. 686), zuletzt geändert durch Artikel 3 des Gesetzes vom 21. Dezember 2015 (BGBl. I S. 2490).

5 Kopp & Ramsauer 2005, § 10(18); Schwarz 2013, § 10(16).

6 In cases of building permits: BGH, NVwZ 1993, 299; BGH, NVwZ 1994, 405.

jurisprudence of the European Court of Human Rights (ECtHR) is strict in protecting this fundamental right. Germany has repeatedly been condemned by the ECtHR for excessively long court procedures,[7] even though the right to a court ruling in reasonable time is considered part of the rule of law and some *Länder* constitutions have explicitly laid down a right to an efficient (*zügig*) procedure.[8] Only recently has the German government published a proposal for the compensation of those who have experienced unduly long (court) procedures.

Having said that, it is certainly true that an efficient and speedy procedure is not the only - and not necessarily the most important - indicator of quality. The outcome of the procedure must also be lawful and just. A difficult process of weighing and balancing interests has to be conducted by the authorities, particularly when a number of different private and/or public interests are concerned. Moreover, in environmental cases the decision-making process has to take into account the protection of the environment. Complex cases naturally need more time to be decided. It is a banal truth that overly speedy decision-making may lead to bad decisions. In this respect, efficiency is not to be equated with speed. It is precisely in this field of tension between efficiency and speed that the discussion of faster decision-making processes and general discussion of 'deregulation' is to be found. Administrative rules and the related practical conditions to be applied should pave the way to find an appropriate balance between these conflicting interests.

3. General Measures to Speed Up Administrative and Judicial Procedures

3.1. *Provisions in the Administrative Procedure Act*

Article 10(2) of the German Administrative Procedure Act[9] sets out a basic condition which applies to all procedures: the procedure has to be performed simply, appropriately and efficiently.

In the 1990s, this rule was expanded by adding a whole chapter to the Act which aimed at speeding up the procedures: it was entitled 'acceleration of licensing procedures' (*Beschleunigung von Genehmigungsverfahren*). This chapter only applied in cases where a licensing procedure was under discussion. According to the explanatory statement of the legislator, the amendment aimed at indicating to the competent authorities that they should speed up the procedure.[10] In Article 71b-e some more or less self-evident advice to the competent authority was given, such as to terminate the procedure in an 'appropriate time', to provide advice to the applicant or to send the relevant application documents delivered by the applicant

7 ECtHR, *Deumeland* v. *Federal Republic of Germany*, Judgment of 29 May 1986, Application No. 9384/81.

8 Lau 2010, p. 358.

9 Verwaltungsverfahrensgesetz in der Fassung der Bekanntmachung vom 23. Januar 2003 (BGBl. I S. 102), zuletzt geändert durch Artikel 1 des Gesetzes vom 20. November 2015 (BGBl. I S. 2010).

10 Huck 2010, § 71a(17).

to the other administrative bodies involved in the decision simultaneously. The legislator created the innovative notion of a parallel procedure (*Sternverfahren*) for this latter practice. Despite the fact that these rules may be regarded as 'symbolic legislation', this legislation underlined the notion that the real potential of speeding up administrative decision-making processes lies much more in sound administrative management than in sophisticated legal provisions. In 2008 the legislator came to the same conclusion and abolished most of the provisions enacted in 1996.[11]

3.2. *Elimination of Preliminary Administrative Objection Proceedings*

Traditionally, the claimant has to go through preliminary administrative objection proceedings before he or she can present his or her case to the court (Art. 68 Administrative Court Procedure Act).[12] This may be considered a type of administrative 'self-control'. The advantage for the claimant is that these proceedings are much less costly than court proceedings and that the administration may also consider the appropriateness of a decision and not only its legality. In some sectors this preliminary procedure is quite effective; in others, particularly when intensive investigations have already been undertaken prior to the decision, the chance that the administration would modify its own decision is rather limited. For these reasons, the preliminary procedure has been repealed bit by bit over the years. At the federal level a number of sectoral laws eliminated the preliminary procedure, such as under Article 14(7) of the genetic engineering law[13] in cases of dissemination permits for genetically modified organisms (GMOs).

At the *Länder* level it can be seen that most by-laws passed on the basis of Article 68(1)(2) Administrative Court Procedure Act[14] produced a large number of exceptions to the rule of preliminary objection proceedings. In fact, only six *Länder* did not act on the basis of this option.[15]

3.3. *Elimination of Suspensive Effect*

In contrast to some other countries like the Netherlands, a remedy against an administrative act (be it the administrative objection or the action before the court)

11 Huck 2010, § 71a(18). The old articles have been now replaced by a chapter transposing Directive 2006/123/EC of the European Parliament and of the Council of 12 December 2006 on services in the internal market, [2006] OJ L 376/36.

12 Verwaltungsgerichtsordnung in der Fassung der Bekanntmachung vom 19. März 1991 (BGBl. I S. 686), zuletzt geändert durch Artikel 3 des Gesetzes vom 21. Dezember 2015 (BGBl. I S. 2490).

13 Gentechnikgesetz in der Fassung der Bekanntmachung vom 16. Dezember 1993 (BGBl. I S. 2066), zuletzt geändert durch Artikel 55 der Verordnung vom 31. August 2015 (BGBl. I S. 1474).

14 Verwaltungsgerichtsordnung in der Fassung der Bekanntmachung vom 19. März 1991 (BGBl. I S. 686), zuletzt geändert durch Artikel 3 des Gesetzes vom 21. Dezember 2015 (BGBl. I S. 2490).

15 Erbguth 2009, p. 925.

has a suspensive effect under Article 80(1) Administrative Court Procedure Act.[16] As a result, a claimant who brings a claim against a licence of an industrial plant in his or her neighbourhood could stop the plant by just lodging the complaint. In spite of the fact that usually in such cases the administration may overrule this effect by an administrative act, determining that the operation or building of the plant is in the private or common interest, most sectoral laws dealing with infrastructure projects today have abolished this suspensive effect. This is the case, for example, under Article 18e(2) of the German general railway law[17] concerning planning permits (*Planfeststellungsbeschluss*) for the construction or modification of railway lines, Article 17e(2) of the law on long distance roads[18] or Article 10(6-8) of the air traffic law[19] (on airport licences).

3.4. *Restriction of the Right of Appeal*

According to the sixth amendment of the Administrative Court Procedure Act[20] in 1996, the right to appeal (on questions of fact and law, *Berufung*) against decisions of first instance administrative courts was restricted. Article 124a[21] provides that an appeal is only admissible if permission for the application is granted by the administrative court. If permission is not granted a claimant may apply to be heard by the Higher Administrative Court.

3.5. *Federal Administrative Court as First and Last Instance*

The classical judicial control system in Germany has three levels: Administrative Court (*Verwaltungsgericht*), Higher Administrative Court (*Oberverwaltungsgericht* or *Verwaltungsgerichtshof*), and Federal Administrative Court (*Bundesverwaltungs-*

16 Verwaltungsgerichtsordnung in der Fassung der Bekanntmachung vom 19. März 1991 (BGBl. I S. 686), zuletzt geändert durch Artikel 3 des Gesetzes vom 21. Dezember 2015 (BGBl. I S. 2490).

17 Allgemeines Eisenbahngesetz vom 27. Dezember 1993 (BGBl. I S. 2378, 2396; 1994 I S. 2439), zuletzt geändert durch Artikel 1 des Gesetzes vom 28. Mai 2015 (BGBl. I S. 824).

18 Bundesfernstraßengesetz in der Fassung der Bekanntmachung vom 28. Juni 2007 (BGBl. I S. 1206), zuletzt geändert durch Artikel 466 der Verordnung vom 31. August 2015 (BGBl. I S. 1474).

19 Luftverkehrsgesetz in der Fassung der Bekanntmachung vom 10. Mai 2007 (BGBl. I S. 698), zuletzt geändert durch Artikel 21 des Gesetzes vom 19. Februar 2016 (BGBl. I S. 254).

20 Sechstes Gesetz zur Änderung der Verwaltungsgerichtsordnung und anderer Gesetze (6. VwGOÄndG) vom 1. November 1996 (BGB1 S. 1626).

21 Art. 124a VwGO reads as follows: '(1) The administrative court shall admit the appeal on points of fact and law in the judgment if the grounds of section 124, subsection 2, No. 3 or No. 4 apply. The Higher Administrative Court shall be bound by the admission. The administrative court shall not be empowered to not admit the appeal on points of fact and law.' The relevant subsection in Art. 124 reads as follows: '(2) The appeal on points of fact and law shall only be admitted [...] 3. if the case is of fundamental significance, 4. if the judgment derogates from a ruling of the Higher Administrative Court, of the Federal Administrative Court, of the Joint Panel of the supreme courts of the Federation or of the Federal Constitutional Court, and is based on this derogation, (...)'. Translation by N. Mussett, German Federal Ministry of Justice, 2014, <www.gesetze-im-internet.de/englisch_vwgo/englisch_vwgo.html#p0582>.

gericht). Speeding up court procedures was already an issue in a proposal made by the German Federal Council (*Bundesrat*) in 1983. A first amendment of the Administrative Court Procedure Act in 1985[22] eliminated the first instance for certain infrastructure projects and large industrial plants (like electrical power plants with a thermal output of more than 300 megawatts or large waste incineration plants). The legislator considered that the length of court procedures was too great where such large investment projects were concerned and that this would hinder planning security and have a negative effect on the protection of legal rights. At that time the law was subject to time limits, but with the fourth amendment of the Administrative Court Procedure Act,[23] which came into effect on 1 January 1991, these rules were made unlimited and incorporated in Article 48 of the Administrative Court Procedure Act.[24]

The law on the acceleration of traffic infrastructure went one step further. It concentrates the competence of judicial review in certain cases only on the *Bundesverwaltungsgericht* in the first and last instance. Actually the law applied only for certain highway projects connecting the new *Länder* with Western Germany;[25] later it was extended to other projects. In addition, the German Infrastructural Planning Procedures Act (*Infrastrukturplanungsbeschleunigungsgesetz*)[26] now covers overall 22 railway-, 57 road- and 6 waterways where the Federal Administrative Court is the only competent court.[27]

4. Measures to Speed Up Licensing Procedures under the Federal Emission Control Act and Infrastructure Planning Procedures

4.1. *The Relationship between Licensing Requirements and Length of Procedures*

In Germany, there are two different types of licensing procedures for industrial plants under the Federal Emission Control Act:[28] a simplified procedure without public participation and a procedure with public participation. The installations requiring a permit are listed in the fourth Ordinance on the Implementation of the

22 On its history, see: Bier & Panzer 2014, § 48(1).

23 Viertes Gesetz zur Änderung der Verwaltungsgerichtsordnung vom 17. Dezember 1990 (BGBl. I 1990, 2809).

24 Verwaltungsgerichtsordnung in der Fassung der Bekanntmachung vom 19. März 1991 (BGBl. I 686), zuletzt geändert durch Artikel 3 des Gesetzes vom 21. Dezember 2015 (BGBl. I S. 2490).

25 Verkehrswegeplanungsbeschleunigungsgesetz, see: Steinberg, Berg & Wickel 2000, p. 88; Backes, *et al.* 2010, p. 138.

26 Gesetz zur Beschleunigung von Planungsverfahren für Infrastrukturvorhaben vom 9. Dezember 2006 (BGBl. I p. 2833).

27 Erbguth 2009, p. 926.

28 Bundes-Immissionsschutzgesetz in der Fassung der Bekanntmachung vom 17. Mai 2013 (BGBl. I S. 1274), zuletzt geändert durch Artikel 76 der Verordnung vom 31. August 2015 (BGBl. I S. 1474).

Federal Emission Control Act.[29] It is important to note that in practice the overwhelming majority of procedures are simplified procedures without public participation. This is due to the fact that the regulator listed more and more plants in this category but also because the majority of licensing procedures concern modifications of existing plants that are usually privileged to undergo a simplified procedure. Thus, between 1997 and 2004 in Nordrhein-Westfalen - the federal state with by far the most industrial plants in Germany - the average number of procedures with public participation is under 10 percent of the overall procedures, as the following table[30] shows:

Category	Licensing procedures in NRW 1997-2004		
		Public procedures	
	Number	Number	%
1	1115	79	7.1
2	999	40	4.0
3	1016	64	6.3
4	1493	41	2.7
5	328	22	6.7
6	125	12	9.6
7	776	75	9.7
8	1778	60	3.4
9	443	30	6.8
10	481	2	0.4
Total	**8554**	**425**	**56.7**

Empirical evidence shows that in cases where public participation is required, the impact on the speed of the procedure is rather limited; it tends to be more influenced by the participation of other administrations and by the fact that the dossier of the applicant is not satisfactory and needs to be supplemented.[31] Thus, public participation has no significant impact on the length of the procedure in most cases.

Moreover, the general question of whether planning procedures have any impact on the investment decisions of companies seem to be largely overestimated in the public debate. Empirical research carried out in 1990 concluded that the duration of procedures is not decisive: companies rated this criterion the 16th most important out of 19 possible answers. Rather, a healthy environment was considered to be an important factor.[32] Other empirical evidence supports the thesis that there is no relevant relationship between investment decisions and the duration of procedures.[33] This fact is all the more interesting as all legislative and regulatory measures taken to 'deregulate' administrative procedures were based on the

29 Vierte Verordnung zur Durchführung des Bundes-Immissionsschutzgesetzes (Verordnung über genehmigungsbedürftige Anlagen) in der Fassung der Bekanntmachung vom 2. Mai 2013 (BGBl. I p. 973, 3756).

30 Baum 2005.

31 SRU 2007, p. 157 *et seq.*; Gebers *et al.* 1996.

32 Steinberg *et al.* 1991, p. 34.

33 SRU 2007, p. 138.

assumption - unsupported by empirical evidence - that there is a causal relationship between these two factors.

4.2. *Measures Taken to Speed Up Licensing Procedures*

4.2.1. Reduced Need for Licences under the Federal Emission Control Act[34]

The easiest way to 'accelerate' a procedure is to eliminate the obligation of acquiring permission. When no such procedure is required the question of duration is obsolete. In fact, in recent years the regulator released a number of industrial plants from the obligation to acquire permission under the Federal Emission Control Act[35] by removing them from the list in the respective regulation. Thus in 2007, by virtue of Article 3 of the law on reducing and accelerating planning permission procedures[36] 30 types of installations were made exempt from the requirement. These installations still have to apply for a building permit but there is no licensing procedure under the Federal Emission Control Act[37] and thus the environmental impact is given less consideration. There is indeed evidence that the overall number of planning permission procedures under the Federal Emission Control Act[38] is decreasing.[39]

Another element of deregulation in this context is the increasing importance of the notification compared to permission. In cases of simple modification of the installation without negative impact on the environment, the operator of the plan is not obliged to run through a procedure for permission; rather, he simply has to notify the modification to the authority (Art. 15 Federal Emission Control Act).[40] The difference is that after a month the operator is allowed to put into force the modification even if the authority has not replied to his notification.

4.2.2. From Public Procedure to 'Simplified' Procedure

Another method of speeding up procedures is to modify the type of procedure and move installations which require public participation to the list of simplified procedures. The aforementioned law of 2007 transferred 15 types of installation to

34 Bundes-Immissionsschutzgesetz in der Fassung der Bekanntmachung vom 17. Mai 2013 (BGBl. I S. 1274), zuletzt geändert durch Artikel 76 der Verordnung vom 31. August 2015 (BGBl. I S. 1474).

35 *Ibid.*

36 Gesetz zur Reduzierung und Beschleunigung von immissionsschutzrechtlichen Genehmigungsverfahren vom 23. Oktober 2007 (BGBl. I S. 2470). See on this Küppers & Schulze 2007, p. 2.

37 Bundes-Immissionsschutzgesetz in der Fassung der Bekanntmachung vom 17. Mai 2013 (BGBl. I S. 1274), zuletzt geändert durch Artikel 76 der Verordnung vom 31. August 2015 (BGBl. I S. 1474).

38 *Ibid.*

39 SRU 2007, p. 147. For example, in the State Hessen between 1995 and 2005 the number of procedures decreased by 47% and in Northrhein-Westfalia by 15%.

40 Bundes-Immissionsschutzgesetz in der Fassung der Bekanntmachung vom 17. Mai 2013 (BGBl. I S. 1274), zuletzt geändert durch Artikel 76 der Verordnung vom 31. August 2015 (BGBl. I S. 1474).

the second type (without public participation).[41] The latest modification in this respect took place in 2009.[42]

4.2.3. Reducing the Number of Public Hearings

The public hearing (*Erörterungstermin*) used to be a crucial element of the public participation procedure. The public hearing was compulsory whenever objections against the project were lodged to the competent authority during the procedure. The revision of Article 10(6) Federal Emission Control Act[43] in 2007 transformed the compulsory character of the public hearing into a discretionary decision of the competent authority.[44] Public hearings had already been abolished by this time by some sectoral laws.[45]

4.2.4. Loss of Standing in Case of Non-Participation

A far-reaching and debatable rule in German administrative law is the so-called *materielle Präklusion*. The rule provides that a claimant loses standing to bring a claim in cases when a participation right was not used by the claimant. If a public procedure takes place and the person does not lodge an objection during the administrative procedure, this objection cannot be brought forward in a later court procedure; thus, the claimant will lose the right to bring a claim against the (for example) permit (in the case it is issued). This rule is not only enshrined in Article 10(3)(5) Federal Emission Control Act[46] but also applies to all infrastructure planning procedures, according to Article 73(4)(3) of the Administrative Procedure Act (*Verwaltungsverfahrensgesetz*).[47]

The compliance of this rule with EU law became more and more doubtful, in particular after the Court of Justice of the European Union (CJEU) held in a Swedish case that:

> 'participation in an environmental decision-making procedure under the conditions laid down in Articles 2(2) and 6(4) of Directive 85/337 is separate and has a different

41 Gesetz zur Reduzierung und Beschleunigung von immissionsschutzrechtlichen Genehmigungsverfahren vom 23. Oktober 2007 (BGBl. I S. 2470).

42 Gesetz zur Bereinigung des Bundesrechts im Geschäftsbereich des Bundesministeriums für Umwelt, Naturschutz und Reaktorsicherheit vom 11. August 2009 (BGBl. I 17.8.2009).

43 Bundes-Immissionsschutzgesetz in der Fassung der Bekanntmachung vom 17. Mai 2013 (BGBl. I S. 1274), zuletzt geändert durch Artikel 76 der Verordnung vom 31. August 2015 (BGBl. I S. 1474).

44 Jarass 2015, § 10(79).

45 Gentechnikgesetz in der Fassung der Bekanntmachung vom 16. Dezember 1993 (BGBl. I S. 2066), zuletzt geändert durch Artikel 55 der Verordnung vom 31. August 2015 (BGBl. I S. 1474), § 18(3).

46 Bundes-Immissionsschutzgesetz in der Fassung der Bekanntmachung vom 17. Mai 2013 (BGBl. I S. 1274), zuletzt geändert durch Artikel 76 der Verordnung vom 31. August 2015 (BGBl. I S. 1474).

47 Verwaltungsverfahrensgesetz in der Fassung der Bekanntmachung vom 23. Januar 2003 (BGBl. I S. 102), zuletzt geändert durch Artikel 1 des Gesetzes vom 20. November 2015 (BGBl. I S. 2010).

> purpose from a legal review' and that therefore 'participation in the decision-making procedure has no effect on the conditions for access to the review procedure'.[48]

However, the German Federal Administrative Court decided shortly after that decision the CJEU ruling could not be interpreted against the *Präklusion* and that the rule was in compliance with EU law.[49]

The recent decision of the CJEU in *Commission* v. *Germany*[50] will phase out the *Präklusion* in environmental cases. According to the CJEU, Article 11(1) of the EIA Directive[51]

> 'lays down no restriction whatsoever on the pleas which may be relied on in support of such a review. [...] That consideration meets the objective pursued by that provision of ensuring broad access to justice in the area of environmental protection'.[52]

It was only a week after this ruling when the German Federal Administrative Court put the final nail in the coffin of the *Präklusion*.[53] In the *Altrip* case, a case dealing with a watershed as part of a flood protection strategy, the German court came to the conclusion that the relevant rule in the law of the *Land* Rhineland-Palatinate could not be applied due to the ruling of the CJEU in *Commission* v. *Germany*.[54]

Once again, the German legislator had been overruled by the CJEU. In order to avoid a situation where two different standards apply - one for cases based on EU law and one for cases with pure national impact - the legislator should reconsider the whole concept of *Präklusion* in German administrative law.

4.3. *Measures in Infrastructure Planning Procedures*

A number of measures which have already been discussed in section 3 also have an impact on planning procedures because the Administrative Procedure Act[55] is also applicable to this type of procedure. Apart from this, legislative measures have been taken in recent years to strengthen the legal effect of planning permits (*Planfeststellungsbeschluss*). This type of permit is used for large infrastructure projects, such as roads, waterways, airports, landfills, and so on. According to

48 Case C-263/08, *Djurgården-Lilla Värtans Miljöskyddsförening* v. *Stockholms kommun genom dess marknämnd*, EU:C:2009:63.

49 BVerwG, Urt. 9A v. 14.7.2011, DE:BVerwG:2011:140711U9A14.10.0.

50 Case C-137/14, *European Commission* v. *Federal Republic of Germany*, EU:C:2015:683.

51 Directive 2011/92/EU of the European Parliament and of the Council of 13 December 2011 on the assessment of the effects of certain public and private projects on the environment, [2011] OJ L 26/1.

52 Case C-137/14, *European Commission* v. *Federal Republic of Germany*, EU:C:2015:683, para. 77.

53 At least for cases based on the Directive 2014/52/EU of the European Parliament and of the Council of 16 April 2014 amending Directive 2011/92/EU on the assessment of the effects of certain public and private projects on the environment, [2014] OJ L 158/77.

54 BVerwG, Urt. 7C v. 22.10.2015, DE:BVerwG:2015:221015U7C15.13.0.

55 Verwaltungsverfahrensgesetz in der Fassung der Bekanntmachung vom 23. Januar 2003 (BGBl. I S. 102), zuletzt geändert durch Artikel 1 des Gesetzes vom 20. November 2015 (BGBl. I S. 2010).

Article 76 and following articles of the Administrative Procedure Act[56] the legal effect of an approved plan goes far beyond the effect of a licence issued under the Federal Emission Control Act.[57] Thus, the law largely provides for rules which allow formal infringements of the law to be remedied by the competent authority after the decision has been taken. The law determines the principle of 'maintenance of the plan' in order to avoid the ex post annulment of the plan as much as possible if there is any violation of the law. Even in cases where the plan is not in compliance with substantive law, the court is to determine (or to oblige the authority to do so) a supplementary measure so as to 'repair' the plan instead of annulling it. In fact, the possibility of challenging this type of administrative decision is nearly impossible. A claimant might achieve a modification of the plan (*Planergänzung*), but the legal doctrine (and the law in force) provides for a very high protection of the plan.

Furthermore, these procedures are highly complex; reducing delays therefore has an impact on the claimant's opportunity to prepare his case.

5. The Paradigm Shift after 'Stuttgart 21'

In the period up to early 2011, the political and legal measures taken to frame the administrative procedures aimed at restricting participatory rights; they clearly laid the emphasis more on speed than on quality. In 2011, a local planning conflict basically changed the attitude of political representatives. 'Stuttgart 21' is a railway and urban development project in the city of Stuttgart in Germany. The highly controversial project led to a political crisis for the regional government of Baden-Württemberg and after the election in March 2011 a *Ministerpräsident* of the Green Party governed (for the first time) that German *Land*, one which was known to be conservative rather than politically open.

At the same time (early 2011) the nuclear accident in Fukushima turned the German debate on nuclear energy upside-down. Angela Merkel's Conservative Party decided – only a few months after having considerably prolonged the phase-out dates of the nuclear power plants foreseen in the Act of the red-green coalition voted on in 2002 (*the Ausstiegsgesetz*) – to end the nuclear path and to more or less re-enact the *Ausstiegsgesetz* of 2002. A number of new laws accompanied the *Energiewende* aiming at building Germany on renewable energy. The main problem with this accelerated approach is the insufficiency in the grid. Therefore, a law in order to speed up the enlargement and modernization of the electricity transport system was set into force (*Netzausbaubeschleunigungsgesetz* – NABEG).[58] As there are a number of local NGOs protesting against new transport lines the public resistance risks becoming a major obstacle to the *Energiewende*. It is interesting to see that the 'new' approach to this is not to decrease, but to increase public participation. To that

56 *Ibid.*

57 Bundes-Immissionsschutzgesetz in der Fassung der Bekanntmachung vom 17. Mai 2013 (BGBl. I S. 1274), zuletzt geändert durch Artikel 76 der Verordnung vom 31. August 2015 (BGBl. I S. 1474).

58 Netzausbaubeschleunigungsgesetz Übertragungsnetz vom 28. Juli 2011 (BGBl. I S. 1690), zuletzt geändert durch Artikel 6 des Gesetzes vom 21. Dezember 2015 (BGBl. I S. 2490).

extent, the law provides in Article 9(3)[59] for public participation in the general planning of the energy network on the federal level (*Bundesnetzplan*).[60] This is a new approach indeed but on the other hand the law does not provide for access to the courts as far as this plan is concerned.[61] Access to the courts is only given to challenge the final planning permit, and in this procedure the previous general plan can be examined implicitly by the judge.

In this context two further amendments of the Administrative Procedure Act[62] have to be noted: Article 25(3) provides for 'early participation' and Article 27a, in force since 7 June 2013, obliges the authority to publish the documents of the planning procedure on the internet (and not only in the office of the authority). In the new debate on further improving these participation rules proposals were made to make the early participation compulsory in planning procedures and to enlarge the scoping phase under the EIA legislation.[63] It has been also suggested that the time limits provided for the participation phase in the procedure should be prolonged.[64]

It seems that also on the regional and local level new forms of public participation in decision-making procedures have a 'renaissance' today, such as the participation in legally not binding, preparatory procedures[65] or planning workshops for urban planning projects at the local level.

6. The Impact of Accelerating Measures on the Quality of Decisions and on the Protection of Legal Rights of Third Parties

The extent to which the number of measures taken in the period from the late 1980s until 2011 has had an impact on the quality of decisions in terms of environmental protection is difficult to evaluate. There is no empirical data available to assess this – a fact that has been regretted also by the General Advisory Council of the German Minister for the Environment.[66] Generally speaking, there seems to be a relationship between the quality of decisions and the judicial control system. Administrative acts that can be challenged before the courts are better prepared and motivated by the authorities; in this way environmental law is better enforced by the administration.[67] Measures that create obstacles to effective judicial control[68] may lower the level of enforcement of environmental legislation.

59 *Ibid.*

60 The law transferred this competence from the *Länder* level to the Regulatory Agency (*Bundesnetzagentur*) at the Federal level.

61 See for a critical appraisal of this concept: Durner 2011, p. 853.

62 Verwaltungsverfahrensgesetz in der Fassung der Bekanntmachung vom 23. Januar 2003 (BGBl. I S. 102), zuletzt geändert durch Artikel 1 des Gesetzes vom 20. November 2015 (BGBl. I S. 2010).

63 Dolde 2013, p. 773. The debate concerns a wide range of procedures, see recently for the determination of *Flugrouten* to airports: Reinhardt & Mutert 2016, p. 84.

64 Dolde 2013, p. 773.

65 Sarcinelli, Köning & König 2011, concerning the reform of the local administration system.

66 SRU 2007, p. 153.

67 De Sadeleer, Roller & Dross 2005, p. 175. The original study is also published on the website: <http://ec.europa.eu/environment/aarhus/pdf/accesstojustice_final.pdf>.

Indeed some authors estimate that the accelerating measures in Germany have had a considerable (negative) impact on the protection of legal rights in environmental cases.[69] Whereas some industrial lobbyists still argue in favour of further 'deregulation' measures, the contrasting argument of some legal scholars is that there is no longer a balance between safeguarding the function of administrative procedures on the one hand and speeding them up on the other hand.[70]

Another indirect negative effect is linked to the time limits for the decision prescribed by law as well as time limits set by the competent authority for opinions to be provided by other administrative bodies that are involved in the decision-making. Although these instruments have undoubtedly had a positive accelerating effect, it has also had the negative effect that the authorities changed priorities. They deal more efficiently with licensing cases and push other issues like surveillance and compliance control after the licence has been issued further down the list of priorities.[71] This is particularly the case if the resources of the administration are not improved but rather, as has been the case in the last years, reduced.[72]

As far as the quality of environmental licences is concerned, a closer look reveals an ambiguous picture. Firstly, it can be generally noted that the quality of administrative decisions in environmental licensing procedures has increased since environmental legislation commenced in Germany in the 1970s. It could happen that a licence for a chemical plant issued in the 1960s consisted of only two pages without any substantial or detailed measures prescribed to protect the environment; objections in procedures lodged by third parties were also rare. As empirical research on the Environmental Impact Assessment in Germany shows, there is some evidence that participation rights have a positive impact on the quality of the decisions: this is also the opinion of civil servants involved in the proceedings.[73]

In the 1980s, the powerful environmental movement actively used the procedural rights provided by the laws. The authorities were in most cases generally not prepared to effectively deal with this new situation and sometimes tried to hinder the effective use of these rights.[74] This may be one reason why procedures took longer in this period but, as a positive effect, the quality of decisions improved and more environmental protective conditions were included in the permits. The relative success of these participation rights in the 1980s and 1990s might be considered one motivation for the regulator's reaction aiming at reducing these rights.

68 Like the *Präklusion* or reduced delays for lodging complaints.

69 Explicitly Erbguth 2009, p. 921 *et seq.*, who highlights the cumulative effect of the amount of measures undertaken in the last two decades.

70 Erbguth 2009, p. 925. The Advisory Council on the Environment also issued some critical remarks on this.

71 Lübbe-Wolff 1995, p. 57 *et seq.*; SRU 2007, p. 152.

72 SRU 2007, p. 64.

73 See on this the comprehensive study of Führ *et al.* 2008, p. 84 *et seq.*

74 Very instructive case studies can be found in: Führ 1989, p. 34 *et seq.*

7. Conclusion

In recent decades and unlike the situation in Germany, information, participation and access to justice has largely evolved in EU law. One might say that EU law assumed the function of a 'safety net' for participation rights in Germany. Since 2011, there has been a national debate and legal revision in Germany to improve public participation.

This is also true for access to the courts where traditionally the legal doctrine in Germany has been very restrictive as far as the legal standing of individual persons is concerned.[75] It is interesting to see that this restrictive approach has been partly adopted by the Netherlands' 'crisis' legislation.[76] Moreover, the claims of NGOs were restricted in Germany for a long time, although there were clear obligations to open the law for claims brought by NGOs under the Aarhus Convention and the implementing EU directives.

In the last five years we can observe a paradigm shift towards improved public participation and to enhanced access to the courts in environmental matters in German law. This has been strongly supported by EU law, and by a new movement of citizen resistance against infrastructure projects. Whether this will lead to a fundamental change in the perception of the value of public participation is an open question. Although some doubts may be justified, the spread of the debate is rather broad and the issue has been taken up by the honourable 'Deutsche Juristentag' where a number of reform proposals have been made.[77] The fact that participation in the procedure has an intrinsic value and a democratic legitimating function is also stressed.[78] It seems that the basis for a 'new' perspective on 'speed and quality' has been built.

[75] Roller 2010, p. 30.
[76] Backes & Jansen 2010, p. 23.
[77] Stender-Vorwachs 2012, p. 1061; Dolde 2013, p. 769.
[78] Renn *et al.* 2014, p. 281.

BIBLIOGRAPHY

Backes & Jansen 2010
Backes, C.W. & Jansen, S., 'Quality and Speed of Administrative Decision-Making Proceedings: Tensions or Balance?', *ELNI-Review*, 2010, p. 23-29.

Backes et al. 2010
Backes, Ch.W., Chevalier, E., Jansen, A.M.L., Eliantonio, M.E., Poortinga, M.A., Seerden, R.J.G.H., *Snellere besluitvorming over complexe projecten vergelijkend bekeken*, Den Haag: WODC 2010, available at: <www.wodc.nl/images/volledige-tekst_tcm44-236321.pdf>.

Baum 2005
Baum, A., *Immissionsschutzrechtliche Genehmigungsverfahren – Entwicklung der Verfahrensdauer und der Beteiligungsrechte im Zeitraum von 1996 bis 2004*, Diplomarbeit Fachhochschule Bingen 2005.

Bier & Panzer 2014
Bier, W. & Panzer N., '§ 48 VwGO', in: F. Schoch, J.P. Schneider & W. Bier (eds.), *Verwaltungsgerichtsordnung: VwGO Loseblatt-Kommentar*, München: C.H. Beck 2014.

De Sadeleer, Roller & Dross 2005
De Sadeleer, N., Roller, G. & Dross, M., *Access to Justice in Environmental Matters and the Role of NGOs, Empirical Findings and Legal Appraisal*, Groningen: Europa Law Publishing 2005.

Dolde 2013
Dolde, K.P., 'Neue Formen der Bürgerbeteiligung?', *Neue Zeitschrift für Verwaltungsrecht*, 2013, p. 769-775.

Durner 2011
Durner, W., 'Die aktuellen Vorschläge für ein Netzausbaubeschleunigungsgesetz', *Das Deutsche Verwaltungsblatt*, 2011, p. 853-858.

Erbguth 2009
Erbguth, W., 'Abbau des Verwaltungsrechtsschutzes', *Die Öffentliche Verwaltung*, 2009, p. 921-932.

Führ 1989
Führ, M., *Sanierung von Industrieanlagen*, Düsseldorf: Werner 1989.

Führ et al. 2008
Führ, M., Bizer, K., Dopfer, J., Schlagbauer, S., Bedke, N., Belzer, F., Mengel, A., v. Kampen, S. & Kober, D., *Evaluation des UVP-Gesetzes des Bundes – Auswirkungen des UVPG auf den Vollzug des Umweltrechts und die Durchführung von Zulassungsverfahren für Industrieanlagen und Infrastrukturmaßnahmen*, Darmstadt: Sonderforschungsgruppe Institutionenanalyse 2008.

Gebers & et al. 1996
Gebers, B. Gebers, B., Jülich, R., Küppers, P. & Roller, G., *Bürgerrechte im Umweltschutz*, Freiburg: Öko-Institut Verlag 1996.

Huck 2010
Huck, W., '§ 71 a VwVfG' in: J. Bader & M. Ronellenfitsch (eds.), *Verwaltungsverfahrensgesetz: VwVfG Kommentar*, München: C.H. Beck 2010.

Jarass 2015
Jarass, H.D., *Bundes-Immissionsschutzgesetz: BImSchG Kommentar* (11th edition), München: C.H. Beck 2015.

Knospe 2010
Knospe, A., 'Mehr Bürokratie wagen!', *Zeitschrift für Rechtspolitik*, 2010, p. 43-46.

Kopp & Ramsauer 2005
Kopp, O. & Ramsauer U., *Verwaltungsverfahrensgesetz: VwVfG Kommentar*, München: C.H. Beck 2005.

Küppers & Schulze 2007
Küppers, P. & Schulze F., 'Erneute Einschränkung von Umweltstandards und Öffentlichkeitsbeteiligung: Bundestag verabschiedet dasGesetz zur Reduzierung und Beschleunigung von immissionsschutzrechtlichen Genehmigungsverfahren', *KGV-Rundbrief*, 2007, p. 2.

Lau 2010
Lau, M., 'Überlange Dauer Eines Verwaltungsgerichtlichen Verfahrens', *Neue Zeitschrift für Verwaltungsrecht*, 2010, p. 358-359.

Lübbe-Wolff 1995
Lübbe-Wolff, G., 'Beschleunigung von Genehmigungsverfahren auf Kosten des Umweltschutzes', *Zeitschrift für Umweltrecht*, 1995, p. 57-62.

Reinhardt & Mutert 2016
Reinhardt, A.S., & Mutert, T., 'Flugrouten: Mehr Öffentlichkeitsbeteiligung – bessere Entscheidungen', *Zeitschrift für Umweltrecht*, 2016, p. 84-90.

Renn et al. 2014
Renn, O., Köck, W., Schweizer, P.-J., Bovet, J., Benighaus, C., Scheel, O. & Schröter, R., 'Öffentlichkeitsbeteiligung bei Vorhaben der Energiewende', *Zeitschrift für Umweltrecht*, 2014, p. 281-288.

Roller 2010
Roller, G., 'Locus Standi for Environmental NGOs in Germany: the (Non)-implementation of the Aarhus Convention by the "Umweltrechtsbehelfsgesetz", *ELNI-Review*, 2010, p. 30-35.

Sarcinelli, Köning & König 2011
Sarcinelli, U., Köning, W. & König, U., *Bürgerbeteiligung in der Kommunal- und Verwaltungsreform*, Bundeszentrale für politische Bildung, 2011, available at: <www. bpb.de/apuz/33491/buergerbeteiligung-in-der-kommunal-und-verwaltungsrefor m?p=all>.

Schwarz 2013
Schwarz, K., '§ 10 VwVfG', in: M. Fehling, B. Kastner & R. Srömer (eds.), *Verwaltungsrecht* (3rd edition), Baden-Baden: Nomos 2013.

SRU 2007
SRU, *Umweltverwaltungen unter Reformdruck: Herausforderungen, Strategien, Perspektiven, Sondergutachten*, Berlin: Erich Schmidt 2007.

Steinberg, Berg & Wickel 2000
Steinberg, R., Berg, T. & Wickel, M., *Fachplanung*, Baden-Baden: Nomos 2000.

Steinberg et al. 1991
Steinberg, R., Allert, H.-J., Grams, C & Scharioth, J., *Zur Beschleunigung des Genehmigungsverfahrens für Industrieanlagen - Eine empirische und rechtspolitische Untersuchung*, Baden-Baden: Nomos 1991.

Stender-Vorwachs 2012
Stender-Vorwachs, J., 'Neue Formen der Bürgerbeteiligung?', *Neue Zeitschrift für Verwaltungsrecht*, 2012, p. 1061-1066.

Roberto Caranta

THE QUEST FOR QUALITY AND SPEED IN ITALIAN ADMINISTRATIVE LAW OR THE TALE OF SOME ELUSIVE TARGETS[1]

1. Introduction

In 1979, Massimo Severo Giannini, a leading scholar in administrative law then serving as a Minister, drafted a report lamenting the overall inefficiency of the Italian bureaucracy.[2] He was pressed into resignation and no changes took place. Italy was then at the height of its quasi-planned economy, with a swollen public sector made bigger by wave after wave of nationalizations and by a tendency to rescue and make into a public undertaking any failing or near bankrupt enterprise of less than minimal size.[3] Efficiency had never been a serious concern. Ballooning public deficit coupled with 'competitive' devaluation of the *Lira* (a currency whose fall was not really mourned) were the default answers to the inevitable problems that ensued.[4] The 'clean hands' probe exposed the fact that the Italian system was not just inefficient, but deeply corrupt (which should not have come as a surprise).[5] With the benefit of hindsight one can say that while following the French pattern of the administrative nation state, Italy had failed to permanently incorporate into its institutional fabric those French characteristics which could warrant an acceptable degree of efficiency (and integrity).[6] As has been noted, the meritocratic system for recruiting officials was weak to say the least; the Italian Council of State (*Consiglio di Stato*) 'never attained the prestige and authority of its French counterpart', and the prefects soon became 'a political instrument of the government'.[7]

1 I want to thank Dr. Massimo Lanfranco for his comments; all remaining errors are my own.
2 Giannini 1979, p. 289.
3 Cerulli Irelli 2006, p. 747; Guarino 1992, p. 35.
4 For a take on the consequences this had on the development of administrative law, see: Irelli 2006, p. 747 *et seq.*
5 Which is undisputed, even if the problem has been assessed differently: contrast Vannucci & Della Porta 2007, p. 830; Burnett & Mantovani 1998.
6 Mattarella 2010, p. 1009.
7 Cassese 2010, p. 994 *et seq.*; Mattarella 2010, p. 1010 *et seq.*

Growing competitive pressure after the Single European Act was to change the situation.[8] The European Commission became serious about state aid - an indispensable lifeline for the inefficiently run public conglomerates which then made up the majority of the Italian economy. At a more generally encompassing level, the belated completion of the single - and later internal - market inevitably exposed a non-competitive economic system to ever growing challenges, making changes a life or death necessity. Moreover, the desire to enter the (then) future monetary union, which meant meeting the 'Maastricht criteria', brought about the need to finally curb the public debt. Speed and quality - or, to put it in one word, efficiency - in administrative decision-making procedures were values Italy could no longer ignore.[9]

Inevitably an era of reform started in the 90s, and is ongoing. This is because very deep and radical changes were needed to bring the Italian system closer to quality and speed. Suffice it to say that the most important piece of legislation, the Law of 7 August of 1990, No. 241 (*Nuove norme in materia di procedimento amministrativo e di diritto di accesso ai documenti amministrativi*)[10] to which we will revert often, had to enact such a basic principle as the duty of public bodies to have administrative procedures result in an explicit decision: Italian administration tended to drag out administrative procedures until they came to a grinding halt without any decision being taken. This was a way for public officials to escape their responsibilities. Misfeasance could make them liable, but under the old system nonfeasance was less prone to attract negative consequences. It was even worse than that. The Italian administration came to abuse the centuries old 'the law will be obeyed but not complied with' (*se obedece pero no se cumple*) Spanish principle as a way to 'prod' concerned individuals and firms to bribe their way to an administrative decision meeting their demands. The system was almost inefficient by design, because it allowed public officials to exact extra money for doing their job. Unsurprisingly, the reforms have been met with considerable resistance.[11]

Another reason for the ongoing reform process is of course that the initial reforms were not radical enough and were loosely implemented if not ignored at lower bureaucratic levels (that is not to say that they were followed by 'counter-reforms' aimed at or diluting their effects).[12] To give an example, reforms aimed at removing elected officials from the decision-making processes by giving power to the top-ranking civil servants to decide on the award of procurement contracts, and on similar measures where the risks of corruption are high, were countered by reforms changing the selection method of top-ranking bureaucrats. The meritocratic system inherited from France was changed into the 'spoil' system, effectively binding the career of high bureaucrats to the goodwill of the politicians.[13]

8 Single European Act [1987] OJ L 169/1.

9 Franchini & Paganetto 2002; Della Cananea 1998; D'Alberti 2008, p. 63 *et seq.*

10 L. 7 agosto 1990, n. 241 (Nuove norme in materia di procedimento amministrativo e di diritto di accesso ai documenti amministrativi).

11 See also the analysis by Savino 2003, p. 2169 *et seq.*

12 Della Cananea 2003, p. 571; Merusi 2010, p. 947 *et seq.* elaborates on the 'trial and error' approach to reform.

13 Marino 2009, p. 249; Dormagen 2004, p. 59; Caranta 2003, p. 399.

It is fair to say, however, that the acceleration of globalization trends coupled with the incumbent financial crisis are setting the efficiency bar higher and higher at the same time that Italy is scrambling to improve its record. This has also led to some form of reform inflation. Statutes are being rewritten yearly - if not more often - with the same provisions being amended again and again. Cynically speaking, reform has become a rite to appease EU institutions and international investors. Italy passed, and again the year after with much emphasis, those administrative laws that 'markets' are demanding. This legislation is adopted through legislative instruments adopted by the government to face situations requiring fast action (*decreti legge*). *Decreti* need to be approved - and may be amended - by the two houses of the Parliament within two months. The legislative technique chosen leads to poor drafting quality. *Decreti* are often hastily drafted and quality worsens with Parliament adding pork barrel and pet projects when amending them. This is not compensated sufficiently by the fancy short titles by which these pieces of legislation have become known.[14]

At the height of the crisis, Berlusconi tried to save Italy (and himself) with a *Manovra bis*. *Manovra* is the traditional name for a mix of spending cuts and tax hikes often blessing Italians at the end of the year and (*bis*) possibly during the summer holidays.[15]

He did not succeed. The prolific saviour was Monti who printed much legislation. Not counting provisions on fiscal matters and the job market and statutes I must surely have forgotten, he started with what became known as 'Save Italy' (*Manovra salva Italia*).[16] However, Italy was not saved in a day: after a few months we had the more optimistically christened 'Grow, Italy, Grow!' (*Cresci Italia*) decree;[17] one decree on simplification and growth;[18] a similarly positively marketed legal instrument known as the 'Growth decree' (*Decreto sviluppo*);[19] and one more in the same vein but dubbed thinking of Millenials as 'Growth decree 2.0' (*Decreto Crescita 2.0*).[20] One is reminded of how wonderful the Italian language is for having two words (*sviluppo* and *crescita*) whereas English has to make do with one (growth). True *sviluppo* may also be translated as development but as Italy was not under- or less developed here the idea was just the same: GDP growth.[21] Finally the Monti's battery of *decreti legge* aptly included one on spending review which was

14 The quality of legislation in this area is analysed by Bombardelli 2015, p. 993 *et seq*.

15 D.l. 13 agosto 2011, n. 138; L. 14 settembre 2011, n. 148 (Ulteriori misure urgenti per la stabilizzazione finanziaria e per lo sviluppo).

16 D.l. 6 dicembre 2011, n. 201; L. 22 dicembre 2011, n. 214 (Disposizioni urgenti per la crescita, l'equità e il consolidamento dei conti pubblici).

17 D.l. 24 gennaio 2012, n. 1; L. 24 marzo 2012, n. 27 (Disposizioni urgenti per la concorrenza, lo sviluppo delle infrastrutture e la competitività - Cresci Italia).

18 D.l. 9 febbraio 2012, n. 5; L. 4 aprile 2012, n. 35 (Disposizioni urgenti in materia di semplificazione e di sviluppo).

19 D.l. 22 giugno 2012, n. 83; L. 7 agosto 2012, n. 134 (Recante misure urgenti per la crescita del Paese).

20 D.l. 18 ottubre 2012, n. 179; L. 17 dicembre 2012, n. 221 179 (Ulteriori misure urgenti per la crescita del Paese).

21 Think again of D.l. 22 giugno 2012, n. 83 (Recante misure urgenti per la crescita del Paese), where *crescita* is summed up as *sviluppo*.

nicknamed in English to make sure that the international markets understood the message without the pain of a translation.[22]

The growth in legislation has not stopped after Monti's time. Most of those statutes needed implementing legislation which was often delayed.[23] The present government also has a penchant for positive spin and could not do without a decree on growth.[24] With the crux of the crisis behind us, the Renzi government is also trying for some more structural and overdue reforms of the public sector.[25] Possibly of more lasting impact is the recent statute - also known as *Riforma Madia*, the name of the relevant minister - giving the government the power to reorganize public administration but also directly changing some of the provisions in Law of 7 August 1990.[26]

Against this very complex - and seismic - background, the focus of this paper will first be on provisions of general application to administrative decision-making proceedings laid down in the Law of 7 August 1990.[27] It will then shift to the rules for emergency situations and to more specific rules for major infrastructure projects. Finally, judicial review will be considered.

Due to wording constraints, some more general issues on the overall efficiency of the Italian administration will only be touched upon in this article. This will be the case particularly with reference to constitutional reforms aimed at making the overall institutional machinery of the Italian Republic more efficient. Institutional issues - such as measures to avoid duplication and conflicts of competences will not be addressed. The role of oversight bodies will be mentioned only in passing. Suffice it to say that the issues of widespread and sometimes endemic corruption on the one hand and of carefree spending have been fought by reinforcing the role of the Court of Auditors and more recently by strengthening that of the ANAC.[28] This, however, has often led to more compliance mechanisms and red tape which are certainly not conducive to speed and their impact on efficiency is doubtful.

22 D.l. 6 luglio 2012, n. 95; L. 7 agosto 2012, n. 135 (Disposizioni urgenti per la revisione della spesa pubblica con invarianza dei servizi ai cittadini nonché misure di rafforzamento patrimoniale delle imprese del settore bancario).

23 Bombardelli 2015, p. 1002.

24 D.l. 24 giugno 2014, n. 91; L. 11 agosto 2014, n. (Disposizioni urgenti per il settore agricolo, la tutela ambientale e l'efficientamento energetico dell'edilizia scolastica e universitaria, il rilancio e lo sviluppo delle imprese, il contenimento dei costi gravanti sulle tariffe elettriche, nonché per la definizione immediata di adempimenti derivanti dalla normativa europea); the mixed bag approach was here already apparent in the long title, which refers to agriculture, the environment, energy saving and so on.

25 New measures for simplification and transparency have been adopted in 2014. D.l. 24 giugno 2014, n. 90; L. 11 agosto 2014, n. 114 (Misure urgenti per la semplificazione e la trasparenza amministrativa e per l'efficienza degli uffici giudiziari); see also the Government action plan at: <http://ec.europa.eu/europe2020/pdf/csr2015/nrp2015_italy_it.pdf>.

26 L. 7 agosto 2015, n. 124 (Deleghe al Governo in materia di riorganizzazione delle amministrazioni pubbliche).

27 L. 7 agosto 1990, n. 241 (Nuove norme in materia di procedimento amministrativo e di diritto di accesso ai documenti amministrativi).

28 <www.anticorruzione.it/portal/public/classic/>.

2. General Provisions Aimed at Speed and Quality in the Decision-Making Process

A number of very different reform initiatives were taken in Italy over the past 25 years to speed up the decision-making process.[29] They range from organizational measures – such as single contact points, collegiate decision-making processes, and terms for taking decisions, to measures aimed at simplification through provisions variously reducing not just the red tape but the competencies and powers of public authorities, and lately of the use of IT instruments (Art. 3 *bis* of the Law of 7 August 1990, introduced in 2005),[30] and the dissemination of best practices.[31]

If speed is easily understood as the time needed to take a decision, quality is more complicated (and time itself may be one component when assessing quality). One approach to quality moves from the distinction between policy design on the one hand (the choice of both the priorities and the means theoretically available to meet those ends having been granted precedence), and on the other hand policy delivery (putting into actual effect the choices made). Given this, two different approaches are possible for the question of how quality may be assessed? If the ends prioritized at policy design level are measurable to the degree they are met, quality is simply the degree reached in policy delivery. In this context, a 100 percent delivery rate will signal an excellent output legitimacy. However, quite often the targets are not really measurable. If so, quality cannot be assessed without considering the people's preferences again at the stage of policy delivery. In this case, the people must be involved in policy delivery also for the sake of output legitimacy – or, and which may be preferred – *ex post* accountability.[32]

On this basis it must be said that only limited attention has been paid in Italian legislation to the possible tools to improve the measurability of the outputs from administrative action.[33] This is notwithstanding the 2001 constitutional reform which basically required costs for the delivery of essential civil and social services to be measured so that resources might be transferred to poorer areas. Implementing legislation was drafted late and the actual application is patchy and essentially limited to the health sector.[34] In the end it is difficult to claim that

> '[T]he main reason for promoting administrative reform were the rediscovery, affirmation, and diffusion of markets and consumer advocacy. The user is no longer an *administré*, but a customer who has to be satisfied. Thanks to the free market philosophy, administrative reforms have changed from being policies involving the

29 Mattarella 2010, p. 1037 *et seq*.

30 L. 7 agosto 2015, n. 124 (Deleghe al Governo in materia di riorganizzazione delle amministrazioni pubbliche), Art. 1.

31 Legislation in this sector benefited from early research, most notably: Masucci 2000; Masucci 1993.

32 Caranta 2011a, p. 178 *et seq*., departing from the idea that any form of government *by* the people amounts to input legitimacy; the idea is instead followed by Verbruggen 2009, p. 432.

33 D.legisl. 27 ottubre 2009, n. 150 (Attuazione della legge 4 marzo 2009, n. 15, in materia di ottimizzazione della produttivita del lavoro pubblico e di efficienza e trasparenza delle pubbliche amministrazioni); Grandis 2010, p. 23 *et seq*.

34 Santoro 2015, p. 99.

public sector internally to interventions aimed at improving the efficiency and effectiveness of services for citizens'.[35]

Historically, Italian administrative law has focused on the decisions taken rather than on the overall performance of administrative authorities. Concerning decisions, administrative law mainly focused - and still focuses - on legality and budgetary issues. Italian administrative law is geared toward checking whether legal and budgetary rules have been complied with. Whether anything good has come out of the procedure is not a concern from the legal point of view. Let us borrow the distinction between input and output control mechanism. The former is established when citizens are sufficiently involved in policy choices ('government *by* the people'). The latter depends on serving the citizens' interests, or put in another way, in public policies being effective ('government *for* the people'). Italian administrative - and constitutional - law rather relies on the former.[36] Italy very much conforms to Max Weber's theoretical model of the rule-based bureaucratic state according to which compliance with the rules provides the legitimacy for the exercise of official powers.[37] In some sectors, however, the pressure for decisions of substantive high quality has led to the establishment of independent administrative authorities with wide ranging regulation powers (a solution that is impossible to generalize due to the high costs it entails).[38]

Concerning quality, Italian legislation over the last 25 years has therefore mainly focused on accrued participation of the concerned parties as a way to come at decisions which are shared - or at least shared to a certain extent - by their addressees. Since a possible trade-off between quality and speed is often discussed when considering participation rules, this paper will focus on this aspect.

3. Measures Taken to Speed Up Decision-Making Procedures

Starting with organizational measures, (and skipping IT instruments whose effects are self-evident)[39] since 1998 Italian legislation has provided for a single contact point (*sportello unico per le attività produttive*) in each municipality.[40] In this way, Italy anticipated - almost a decade in advance - the requirement for a single contact point, later laid down in Article 6 of Directive 2006/123/EC.[41] The measure was taken specifically with a view to make it easier for firms entangled in bureaucratic red tape to start business by addressing a single office instead of different public

35 See, writing about global trends, Cassesse 2010, p. 1004.
36 For the distinction see Scharf 1999, p. 6 *et seq.*
37 For example, Schneider 2007, p. 89 *et seq.*
38 For an overview see Caranta 2004, p. 93 *et seq.*
39 Calvani 2009a, p. 23 *et seq.*
40 D.P.R. 20 ottobre 1998, n. 447 (Regolamento recante norme di semplificazione dei procedimenti di autorizzazione per la realizzazione, l'ampliamento, la ristrutturazione e la riconversione di impianti produttivi, per l'esecuzione di opere interne ai fabbricati, nonché per la determinazione delle aree destinate agli insediamenti produttivi, a norma dell'articolo 20, comma 8, della legge 15 marzo 1997, n. 59).
41 Directive 2006/123/EC of the European Parliament and of the Council of 12 December 2006 on services in the internal market, [2006], OJ L 376/36.

administration departments with powers related to specific activities. It is to be noted, however, that the single contact point has in no way absorbed the disparate powers spread among different authorities. It is merely a point to obtain information and to have the procedure started, but the rest of the procedure, including fact finding and taking the decision or decisions, rests with the authority - or authorities - ordinarily competent.[42]

This is why the different 'conferences' among competent authorities are more relevant as a tool for efficient decision-making. 'Services conferences' (*conferenze di servizi*) bring together all the different public administration departments involved in one procedure. The Italian public administration is very much compartmentalized, structured in many different administration departments with unobvious or overlapping competencies. Even when only one authority has the power to take a decision - which is not always the case, examples are given where two or more public authorities must agree on the final decision - it usually has to act after having secured the agreement or heard the advice (often binding) of one or more different public administration departments.

For instance, in the case of building permits for buildings listed as part of the national heritage, the municipality responsible for the permits must first get the authorization (*nulla osta*) from the superintendent on historic sites and buildings (an institution of the state).[43] Traditionally legislation arranged interaction between different public administration bodies in sequence mode, one authority intervening after the other. The resulting process was quite lengthy in even the best scenario (over a year), and each and every authority involved enjoyed the power to grind the process to halt by dragging its feet.

The idea behind *conferenze di servizi* is to have all the public authorities involved meeting together and working together to iron out differences.[44] Moreover, concerned parties are normally invited to attend the *conferenze*, and have speaking (but no voting) rights. This on its own is not enough to guarantee speed, and *conferenze di servizi* may potentially go on indefinitely if it is reconvened again and again. In the past 25 years the legislation has failed to provide a solution in different devices, such as: giving to the highest authority (such as the Council of Ministers for state-led projects) the power to take a decision if the *conferenze* cannot come to an agreement; waiving the requirement of unanimity providing that a decision can be made with the agreement of those participants' authorities representing the most relevant (public) interests; listing a growing number of interests (like security, protection of the environment, and so on) which cannot be

42 Normally it is still decisions (plural) but in specific areas a single decision is foreseen, to be taken together by the competent administrations in a *conferenza di servizi* (to be discussed below): for example, for the authorization of alternative energy production plants, D.legisl. 29 dicembre 2003, n. 387 (Attuazione della direttiva 2001/77/CE relativa alla promozione dell'energia elettrica prodotta da fonti energetiche rinnovabili nel mercato interno dell'elettricità), Art. 12.

43 D.legisl. 22 gennaio 2004, n. 42 (Codice dei beni culturali e del paesaggio), Art. 10; this also applies to authorization for wind farms in so far as the cultural heritage may be affected: C.g.a. 22 luglio 2014, n. 435; 440.

44 Cons. St., Sez. VI, 3 marzo 2010, n. 1248.

overcome by majority decisions.[45] The provisions of the Law of 7 August 1990, lay down a general legislative framework for *conferenze di servizi*, but *ad hoc* legislation is applicable in specific areas.

While *conferenze di servizi* have become a major working tool for Italian public authorities at both central and local level, the main difficulty still persists: to find acceptable ways out of a potentially blocking unanimity rule.[46] Article 6 of the *Riforma Madia* is another shot for the government, giving it 12 months to enact new rules. One interesting aspect is the provision that only one authority must be chosen to represent all of state administration in the conference, therefore reducing the risk of conflicting positions.[47]

The provision for the pre-fixation of the duration of each and any administrative proceeding was first introduced by Article 2 of the Law of 7 August 1990.[48] If the duration is not already provided in the applicable laws or implementing legislation (which is often the case with reference to sanctioning provisions), it must be enacted and made public by the competent public authority with reference to the specific procedure. If no time has been established there is a default duration of 30 calendar days provided by Article 2 (which has been amended a few times). Needless to say, many public administration departments have tried giving themselves fairly generous times for decision-making.[49] The 2005 reform therefore provided that the duration should in principle not exceed 90 calendar days.[50] Generally speaking, and an exception being the implicit positive decision (*silenzio-assenso*), to which we will revert, the passing of the deadline does not deprive the administration of the power to act.[51]

Under the new (2005) Article 10 *bis*, the time runs again in case the concerned party, having been notified of a potential negative decision, submits new documents or memos. The provision stems from a strongly perceived need to involve the concerned party and to pursue any possibility to reach an agreed outcome to the procedure. Article 2 *bis* has been grafted into the Law of 7 August

45 The provisions of what originally was l. 7 agosto 1990, n. 241 (Nuove norme in materia di procedimento amministrativo e di diritto di accesso ai documenti amministrativi), Art. 14, were later developed in a total of six articles (up to 14 *quinquies*), which in turn have been changed a number of times.

46 For an overview see Sciullo 2011, p. 1138; and (though it is to be updated) with recent legislation such as Art. 49, d.l. 31 maggio 2010, n. 78, (Misure urgenti in materia di stabilizzazione finanziaria e di competitivita' economica); L. 30 luglio 2010, n. 122 (Conversione in legge, con modificazioni, del d.l. 31 maggio 2010, n. 78); Sandulli 2003, p. 1303 *et seq.*

47 L. 7 agosto 2015, n. 124 (Deleghe al Governo in materia di riorganizzazione delle amministrazioni pubbliche).

48 L. 7 agosto 1990, n. 241 (Nuove norme in materia di procedimento amministrativo e di diritto di accesso ai documenti amministrativi).

49 Cons. St., A.G., 9 febbraio 1995, n. 3, Cons. St. 1995, I, 1728.

50 See generally Mastrodomenico 2009, p. 39 *et seq.*

51 Cons. St., Sez. IV, 10 giugno 2010, n. 3695.

1990 by the Law of 18 June 2009, No. 69,[52] providing the right to sue for damages in case the deadline for coming to a decision is not met.[53]

Article 23 of the Law of 18 June 2009[54] provides for the dissemination of best practices focusing on speed and efficiency, including top quality services as shown by users' satisfaction and reductions in the litigation.[55]

Simplification measures have also been around since 1990, and possibly before, with Article 1(2) of the Law of 7 August 1990[56] providing that no procedural step or requirement going beyond what is required under the applicable legislation should be imposed if not strictly necessary.[57] These measures have been strengthened from time to time.[58] The pressure is so strong that Parliament is expected to pass on a yearly basis a law erasing from the statute book procedural requirements and entire proceedings which have lost their *raison d'être*. Measures stopping short from fully abolishing an administrative procedure can be arranged in a *crescendo*:

- Since 1968, some legislative rules provide for sworn declarations taking the place of certificates as evidence of status and personal conditions (such as place of birth and personal income). The matter is today ruled in Article 18 of the Law of 7 August 1990.[59] The decision- maker who has received the sworn declaration is expected to check (at least on a sample basis) the truth of the sworn declarations by enquiring with the competent public authority for certification. Wider recourse to IT (encouraged by Art. 3 *bis* of the Law of 7 August 1990)[60] should make it easier to police declarations. Providing a false declaration is in any case a criminal offence. Today the matter has a more detailed regulation in Article 46 f. of D.P.R. of 28 December 2000, No. 445,[61] the consolidated implementing legislation on administrative documents, which has had a few amendments since its entry into force.

52 L. 7 agosto 1990, n. 241 (Nuove norme in materia di procedimento amministrativo e di diritto di accesso ai documenti amministrativi), l. 18 giugno 2009, n. 69 (Disposizioni per lo sviluppo economico, la semplificazione, la competitivita' nonche' in materia di processo civile).

53 The provision is now part of the Administrative Judicial Procedural Code: see Caranta 2011b, p. 649 *et seq*.

54 L. 18 giugno 2009, n. 69 (Disposizioni per lo sviluppo economico, la semplificazione, la competitivita' nonche' in materia di processo civile), Art. 23.

55 See generally Grandis 2010, p. 23-28.

56 L. 7 agosto 1990, n. 241 (Nuove norme in materia di procedimento amministrativo e di diritto di accesso ai documenti amministrativi).

57 Generally Savino 2003, p. 2265 *et seq*.

58 A comprehensive analysis is due to Bombardelli 2015, p. 985 *et seq*. Reference to older case law and scholarly works in Caranta & Protto 2002, p. 203.

59 L. 7 agosto 1990, n. 241 (Nuove norme in materia di procedimento amministrativo e di diritto di accesso ai documenti amministrativi).

60 *Ibid*.

61 D.P.R. of 28 dicembre 2000, n. 445 (Testo unico delle disposizioni legislative e regolamentari in materia di documentazione amministrativa).

- Under Article 16 of the Law of 7 August 1990,[62] in case advisory boards fail to provide their advice within 20 (reduced from 45 in 2009) calendar days after being asked by the competent authority, this authority may choose to come to a decision without any prior advice. Recourse to this possibility was quite limited for the additional responsibility it will bring over the shoulders of the decision maker. In 2009 the provision was amended to the effect that the public administration must decide after the expiry of the deadline if the advice is not compulsory; in this case, any possible liability for the official having taken the decision is waived. Under Article 17, in case the decision maker is to have recourse to technical expertise beyond its capacity, it may give the technical advising body a deadline to answer (a default 90 calendar days deadline is provided). If the deadline is not met, the decision maker can address itself to other public law entities, universities being expressly therein. The powers conferred under Articles 16 and 17 do not apply in case the environment, urban planning, or human health are at stake; the idea behind this and similar provisions which will be referred to later is that some general interests are so relevant that *a posteriori* controls would not be adequate to effectively safeguard such interests.[63]

- Article 19 of the Law of 7 August 1990[64] provided for a declaration on the commencement of activity (*denuncia*, later *dichiarazione, di inizio attività*) (DIA). While in 1990 DIA was to be specifically foreseen by implementing bylaws to be adopted by the government, since then successive waves of reform have transformed it into a fairly general tool.[65] Nowadays, when an activity is conditioned upon the granting of a licence, authorization, permission, or any other decision by the public administration whatever its name, the interested party may submit a sworn declaration that he/she meets all the legal requirements for the activity along with the documents proving this and start

62 L. 7 agosto 1990, n. 241 (Nuove norme in materia di procedimento amministrativo e di diritto di accesso ai documenti amministrativi).

63 The rationale is the same as the one behind Art. 9(1)(c) of Directive 2006/123/EC of the European Parliament and of the Council of 12 December 2006 on services in the internal market, [2006], OJ L 376. 'Member States shall not make access to a service activity or the exercise thereof subject to an authorisation scheme unless the following conditions are satisfied: [...] the objective pursued cannot be attained by means of a less restrictive measure, in particular because an a posteriori inspection would take place too late to be genuinely effective'; see also Recital 54 thereof: 'that authorisation schemes should be permissible only where an a posteriori inspection would not be effective because of the impossibility of ascertaining the defects of the services concerned a posteriori, due account being taken of the risks and dangers which could arise in the absence of a prior inspection'; the systematic relevance of the *Bolkenstein* directive (Directive 2006/123/EC of the European Parliament and of the Council of 12 December 2006 on services in the internal market, [2006], OJ L 376) has been stressed by Lazarra 2011, p. 681 *et seq.*; for its implementation in Italy see D.Legisl. 26 marzo 2010 n. 59 (Attuazione della direttiva 2006/123/CE relativa ai servizi nel mercato interno), Art. 10, below in the conclusion.

64 L. 7 agosto 1990, n. 241 (Nuove norme in materia di procedimento amministrativo e di diritto di accesso ai documenti amministrativi).

65 The 1993 reform was analysed by Pajno 1994, p. 40.

the activity. Different standstill periods were provided in previous versions of the provision, but they were progressively reduced and finally eliminated.
It is worth noting that changes were first introduced with reference to administrative procedures concerning business activity. For instance, following the 2009 reform of Article 19,[66] an immediate start was allowed for those activities covered under Directive 2006/123/EC.[67] Article 19 does not apply to those activities for which a limited availability exists because of planning and other requirements. Moreover, besides the usual exclusions (the protection of the environment, urban planning concerns, or the need to protect human health) this provision last amended in 2005, also lists national security, immigration, taxation, the protection of cultural heritage and the necessity to comply with (as known at that time) Community law requirements.[68]
Bearing witness to the relentless reform process, the Decree of 31 May 2010, No. 78, validated by the Law of 30 July 2010, No. 122,[69] has now changed DIA into a certified declaration on the commencement of activity (*segnalazione certificata di inizio attività*) (SCIA). The main change is that having served the notice the person or undertaking may immediately begin the activity concerned.[70] Following the changes in Article 19 introduced by the *Riforma Madia*, within 60 days from being served the notice, the competent authority may forbid the activity for the future or lay down conditions for its continuation.[71] However, under Article 21 *nonies* as changed by the *Riforma Madia*, no foreclosure for administrative action exists if the SCIA was based on criminally false or misleading declarations while - and here the law maker is verging on schizophrenia - withdrawal of authorizations or grants is possible within 18 months. It is presently unclear when the 60 days or 18 months deadline will apply.[72]

- Well before 1990, specific legislation provided for instances where non-decisions were to be taken as implicit positive decisions (*silenzio assenso*). The latest so far - a version of Article 20 of the Law of 7 August 1990,[73] has made *silenzio assenso* the default rule. When the conditions for DIA (now SCIA) are absent, and this is normally the case when the outcome of the decision depends on the making of discretionary choices,[74] the expiry of the deadline

66 L. 7 agosto 1990, n. 241 (Nuove norme in materia di procedimento amministrativo e di diritto di accesso ai documenti amministrativi), Art. 19.
67 Directive 2006/123/EC.
68 See generally Di Gaetano 2009, p. 57 *et seq*.
69 D.l. 31 maggio 2010, n. 78; l. 30 luglio 2010, n. 122 (Misure urgenti in materia di stabilizzazione finanziaria e di competitivita' economica).
70 Lazarra 2011, 689 *et seq*.
71 L. 7 agosto 2015, n. 124 (Deleghe al Governo in materia di riorganizzazione delle amministrazioni pubbliche), Art. 6.
72 *Ibid*.
73 L. 7 agosto 1990, n. 241 (Nuove norme in materia di procedimento amministrativo e di diritto di accesso ai documenti amministrativi).
74 On the specific Italian notion of discretion see Caranta 2008, p. 189 *et seq*.

> set under Article 2 of the law[75] gives rise to an implicit positive decision. Here some exclusions do exist (drafted differently from Art. 19) and the competent authority may still forbid, within the new time limits set by the *Riforma Madia*,[76] any activity pursued in breach of the applicable legal provisions.[77]

It should be plain from what has just been said that speed has been the paramount concern of the Italian legislation in the past 20 years.[78] Simplification measures have become stronger and stronger as the years passed, with DIA being introduced and developed into SCIA and *silenzio assenso* becoming a default option.[79] Few general interests only - the environment, urban planning, health, and of late national security - have been granted a special status, and have not really been affected by the new trends to reduce the binding force of administrative law.[80] It is to be noted that all the provisions discussed are expected to be recast in the near future given that *Riforma Madia* has allowed the government 12 months to do so (and a further 12 months to possibly rework the provisions adopted).[81]

As already mentioned, the most relevant measure taken to improve the quality of administrative decision-making processes is participation with a view to reach an agreement between the parties concerned and the decision-maker.[82]

The Law of 7 August 1990[83] marks the start of a shift from a procedure which is centred on the public authority supposedly vested with the knowledge as to where the general interest lays, to an administration which discovers through the involvement of the participants in the procedure those solutions which are more acceptable to civil society. All those concerned by a possible future decision may take part in the procedure possibly leading to its adoption. This includes public interest groups (Art. 9). Moreover, those whose rights and interests are directly affected and those other concerned parties known or easily acknowledged by the decision-maker are served a notice giving them details of the proceedings being issued (Art. 7). Participants enjoy the right of access and the right to submit

75 L. 7 agosto 1990, n. 241 (Nuove norme in materia di procedimento amministrativo e di diritto di accesso ai documenti amministrativi), Art. 2.

76 L. 7 agosto 2015, n. 124 (Deleghe al Governo in materia di riorganizzazione delle amministrazioni pubbliche), Art. 5.

77 Giovagnoli 2005.; Marinaro 2009, p. 103-115.; Cioffi p. 99 *et seq.*; see, for instance, concerning an authorization to put a menu totem and some plants on the street in front of a restaurant T.A.R. Veneto, Sez. III, 15 maggio 2008, n. 1400; this power is normally used when some other concerned parties lament that the activity is pursued in breach of or absent some legal requirements.

78 Mastrangelo 2009, 19 *et seq.*

79 Forlenza 2005, p. 10, and 42.

80 Sandulli 2001, 585 *et seq.*

81 L. 7 agosto 1990, n. 241 (Nuove norme in materia di procedimento amministrativo e di diritto di accesso ai documenti amministrativi), Art. 21 nonies; L. 7 agosto 2015, n. 124 (Deleghe al Governo in materia di riorganizzazione delle amministrazioni pubbliche), Art. 5.

82 Generally Allegretti 2006, p. 790 *et seq.*

83 L. 7 agosto 1990, n. 241 (Nuove norme in materia di procedimento amministrativo e di diritto di accesso ai documenti amministrativi).

documents and memos to be taken into account in the decision (including in the reasons given for it).[84]

Ideally participation means agreed solutions between the public authority and private actors concerned. Article 11 of the Law of 7 August 1990[85] provided for the possibility of agreements between public administration and private parties as to the use of official discretionary powers (*accordi*). Article 11 stated that, under given and somewhat restrictive conditions, an agreement between the interested parties and the administration could either take the place of the final decision or set out the content of this decision in so far as it was not bound by the law.[86] Article 11 is only one example of an ever increasing trend to substitute the unilateral final decision with an agreement between the citizen and the public administration.

The Law of 11 February 2005, No. 15,[87] has amended Article 11 of the Law of 7 August 1990,[88] effectively widening the scope for *accordi*.[89] *Accordi* have a mixed public-private law regime. They are submitted to the same controls as administrative unilateral decisions and they can be unilaterally terminated by the public party. If so, the private party is entitled to receive compensation. This, however, is in principle limited to costs, but does not cover lost profit. Apart from these special measures, *accordi* are ruled by principles on the law of obligations derived from the Civil Code as long as they are consistent with their peculiar nature.[90]

A new provision was added in 2005. Article 10 *bis* of the Law of 7 August 1990[91] now provides that before rejecting any application, the competent authority must serve the applicant with a statement of the reasons against granting the measure or benefit sought. The applicant then has time to submit (further) documents and memos. The provision aims at making it easier for the decision-maker and the private party to come to a mutually satisfactory agreement and comes at a time when the possibility to reach agreement *in lieu* of the adoption of unilateral measures.[92] In principle, the traditional top-down approach to public administration is giving place to a different bottom-up take geared at stimulating – rather than stopping – entrepreneurial and other forces present in civil society.[93] The same is true in environmental matters. Participation in EIA procedures is seen as an

84 Caranta 2005.

85 L. 7 agosto 1990, n. 241 (Nuove norme in materia di procedimento amministrativo e di diritto di accesso ai documenti amministrativi).

86 Aicardi 1997, p. 1; Bruti Liberati 1996.

87 L. 11 febbraio 2005, n. 15 (Modifiche ed integrazioni alla legge 7 agosto 1990, n. 241, concernenti norme generali sull'azione amministrativa).

88 L. 7 agosto 1990, n. 241 (Nuove norme in materia di procedimento amministrativo e di diritto di accesso ai documenti amministrativi).

89 See, with an eye to the reform process then in progress, Merusi 2004, p. 649; Trimarchi Banfi 2004, p. 661; Cerulli Irelli 2003, p. 244.

90 Greco 2004.

91 L. 7 agosto 1990, n. 241 (Nuove norme in materia di procedimento amministrativo e di diritto di accesso ai documenti amministrativi).

92 Caranta, Ferraris & Rodriquez 2005, p. 376; Bonomo 2009, p. 93 *et seq*.

93 Caranta 2009, p. 114 *et seq*.

instrument for both raising the concerns of the public and for making it potentially possible to overcome them through changes to the project.[94]

The major shortcoming of the legislative provisions on participation in the Law of 7 August 1990 is that their application is confined to procedures ending with individual decisions being taken. Rule-making and planning decisions are still ruled under older and more traditional provisions focusing on representative democracy institutions (such as debates in regional or local councils). Article 1 of the *Riforma Madia* giving power to the government to enact implementing legislation to provide for internet based public enquiries might result in changes to this situation, but their substance and scope will become apparent only after the government act.[95]

The situation is different in matters falling under environmental legislation. EU rules, including those derived from the Aarhus Convention[96] on access to information, public participation in decision-making and access to justice in environmental issues, have been implemented in the Code of environmental legislation.[97] Articles 14 and 24 thereof provide for consultation of the public in SEA and EIA procedures respectively and have not been affected by measures taken to face the financial crisis. However, Article 24 provides for consultation based on the proponent study, which may not allow for early participation when all the options are still available. The issue whether this is in line with the requirements flowing from the Aarhus Convention[98] has not been raised in the case law, which rather focuses on whether specific people had to be served individual notice of the opening of the impact assessment procedure (in principle they did not),[99] or whether the information foreseen by the law had been made available in due manner and time.[100] However, the case law is quite clear in holding that a public authority faced with a negative EIA may consider all the options, including the option of denying the authorization sought after.[101]

Finally independent administrative authorities are increasingly turning to notice-and-comment regulation patterns.[102] Indeed, the role of participation is much strengthened with reference to these authorities.[103]

In Italy efficiency needs can still get the upper hand on participation. Under the new Article 21 *octies* of the Law of 7 August 1990 added in 2005,[104] procedural

94 Cons. St., Sez. V, 2 ottobre 2010, n. 4928.

95 L. 7 agosto 1990, n. 241 (Nuove norme in materia di procedimento amministrativo e di diritto di accesso ai documenti amministrativi), Art. 21 nonies; L. 7 agosto 2015, n. 124 (Deleghe al Governo in materia di riorganizzazione delle amministrazioni pubbliche), Art. 6.

96 Convention on Access to Information, Public Participation in Decision-Making and Access to Justice in Environmental Matters, 2161 UNTS 447; 38 ILM 517 (1999).

97 D.Legisl. 3 aprile 2006 n. 152 (Norme in materia ambientale), Arts. 4 *et seq.*

98 Convention on Access to Information, Public Participation in Decision-Making and Access to Justice in Environmental Matters, 2161 UNTS 447; 38 ILM 517 (1999).

99 Cons. St., Sez. IV, 3 marzo 2009, n. 1213.

100 T.A.R. Friuli Venezia Giulia, Sez. I, 12 marzo 2009, n. 122.

101 Cons. St., Sez. V, 2 ottubre 2010, n. 4928.

102 For example, with reference to the insurance market regulator, Caranta 2006, p. 458 *et seq.*

103 Cons. St., Sez. VI, 27 dicembre 2006, n. 7972; Poto 2007, p. 1139; Frego Luppi 2008, p. 695 *et seq.*

104 L. 7 agosto 1990, n. 241 (Nuove norme in materia di procedimento amministrativo e di diritto di accesso ai documenti amministrativi).

breaches do not need to cause the annulment of the decision taken. Annulment is ruled out in cases of bound competence if the decision taken appears to be right on its substance; the same with the failure to give the notice provided under Article 7, and even in case of discretionary powers, provided that the defendant authority can show that no other decision could have been taken on the given circumstances and that therefore the breach had no effect on the outcome of procedure.[105] The provision was cast along the lines of § 46 of the German Administrative Procedure Act (*Verwaltungsverfahrensgesetz*).[106] That provision makes sense in Germany where courts are more than ready to step into the shoes of the decision-maker.[107] In Italy administrative courts stop well before going into the merits, and this - rather than an improbable sudden love for participation - goes a long way towards explaining the prudence they have so far displayed in the application of the new rule.[108]

Italy no longer relies on controls by higher or just different authorities on the decision taken to safeguard quality in the decision-making processes. These have been very much lessened if not obliterated in the past decade, owing both to strong reserves as to their cost-efficiency ratio (they take time) and to the growing autonomy already recognized at the constitutional level of regional and local authorities.[109]

Other measures expected to enhance quality do not focus on specific procedures, but on the bureaucratic machinery generally considered. As such they fall outside the scope of this paper. A few may be briefly recalled, such as provisions forbidding elected officials to take specific decisions and giving decision-making power to the bureaucratic top echelons, the so-called privatization of the former public servant's status,[110] and the provision of efficiency audits focusing on the overall administrative output rather than on specific decisions.[111]

Doubts are allowed as to the effectiveness of such provisions, quite removed from the legalistic frame of mind still characterizing much of the Italian bureaucracy (not to mention the politicians' and media fascination with ideological discourse, coupled with indifference if not contempt for anything quantifiable and demonstrable).

105 Caranta, Ferraris & Rodriquez 2005, p. 163 *et seq*.
106 Verwaltungsverfahrensgesetz in der Fassung der Bekanntmachung vom 23. Januar 2003 (BGB1. I S. 102), zuletzt geändert durch Artikel 1 des Gesetzes vom 20. November 2015 (BGBl. I S. 2010).
107 See the detailed analysis by Galetta 2003.
108 The case law is quite restrictive in considering whether this condition has been met: see Bonomo 2009, p. 91 *et seq*.
109 See D'Auria 2003, p. 1343.
110 Besides Cassese 2010, p. 994 *et seq*.; please refer to Caranta 2003, p. 399.
111 D.l. 10 ottubre 2012, n. 174; L. 7 dicembre 2012, n. (Recante disposizioni urgenti in materia di finanza e funzionamento degli enti territoriali, nonché ulteriori disposizioni in favore delle zone terremotate nel maggio 2012); Astegiano, Aries & Padovani 2014.

4. Exceptional Rules for Various 'Emergency' Situations

Obviously the concern for speed is heightened in emergency situations. This is already plain from the Constitution.[112] Under Article 77(2) in extraordinary cases, when it is both necessary and urgent, the government may issue provisional measures with the force of law. These measures lose all binding force if not confirmed within 60 days by both Houses of Parliament. Italian governments have a penchant for abusing this power, quite often using flimsy excuses to adopt such measures as a way to force usually slow parliamentary procedures into higher gear.[113]

A similar attitude has been displayed with reference to extraordinary administrative powers in cases of emergency. The Law of 24 February 1992 , No. 225[114] established a national civil protection service.[115] Article 2 thereof distinguishes three kinds of natural or man-made events demanding action, the first two requiring action by the public authorities ordinarily competent, possibly in coordination with them. The third category, instead, covers natural and other disasters which because of their nature have to be addressed through extraordinary means and powers. Under Article 5, an emergency situation is to be declared by decree taken by the Council of Ministers. Once the decree is adopted, state, regional and local authorities may derogate from any legal provision generally in force (*in deroga ad ogni disposizione vigente*) provided the measures taken comply with the general principles of the Italian legal order and with specific provisions - if any - referred to in the enabling legislation.[116] The problem may be whether EU rules are included among those which can be departed from.[117]

The case law seems keen to underline that EU rules themselves allow margins for derogation or adjustment. So, for instance, it was held that legislation allowing the building of a dumping ground within the borders of a natural park in the Naples area did not infringe EU rules on environmental impact assessment.[118] A recent judgment went so far as affirming the validity of an environmental impact assessment made after the works had already started (they concerned a dumping facility for the boats used by illegal immigrants to reach Pantelleria, a small island south of Sicily).[119] The Law of 24 February 1992, No. 225[120] further empowers the government to establish officials acting outside the normally applicable rules to address the situation (*commissari straordinari*).[121] These *commissari* are not bound by urban planning instruments.[122]

112 Costituzione della Republica Italiana (GU n. 298 del 27 dicembre 1947).

113 Celotto & Di Benedetto 2006, p. 1506.

114 L. 24 febbraio 1992 n. 225 (Istituzione del Servizio nazionale della protezione civile).

115 Tedeschini & Ferrelli 2010; Meoli 2003, p. 2145.

116 Cons. St. Sez. VI, 10 febbraio 2015, n. 701; Cons. St., Sez. VI, 6 settembre 2010, n. 6464.

117 Enabling legislation usually refers to the need to comply with EU rules: Cons. St., Sez. IV, 13 gennaio 2009, n. 199.

118 T.A.R. Lazio, Sez. I, 18 gennaio 2010, n. 319.

119 T.A.R. Sicilia, Palermo, Sez. I, 20 gennaio 2010, n. 583.

120 L. 24 febbraio 1992 n. 225 (Istituzione del Servizio nazionale della protezione civile).

121 See the situation leading to Case C-525/03 *Commission of the European Communities* v. *Italian Republic*, ECLI:EU:C:2005:648; and especially the conclusions by AG Jacobs: Opinion of →

This legislation might easily be considered a reasonable approach to extraordinary and unforeseeable circumstances. The problem is, recourse is had to it quite ordinarily: any time the government wants or pretends to want to address some issue of any political relevance.[123] Just to give an example, an emergency situation was declared in 2010 with reference to immigration from non-EU countries (hardly an unforeseeable issue).[124] Moreover, a 2001 decree later passed into law by the Law of 14 July 2001, No. 12 extended the same regulatory framework to major events (*grandi eventi*), such as the Olympics, any football championship, a G8 or such, is organized, and this quite independently from an emergency situation.[125] The idea is that nothing relevant or less than trivial can be accomplished by complying with the ordinary rules.[126] Quite often the same officials that would be competent under normal rules - such as for instance the mayors of the concerned municipalities - are named *commissari straordinary* in order to allow them to act outside the provisions normally applicable.[127]

Unsurprisingly, the wide powers given to the *commissari straordinari* may be abused; a blatant case was to pretend to validate retroactively a procurement contract whose illegality was *res judicata*.[128] In another case, a negotiated procedure was used to award a contract whose duration greatly exceeded that of the 'emergency'.[129]

Both the Parliament and the government in Italy share an uninhibited enthusiasm for *ad hoc* legislation in case of urgency brought about by natural disasters and/or sheer incompetence (including but not limited to the inability to organize any major event according to the ordinary procedures). The already quite generous special provisions in the Law of 24 February 1992, No. 225[130] have been widened on more than one occasion. Legislative measures adopted after the Abruzzo earthquake or the Naples waste crisis, just to mention a couple of the most recent measures, share two characteristics with previous legislative interventions, namely that one person is named to act in the place of the bodies ordinarily competent (*commissario straordinario*) and that he/she is dispensed from the application of ordinary rules (including but not limited to public procurement rules).[131]

Advocate General F.G. Jacobs in Case C-525/03 *Commission of the European Communities* v. *Italian Republic*, ECLI:EU:C:2005:343.

122 Cons. St., Sez. IV, 24 aprile 2008, n. 1859.

123 The Court of Auditors had to criticize 'special' measures taken by the Prime Minister whose aim was to relaunch Italy's image as a tourist destination: 'Conti, C, Sez. 1 dicembre 2009, n. 23', *Gior. dir. amm.*, 2010, p. 410.

124 D.P.C. 19 dicembre 2010, further extending the effects of a series of previous decrees.

125 Chianale 2010; Capantini 2010, p. 171 *et seq.*

126 Only recently the Court of Auditors tried limit to this tendency, arguing that only those events entailing risks for the people or the environment may be dealt with in this way: 'Conti, C, Sez. 2 marzo 2010, n. 5', *Giorn. dir. amm.*, 2010, 636; Capantini 2010, p. 185 *et seq.*

127 The point is stressed by Chianale 2010; Capantini 2010, p. 53 *et seq.*

128 Cons. St. Sez. VI, 3 marzo 2008, n. 796, in *Foro it.*, 2009, III, 250.

129 Cons. St., Sez. V, 16 giugno 2009, n. 3903.

130 L. 24 febbraio 1992 n. 225 (Istituzione del Servizio nazionale della protezione civile).

131 See the analysis by Chieppa 2010, p. 680 *et seq.*

These measures are of a limited interest as possible examples for adoption, since the consistency of most of them with EU rules (including environmental and public procurement rules) could very well be plunged into doubt.[132] Moreover, their applicability is in principle limited in time and space.

Take, for instance, *decreto legge* of 23 May 2008, No. 90, then the Law of 14 July 2008, No. 123 addressing the Naples waste crisis. This provided for the naming of a new undersecretary of state specifically charged with the problem.[133] The measure was qualified as not just extraordinary but as something which could not be done again and a deadline for the expiration of the position was set on December 31, 2009.[134] The undersecretary was given authority not to apply procurement rules when awarding contracts and with the compliance with the rules on expropriation (Art. 2). As a good measure Article 18 listed several dozens of statutes and statutory instruments which the undersecretary and his delegates could depart from. These range from accounting rules to environmental law, and the Law of 7 August 1990, No. 241,[135] is listed among them, all its provisions possibly being departed from.[136]

The powers given to the usual *commissari straordinari* are far ranging, and include the power to take over the management of waste disposal facilities.[137] According to its title, Article 13 provides for specific measures for the information and participation of civil society. To be accurate, however, no participation rights are given, and the provision is more concerned with top down measures aimed at making the people aware of the needs for proper waste disposal. It is worth noting that even the possibility not to apply the law does not end all complications. The *commissari straordinari* often exercise their powers in areas which should belong to regional and local authorities, meaning conflicts may easily arise.[138]

Somewhat similar measures were adopted after the earthquake in Abruzzo. Article 1 of *decreto legge* of 28 April 2009, No. 39, later the Law of 24 June 2009, No. 77, again provides for the naming of a dedicated officer and wide ranging powers, including the recourse to negotiated procedures in public procurement for the construction of temporary shelters: specific provisions are adopted to reclassify the resulting rubbles in a different waste category with the aim at making rubble removal and disposal easier.[139] The statute also provided to have the soon to be held G8 meeting moved to Abruzzo, and for renegotiation of the procurement contracts already passed with reference to the location previously chosen.

132 See again Capantini 2010, p. 18 *et seq.*; the case law had to recall that emergency situations by themselves are not sufficient to derogate from public procurement rules: 'T.A.R. Lazio, Roma, Sez. I, 18 febbraio 2009, n. 1656'; Mezzotero 2009, p. 2242.

133 D.l. 23 maggio 2008, n. 90; l. 14 luglio 2008, n. 123 (Misure straordinarie per fronteggiare l'emergenza nel settore dello smaltimento dei rifiuti nella regione Campania e ulteriori disposizioni di protezione civile).

134 *Ibid.* Art. 1(2).

135 L. 7 agosto 1990, n. 241 (Nuove norme in materia di procedimento amministrativo e di diritto di accesso ai documenti amministrativi).

136 See critically Chieppa 2010, p. 680 *et seq.*

137 Cons. St. Sez. IV, 26 gennaio 2010, n. 290,

138 'T.A.R. Campania, Napoli, Sez. V, 18 maggio 2009, n. 2689', *Foro it.*, 2009, p. 564.

139 D.l. 28 aprile 2009, n. 39, l. 24 giugno 2009, n. 77 (Interventi urgenti in favore delle popolazioni colpite dagli eventi sismici nella regione Abruzzo nel mese di aprile 2009 e ulteriori interventi urgenti di protezione civile).

Taken together these measures show the existence of a special body of rules, however, having a rather wide area of application. Italy seems unable to manage major problems through the ordinary rules. Recourse to special rules instead of reform to the ordinary rules is to be explained by the fact that these days many ordinary rules transpose EU secondary law. As such, they are kept in the statute books, applied to simple situations, and departed from more often than not in 'emergencies', a term given its widest possible meaning.[140]

Of course it may be doubted whether exceptions to EU rules are permissible under EU law.

5. Rules for Major Infrastructural Projects

Specific legislation enacted with reference to major infrastructural projects is somewhat special. The difficulty of simply doing away with EU law on a case-by-case basis in this area led to a number of successive legislative measures which struggled to combine simplicity and compliance with EU law.

A major reform in this area was introduced by D.legisl. 1° August 2002, No. 166.[141] It was amended many times, partly to remedy encroachments on the competencies of the regions present in the original text.[142]

However, considering that a major reason for the delay of project implementation in Italy is due to the scarcity and uncertainty of the available budgetary resources, coupled with a firm tendency to overshoot the original budget plans, the first concern is normally to speed up the existing implementation project rather than to read new and efficient ones. To this end, the government is given the power to look at the state budget and use unused money and to commit to pay for the completion of the works. Apart from financial measures, the main tool to push existing projects to their completion envisaged by Article 2(9) of the Decree of 1 August 2002, No. 166, is - again - the *commissario straordinario*. Somewhat paradoxically, the government has the power to revoke the authority from *commissari* already in office when the infrastructure work they are presiding over is stalled and name new ones. Quality - or more prosaically integrity of the decision process - should somehow be safeguarded by a special audit commission within the works ministry and chaired by a member of the Court of Auditors. The commission is charged with the *ex post* review of the expenses decided by the *commissario* (Art. 2(4)).[143]

140 Salvia 2006, p. 103.

141 Vetro 2003, p. 1066; De Nictolis 2002, p. 1276 *et seq*. An early attempt to pass legislation specific to major works was D.legisl. 3 aprile 1993, n. 96; l. 21 dicembre 2001, n. 443 (Trasferimento delle competenze dei soppressi Dipartimento per gli interventi straordinari nel Mezzogiorno e Agenzia per la promozione dello sviluppo del Mezzogiorno, a norma dell'art. 3 della legge 19 dicembre 1992, n. 488), it somewhat anticipated D.legisl. 1 agosto 2002, n. 166 (Disposizioni in materia di infrastrutture e trasporti), and was amended by it.

142 C. cost., 1 ottobre 2003, n. 303, in *Giur. it.*, 2004, p. 1567; Massa Pinto 2004, p. 30; Dickmann 2004, p. 41.

143 D.legisl. 1 agosto 2002, n. 166 (Disposizioni in materia di infrastrutture e trasporti).

The Decree of 1 August 2002, No. 166,[144] amending the Law of 21 December 2001, No. 443,[145] provides a specific procedure for approval of major infrastructure projects. These are designated - on a yearly basis, though new ones may be added - in a procedure involving ministers and possibly regional governments and ending up in a programme which must take into account the available resources and a number of priorities (including the European infrastructures strategy). The main idea is that the approval of a project by the Council of Ministers takes the place of any other decision necessary for environmental protection, urban planning, or expropriation which may be required by the law to start the implementation of the project (Art. 13(6), amending previous legislation). The complexity of different administrative procedures needing coordination is swept away by giving the decision-making power to the government.[146]

It is worth noting that Article 14 of the same Decree of 1 August 2002, No. 166[147] procuring the necessary work contracts. As a consequence of the financial crisis the Monti government decided to stop the whole procedure and to liquidate the company.[148]

The overall legislation on infrastructure (major or not) was recast by the Decree of 12 April 2006, No. 163, the new Code on public contracts,[149] aimed, *inter alia*, to implement Directives 2004/17/EC and 2004/18/EC on public procurement in the utilities and classic sectors.[150] Article 97 onwards lay down the rules generally applicable to works projects. Article 97 stipulates that projects have to be approved following the rules laid down in the Law of 7 August 1990, No. 241,[151] and more notably those provisions concerning *conferenze di servizi*. Article 98 reaffirms pre-existing rules giving to the approval of a works project the same effects of a both planning permission and a decision authorizing expropriation. Besides, for those infrastructure projects aimed at bettering towns' environmental quality, the approval also implies the amendment to existing urban plans.

Article 161 *et seq.* of the Code for public contracts is expressly devoted to strategic infrastructure and industrial sites (*infrastrutture strategiche e insediamenti produttivi*). It is worth noting that (major) manufacturing sites are dealt with

144 *Ibid.*

145 L. 21 dicembre 2001, n. 443 (Trasferimento delle competenze dei soppressi Dipartimento per gli interventi straordinari nel Mezzogiorno e Agenzia per la promozione dello sviluppo del Mezzogiorno, a norma dell'art. 3 della legge 19 dicembre 1992, n. 488).

146 Mari 2003, p. 1861 *et seq.*; Protto 2002, p. 12 *et seq.*

147 D.legisl. 1 agosto 2002, n. 166 (Disposizioni in materia di infrastrutture e trasporti).

148 Lavori Pubblici, Comunicazioni 8a, 26 giugno 2013, Presidenza del Presidente Matteoli, <www.senato.it/Web/17LavoriNewV.nsf/All/2A3B1EF8A51D5E5CC1257B960073B402?OpenDocument>.

149 D.legisl. 12 aprile 2006, n. 163 (Codice dei contratti pubblici relativi a lavori, servizi e forniture in attuazione delle direttive 2004/17/EC e 2004/18).

150 Directive 2004/17/EC of 31 March 2004 coordinating the procurement procedures of entities operating in the water, energy, transport and postal services sectors [2004] OJ L 134/1; Directive 2004/18/EC of 31 March 2004 on the coordination of procedures for the award of public works contracts, public supply contracts and public service contracts [2004] OJ L 134/114.

151 L. 7 agosto 1990, n. 241 (Nuove norme in materia di procedimento amministrativo e di diritto di accesso ai documenti amministrativi).

infrastructures. Recourse is to be had to the usual *commissari* and *conferenze di servizi* (see Art. 168; however, under Art. 165(5), a ministerial committee acting according to majority rule is preferable to address conflicts at the initial project stage). A reinforced form of cooperation between the different authorities involved is the public-public institutional partnership charged with adopting any necessary measure, including expropriation and the award of contracts, on behalf of the authorities involved (*società publica di progetto*). Again, the decision taken is considered as solving all collateral issues, including urban planning and expropriation (Art. 165). Article 171 places a duty on all utilities providers whose networks may interfere with the projected infrastructure to cooperate in good faith to solve the possible problems already at the project design stage. To improve quality and speed, a role is given to advisors and general contractors (Art. 163(3)(c) and Art. 162(1)(g)). The aim is to benefit from what are perceived as more efficient market participants. This is confirmed by Article 174 *et seq.*, making concessions and project financing the alternative to the general contractor for the implementation of the project.[152]

This general framework has been tampered with by legislative measures often concerning specific projects of project categories.[153] It is due to be reconsidered to implement the 2014 public procurement directives.[154]

6. On Judicial Review

Italy has a dual judicial protection system. Ordinary courts are normally competent when individual rights are at stake. Administrative courts are competent when the applicable legislation does not confer an individual right and when discretionary powers are given to administrative authorities (*interessi legittimi*).[155] However, administrative courts may be given jurisdiction to hear cases involving individual rights, including constitutional rights.[156]

Provided a right or an *interesse legittimo* has been recognized by the law or – as is more often the case with reference to the latter – the case law, access to justice cannot be limited. Under Article 24 of the Constitution,[157] everyone has the right to defend his/her rights and *interessi legittimi* in court, and this cannot be limited or

152 See generally Celotto & Conte 2008.

153 D.l. 12 settembre 2014, n. 133; l. 11 novembre 2014, n. 164 (Misure urgenti per l'apertura dei cantieri, la realizzazione delle opere pubbliche, la digitalizzazione del Paese, la semplificazione burocratica, l'emergenza del dissesto idrogeologico e per la ripresa delle attività produttive).

154 Directive 2014/23/EU of 26 February 2014 on the award of concession contracts [2004] OJ L 94/1; Directive 2014/24/EU of 26 February 2014 on public procurement and repealing Directive 2004/18/EC [2014] OJ L 94/65; Directive 2014/25/EU of 26 February 2014 on procurement by entities operating in the water, energy, transport and postal services sectors and repealing Directive 2004/17/EC [2014] OJ L 94/243.

155 Angeletti 2011, p. 1 *et seq.*

156 Cass., Sez. un., 28 dicembre 2007, n. 27187, *Foro it.*, 2008, p. 766; see generally Rega 2011, p. 56 *et seq.*

157 Costituzione della Republica Italiana (GU n. 298 del 27 dicembre 1947).

excluded under any circumstance.[158] This is true for individuals, but also NGOs, with courts playing a fundamental role in extending standing.[159]

Judicial review is performed in a somewhat peripheral or tangential way, administrative courts stopping well short of acting as appellate bodies going into the merits of the decisions challenged in front of them.[160] The contribution of the courts to the quality of the decisions taken is correspondingly somewhat limited and mainly indirect. The most relevant profile is possibly the review of the reasons given for discretionary decisions, in that it forces the decision-maker to articulate the grounds on which the measure taken is grounded. This notwithstanding, the time needed to get a final judgement in Italy is long enough and the reasonable duration of judicial proceedings is a major issue affecting the speed of administrative action alongside the rights of citizens.[161] Meaningful statistical analysis for judicial review proceedings do not exist, and duration varies very much from one first instance administrative court to the other, and, also for the Council of State (*Consiglio di Stato*), depending on the subject matter of the claim and how active lawyers are.[162] Undigested data published each year tend to show there is quite a backlog.[163]

A number of partially contradictory measures have been enacted in the past ten years, more notably in 2005 and in 2010, when a Code of Judicial Administrative Procedure entered into force,[164] mainly to limit the slowing effects of litigation on administrative action:

- administrative courts have been given the power to decide by providing very short reasons and referring to precedents;[165]
- if interim relief has been requested, they have the power to decide on the merits when they believe they have all the necessary material in front of them;[166]
- in some areas (such as planning and other decisions linked to infrastructure building, public procurements, decisions taken by independent administrative authorities), a fast track procedure has been devised; all the deadlines for the procedure (but, and not without exceptions such as in the case of public procurement, the one to bring the action or to resist to it) are cut in half;[167]
- first instance judgments may be given effect pending appeal;[168]

158 Pizzorusso 1992, p. 607.

159 See also for reference Eliantonio *et al*. 2013, p. 404 *et seq*.

160 Caranta & Marchetti 2009, p. 145.

161 Mirate 2011, p. 865 *et seq*.

162 Under Art. 71 of the Code of Administrative Judicial Procedure, the lawyers for the parties have to specifically ask for the case to be discussed by the court.

163 For instance, there is a backlog of 70.000 claims at the central T.A.R. Lazio in 2014, compared to 30,000 that have been ruled on: see tables at <www.giustizia-amministrativa.it/cdsintra/wcm/idc/groups/public/documents/document/mday/mde5/~edisp/nsiga_3878254.pdf>.

164 D.legisl. 2 luglio 2010, n. 104 (Attuazione dell'articolo 44 della legge 18 giugno 2009, n. 69, recante delega al governo per il riordino del processo amministrativo).

165 Ramajoli 2011, p. 626 *et seq*.; Gagliardi la Gala 2009, p. 149 *et seq*.; Branca 2002, p. 681.

166 Calvani 2009b, p. 142 *et seq*.; Scognamiglio 2007, p. 131 *et seq*.; Gallo 2005, p. 375.

167 Parisio 2011, p. 663 *et seq*.

168 Carella 2009, p. 169 *et seq*.

- costs for bringing judicial review proceedings have risen considerably, even more so in some areas such as the challenge of decisions taken by independent administrative authorities or for public procurements award decisions; in both instances the cost mentioned is EUR 4.000, which could be considered excessive in the case of small contracts award procedures (but the Constitutional Court and, to a large extent, the CJEU have both indicated otherwise);[169]
- ADR procedures have to be set up for actions brought by users of services of general economic interest (Art. 30 of the Law of 18 June 2009, No. 69[170]);[171]
- in the case of formal and/or procedural breaches, administrative courts may nevertheless refrain from quashing the challenged decision if they are satisfied that no other decision could have been taken on the facts of the case.[172]

'Emergency' legislation has tried to limit the delaying effects of litigation, and especially of potentially conflicting judgments from different jurisdictions. To this end, administrative courts, and at first instance the Regional Court of Lazio (*Tribunale amministrativo regionale del Lazio*),[173] have been given jurisdiction to hear cases in which individual rights are at stake,[174] including constitutional rights.[175] At

169 Scoca 2014, p. 1414; De Nictolis 2007, p. 139; a barrage of cases have been brought to the Constitutional Court by first instance courts, lamenting the narrowing of the right to defence. Most of the cases have been disposed of on the basis of technicalities specific to the judicial review of legislation (C. cost., 23 marzo 2012, n. 69; C. cost., 28 ottobre 2011, n. 284; C. cost., 24 giugno 2011, n. 195); however, it was held in C. cost., 6 maggio 2010, n. 164 that the question was not in its remit as the Parliament has a wide discretion in levying taxes and tax like contributions: and that since the sums due are differentiated according to different subject matters, the costs imposed could not be considered manifestly unreasonable (the case concerned public procurement, and at that time the cost was EUR 2000; it is doubtful whether the reasoning would be different now that it is EUR 4000). See also Case C-61/14 *Orizzonte Salute - Studio Infermieristico Associato* v. *Azienda Pubblica di Servizi alla persona San Valentino – Città di Levico Terme and Others*, ECLI:EU:C:2015:655.

170 L. 18 giugno 2009, n. 69 (Disposizioni per lo sviluppo economico, la semplificazione, la competitivita 'nonche' in materia di processo civile).

171 Gallo 2010, p. 501.

172 L. 7 agosto 1990, n. 241 (Nuove norme in materia di procedimento amministrativo e di diritto di accesso ai documenti amministrativi), Art. 21 *octies*.

173 The *Consiglio di Stato* stressed the exceptional nature of the provision, which cannot therefore be applied to measures different to those adopted by the *Commissari straordinari* to address this specific situation: Cons. St., Sez. VI, 24 novembre 2009, n. 7391.

174 D.l. 23 maggio 2008, n. 90; L. 14 luglio 2008, n. 123 (Misure straordinarie per fronteggiare l'emergenza nel settore dello smaltimento dei rifiuti nella regione Campania e ulteriori disposizioni di protezione civile), Art. 14; the choice has entered into L. 7 agosto 1990, n. 241 (Nuove norme in materia di procedimento amministrativo e di diritto di accesso ai documenti amministrativi), Art. 133; see, declining its jurisdiction, Trib. Salerno, 30 gennaio 2008, in *Foro it.*, 2008, 1, 768; the local first instance administrative court too had to decline its jurisdiction: T.A.R. Napoli Sez. I, 27 maggio 2010, n. 9751. T.A.R. Campania, Sez. Salerno, 19 giugno 2008, n. 1987, in *Foro it.*, 2008, III, 590. The Constitutional Court upheld the provision: C. cost., 5 febbraio 2010, n. 35, in *Corriere giur.*, 2010, p. 409. The provision has failed to put all questions at rest: see, affirming the jurisdiction of ordinary civil courts in case of delay in the payments of sums due by the *commissari*, Cass., Sez. un., 11 giugno 2010, n. 14126; Fimiani 2010, p. 1047.

the same time, the deadline for challenging decisions taken by the *commissari straordinari* has been shortened to 30 days.[176]

Further provisions (possibly inconsistent with EU law) were taken with reference to public procurements, those on infrastructure first, then the others, to the effect that remedies available had to be limited to damages, with the exclusion of interim relief and setting aside of the concluded contract. The potential breach has, however, been remedied by Articles 121 and 122 of the 2010 Code,[177] providing for the ineffectiveness of the concluded contract in those situations where Directive 2007/66/EC so requires.[178]

Finally, the all too frequent emergency pieces of legislation tend to include provisions that are limiting the remedies available in some way. For instance, Article 4 of the Decree of 23 May 2008, No. 90,[179] on the Naples waste crises has limited the effects of interim measures to 30 days after which the measures lose their effects even if no decision on the merits has been taken.

7. Conclusion

Italy is a basket case of iterative reforms. The same provisions have been changed, amended, and tinkered with a dozen times or more in the last 25 years. A new wave of reforms is going to be unleashed following the *Madia* reform. True, some of this effort is window dressing for the benefit of international investors, but still it means that reforms are not working. Efficiency is still most elusive. It is submitted that one lesson learned from the Italian reforms just discussed is the need to shrink the province of administrative law, abandoning the pretence of regulating the details of each and every human action, however, minor its implications for the general interest. The regulation and managing resources of the state and other public law entities must be focused on major questions and the most relevant general interests, while leaving minor and trivial issues to the free choice of individuals and ultimately to the market. Many activities should be simply deregulated. Halfway measures - such as *silenzio assenso* or SCIA - alone have not worked.[180]

The time is ripe for change. One relevant adjustment in the spirit of Italian legislation is that it seems to be departing from the idea that entrepreneurs and the other active actors in civil society must be held in check by administrative law to prevent them from harming the general interest in the blind pursuit of their egoistic interests. A long recent history of budget woes topped by the financial crisis has led law-makers to accept that economic actors may contribute to the overall wellbeing

175 Trib. Salerno, 6 maggio 2008, *Corr. merito*, 2008, p. 1005.

176 D.legisl. 2 luglio 2010, n. 104 (Attuazione dell'articolo 44 della l. 18 giugno 2009, n. 69, recante delega al governo per il riordino del processo amministrativo), Art. 119.

177 *Ibid.*

178 Parisio, Gambato Spisani & Pagliari 2011, p. 727 *et seq.*

179 D.l. 23 maggio 2008, n. 90, (Misure straordinarie per fronteggiare l'emergenza nel settore dello smaltimento dei rifiuti nella regione Campania e ulteriori disposizioni di protezione civile).

180 Satta 2010, p. 299.

of the society, and checks in the general interest must strike a proportional balance between overriding public interest and the general interest to development.[181]

This tendency has of course been accelerated by the dire situation in which Italy finds itself. Already on the occasion of the implementation of Directive 2010/123/EC, Article 10(1) of the Decree of 26 March 2010 No. 59,[182] provided that the provision of services constitutes exercise of the fundamental freedom of economic initiative, and as such cannot be limited without appropriate grounds. Under Article 12, this freedom can be limited for overriding reasons of general interest only complying with the principles of both proportionality and non-discrimination. According to Article 14, all existing authorization schemes should be reviewed to check whether they meet these requirements. Even if this is the case, the rules on SCIA laid down in Article 19 of the Law of 7 August 1990, No. 241,[183] do in principle apply.

The review process has not really been a success and a similar exercise has been applied to all authorization schemes affecting economic activities by Article 3 of the Law of 3 August 2011, n. 138, validating the Decree of 13 August 2011, No. 138,[184] and later by Article 1 of the Law of 24 March 2012, No. 27, validating the Decree of 24 January 2012, No. 1,[185] which gives the government the power to list those legislative provisions which must cease to have effect because they unreasonably limit economic freedom.[186]

The iteration of the rules calling for radical simplification bears witness to both the need for a reform focused on speed and to the obstacles to it, quite often the result of vested interests more than of any preoccupation for quality. To this must be added an Italian tendency to address any small problem with legislation providing for administrative procedures. To give a recent example, after precious books were spirited away from some abbeys, legislation on the protection of cultural heritage was changed to the effect that previous authorization is to be required to export any book over 50 years old, whatever its value Some regional articulations of the Ministry for Cultural Heritage are competent to start those proceedings and it is a criminal offence to export such books without prior authorization. As the subject matter is cultural heritage neither *silenzio assenso* nor SCIA apply.[187] Of course antiquarian books are beautiful and desirable and deserve

[181] Lazzara 2011, p. 679 *et seq.*

[182] D.legisl. 26 marzo 2010 n. 59 (Attuazione della direttiva 2006/123/CE relativa ai servizi nel mercato interno).

[183] L. 7 agosto 1990, n. 241 (Nuove norme in materia di procedimento amministrativo e di diritto di accesso ai documenti amministrativi).

[184] D.l. 13 agosto 2011, n. 138; L. 14 settembre 2011, n. 148 (Ulteriori misure urgenti per la stabilizzazione finanziaria e per lo sviluppo).

[185] D.l. 24 gennaio 2012, n. 1; L. 24 marzo 2012, n. 27 (Disposizioni urgenti per la concorrenza, lo sviluppo delle infrastrutture e la competitività - Cresci Italia).

[186] Lazzara 2011, p. 699 *et seq.*

[187] D.l. 19 giugno 2015, n. 78, convertito con modificazioni dalla l. 6 agosto 2015, n. 125 (Disposizioni urgenti in materia di enti territoriali (Disposizioni per garantire la continuita' dei dispositivi di sicurezza e di controllo del territorio. Razionalizzazione delle spese del Servizio sanitario nazionale nonche' norme in materia di rifiuti e di emissioni industriali); Art. 16; a number of directives have been issued by the Ministry, including <www.librari. beniculturali.it/opencms/export/sites/dgbid/it/documenti/Normativa/Circolare48-DGBE →

protection. Only Italian law-makers, rather than providing resources for catalogues and scanning (which have actually been cut dramatically) prefer to add red tape for those willing to act according to the law.[188]

For all the possible simplifications, and there is still much room for that in Italy, major projects will still require the intervention of the public hand. Cooperation from market participants is essential at the project design and much more so at the project implementation stage. Besides the mobilization of market resources and simplification, for which margins do exist, public authorities must strengthen cooperation between themselves. *Conferenze di servizi* and project company (*società di progetto*) are useful tools even if the operational rules laid down for the former certainly need to be fine-tuned to improve their performance.

AP-22ottobre2015.pdf> and <www.librari.beniculturali.it/opencms/opencms/it/documenti/Normativa/CircolareDGBEAP-17dicembre2015.pdf>; this piece of legislation is by itself a remarkable mish-mash of provisions addressing a disparate set of issues.

188 See some of the data in Torno 2015, <www.ilsole24ore.com/art/commenti-e-idee/2015-11-03/perche-libri-antichi-sono-pericolo--073140.shtml?uuid=ACUKvOSB>.

BIBLIOGRAPHY

Aicardi 1997
Aicardi, N,. 'La disciplina generale e i principi degli accordi amministrativi: fondamento e caratteri', *Rivista di diritto pubblico,* 1997, p. 1-59.

Allegretti 2006
Allegretti, U., 'Il valore della Costituzione nella cultura amministrativistica', *Diritto pubblico,* 2006, p. 751-819.

Angeletti 2011
Angeletti, A., 'Le origini del sistema di giustizia amministrativa', in: R. Caranta (ed.), *Il nuovo processo amministrativo,* Torino: Zanichelli 2011, p. 3-28.

Astegiano, Aries & Padovani 2014
Astegiano, G., Aries, C.D. & Padovani, E., *Il nuovo sistema dei controlli interni,* Milano: Kluwer Italia 2014.

Bombardelli 2015
Bombardelli, M., 'Semplificazione normative e complessità nel diritto amministrativo', *Diritto pubblico,* 2015, p. 985-1061.

Bonomo 2009
Bonomo, A., 'L'accelerazione dell'attività amministrativa e gli oneri di comunicazione agli interessati', in: D. Mastrangelo (ed.), *L'alta velocità nell'amministrazione,* Rome: Aracne 2009, p. 85-101.

Branca 2002
Branca, M., 'Brevi note sulla sentenza succintamente motivata', *Consiglio di Stato,* 2002, p. 681-687.

Bruti Liberati 1996
Bruti Liberati, E., *Consenso e funzione nei contratti di diritto pubblico tra amministrazioni e privati,* Milano: Giuffrè 1996.

Burnett & Mantovani 1998
Burnett, S.H. & Mantovani, L., *The Italian Guillotine: Operation Clean Hands and the Overthrow of Italy's First Republic,* Lanham MD: Rowman & Littlefield 1998.

Calvani 2009a
Calvani, A.G., 'L'informatica nella pubblica amministrazione', in: D. Mastrangelo (ed.), *L'alta velocità nell'amministrazione,* Rome: Aracne 2009, p. 23-37.

Calvani 2009b
Calvani, N.A., 'La tutela cautelare urgente' D. Mastrangelo (ed.), *L'alta velocità nell'amministrazione,* Rome: Aracne 2009, p. 125-147.

Capantini 2010
Capantini, M., *I grandi eventi. Esperienze nazionali e sistemi ultrastatali*, Napoli: ESI 2010.

Caranta 2003
Caranta, R., 'Point de vue sur les réformes récentes en matière de fonction publique en Italie', *Conseil d'État*, 2003, EDCE, n° 54, p. 399-413.

Caranta 2004
Caranta, R., 'Independent Administrative Authorities in Italian Law', in: R. Caranta, M. Andenas & D. Fairgrieve (eds.), *Independent Administrative Authorities*, London: BIICL 2004, p. 93-109.

Caranta 2006
Caranta, R., 'Assicurazioni (vigilanza sulle)', in: S. Cassese (ed.), *Dizionario di diritto pubblico*, Milano: Giuffre 2006, p. 458-466.

Caranta 2008
Caranta, R., 'On Discretion', in: S. Prechal & B. van Roermund (eds.), *The Coherence of EU Law. The Search for Unity in Divergent Concepts*, Oxford: Oxford University Press 2008, p. 189-215.

Caranta 2009
Caranta, R., 'The Fall from Fundamentalism in Italian Administrative Law', in: M. Ruffert. (ed.), *The Public-Private Law Divide: Potential for Transformation*? London: BIICL 2009, p. 99-121.

Caranta 2011a
Caranta, R., 'Democracy, Legitimacy and Accountability - is there a Common European Theoretical Framework?', in: M. Ruffert (ed.), *Legitimacy in EU Administrative Law: Reform and Reconstruction*, Groningen: Europa Law Publishing 2011, p. 175-196.

Caranta 2011b
Caranta, R., 'Le controversie risarcitorie', in: R. Caranta (ed.), *Il nuovo processo amministrativo*, Torino: Zanichelli 2011, p. 629-662.

Caranta & Marchetti 2009
Caranta, R. & Marchetti, B., 'Judicial Review of Regulatory Decisions in Italy; Changing the Formula and Keeping the Substance?', in: O. Essens, A. Gerbrandy & S. Lavrijssen (eds.), *National Courts and the Standard of Review in Competition Law and Economic Regulation*, Groningen: Europa Law Publishing 2009, p. 145-171.

Caranta & Protto 2002
Caranta, R. & Protto, M., 'Italy', in: *Comparative Analysis of Administrative Law* (European Public Law Series - Bibliothèque de droit public européen), London, Brussels: Esperia Publications, Bruylant, 2002, p. 203-247.

Caranta, Ferraris & Rodriquez 2005
Caranta, R., Ferraris, L. & Rodriquez, S., *La partecipazione al procedimento amministrativo*, Milano: Giuffrè 2005.

Carella 2009
Carella, M., 'L'ottemperanza alle sentenze dei TAR non passate in giudicato', in: D. Mastrangelo (ed.), *L'alta velocità nell'amministrazione*, Rome: Aracne 2009, p. 169-185.

Caricato 2009
Caricato, F., 'L'accelerazione della tutela avverso i silenzi dell'amministrazione', in: D. Mastrangelo (ed.), *L'alta velocità nell'amministrazione*, Rome: Aracne 2009, p. 103-115.

Cassese 2010
Cassese, S., 'The Rise of the Administrative State in Europe', *Rivista trimestrale di diritto pubblico*, 2010, p. 981-1007.

Celotto & Conte 2008
Celotto, A. & Conte, G.B., 'Gli insediamenti produttivi e le infrastrutture private strategiche per l'approvvigionamento strategico', in: M.A. Sandulli, R. De Nictolis & R. Garofoli (eds.), *Trattato sui Contratti Pubblici* (Vol. IV Le Tipologie Contrattuali), Milano: Giuffrè 2008, p. 2867-2879.

Celotto & Di Benedetto 2006
Celotto, A. & Di Benedetto, E., 'Art. 77', in: R. Bifulco, A. Celotto & M. Olivetti (eds.), *Commentario alla Costituzione*, Torino: Utet 2006, p. 1506-1530.

Cerulli Irelli 2003
Cerulli Irelli, V., 'Note critiche in tema di attività amministrativa secondo modelli negoziali', *Diritto amministrativo*, 2003, p. 217-276.

Cerulli Irelli 2006
Cerulli Irelli, V.C., 'Impresa pubblica, fini sociali, servizi di interesse generale', *Rivista italiana di diritto pubblico comunitario*, 2006, p. 747-790.

Chianale 2010
Chianale, A., *Emergenza! Protezione civile e democrazia*, Milano: Guerini 2010.

Chieppa 2010
Chieppa, R., 'Mario Nigro e la disciplina del procedimento amministrativo', *Rivista trimestrale di diritto pubblico*, 2010, p. 667-684.

Cioffi 2006
Cioffi, A., 'Dovere di provvedere e silenzio assenso della pubblica amministrazione dopo la legge 14 maggio 2005, n. 80', *Diritto amministrativo*, 2006, p. 99-193.

D'Alberti 2008
D'Alberti, M., 'Il diritto amministrativo fra imperativi economici e interessi pubblici', *Diritto amministrativo*, 2008, p. 51-66.

D'Auria 2003
D'Auria, G.D., 'I controlli', in: S. Cassese (ed.), *Trattato di diritto amministrativo. Diritto amministrativo generale*, Milano: Giuffré 2003, p. 1343-1545.

Della Cananea 2003
Della Cananea, G., 'Beyond the State: The Europeanisation and Globalisation of Procedural Administrative Law', *European Public Law*, 2003, p. 563-578.

Della Cananea & Napolitano 1998
Della Cananea, G. & Napolitano, G., *Per una nuova costituzione economica*, Bologna: il Mulino 1998.

De Nictolis 2002
De Nictolis, R., 'La nuova riforma dei lavori pubblici', *Urbanistica e appalti*, 2002, p. 1271-1299.

De Nictolis 2007
De Nictolis, R., 'Il nuovo contributo unificato nel processo amministrativo', *Urbanistica e appalti*, 2007, p. 137-141.

Di Gaetano 2009
Di Gaetano, C., 'La dichiarazione di inizio attività', in: D. Mastrangelo (ed.), *L'alta velocità nell'amministrazione*, Rome: Aracne 2009, p. 57-69.

Dickmann 2004
Dickmann, R, 'I principi di sussidiarietà e di proporzionalità ed il principio dell'intesa per un corretto metodo della legislazione statale di attrazione di funzioni amministrative regionali', *Corriere giuridico*, 2004, p. 41-46.

Dormagen 2004
Dormagen, Y-J., 'Pourquoi il n'y a plus de haute fonction publique en Italie', *Rivista trimestrale di diritto pubblico*, 2004, p. 59-90.

Eliantonio et al 2013
Eliantonio, M., Backes, C.W., Van Rhee, C.H., Spronken, T. & Berlee, A. (eds.), *Standing up for Your Right(s) in Europe*, Cambridge: Intersentia 2013.

Fimiani 2010
Fimiani, P., 'La giurisdizione in materia di rifiuti: dalle Sezioni Unite al nuovo Codice del processo amministrativo', *Urbanistica e appalti*, 2010, p. 1047-1055.

Forlenza 2005
Forlenza, G., 'Un'enfatizzazione del principio di efficacia a scapito delle garanzie di tutela dei cittadini', *Guida al diritto*, 2005, p. 42-46.

Franchini & Paganetto 2002
Franchini, C. & Paganetto L. (eds.), *Stato ed economia all'inizio del XXI secolo*, Bologna: il Mulino 2002.

Frego Luppi 2008
Frego Luppi, S.A., 'Il principio di con sensualità dell'agire amministrativo alla luce della legislazione e della giurisprudenza più recenti', *Diritto amministrativo*, 2008, p. 691-716.

Gagliardi la Gala 2009
Gagliardi la Gala, F., 'La decisione in forma semplificata ed i suoi limiti', in: D. Mastrangelo (ed.), *L'alta velocità nell'amministrazione*, Rome: Aracne 2009, p. 149-157.

Galetta 2003
Galetta, D.U., *Violazione di norme sul procedimento amministrativo e annullabilità del provvedimento*, Milano: Giuffrè 2003.

Gallo 2005
Gallo, C.E., 'Giustizia amministrativa', *Digesto (discipline pubblicistiche)*, 2005, p. 359-378.

Gallo 2010
Gallo, C.E., 'La class action nei confronti della pubblica amministrazione', *Urbanistica e appalti*, 2010, p. 501-507.

Giannini 1979
Giannini, M.S., 'Rapporto sui principali problemi dell'amministrazione', *Il Foro italiano*, 1979, p. 289-314.

Giovagnoli 2005
Giovagnoli, L., *I silenzi della pubblica amministrazione dopo la legge 80/2005*, Milano: Giuffré 2005.

Grandis 2010
Grandis, F.G., 'Luci ed ombre nella misurazione, valutazione e trasparenza delle performance', *Giornale di diritto amministrativo*, 2010, p. 23-28.

Greco 2004
Greco, G., 'Accordi amministrativi tra provvedimento e contratto', in F.G. Scoca, F.A. Roversi Monaco & G. Morbidelli (eds.), *Sistema del diritto amministrativo italiano*, Torino: Giappichelli 2004.

Guarino 1992
Guarino, G., 'Pubblico e privato nella economia. La sovranità tra Costituzione ed istituzioni comunitarie', *Quaderni costituzionali*, 1992, p. 2.

Lazarra 2011
Lazarra, P., 'Principio di semplificazione e situazioni giuridico-soggettive', *Diritto amministrativo*, 2011, p. 679-701.

Marinaro 2009
Marinaro, M., 'Il silenzio assenso' in: D. Mastrangelo (ed.), *L'alta velocità nell'amministrazione. Seminari sullla disciplina acceleratoria dell'attività e dei giudizi amministrativi*, Roma: Aracne editrice 2009, p. 103-114.

Mari 2003
Mari, A., 'Le infrastrutture', in: S. Cassese (ed.), *Trattato di diritto amministrativo. Diritto amministrativo generale*, Milano: Giuffré 2003, p. 1861-1927.

Marino 2009
Marino, C., 'On the Relationship between the Political and Managerial Levels in the Italian Public Administration Reform', *Transylvania Revue of Administrative Sciences*, 2009, p. 249-265.

Massa Pinto 2004
Massa Pinto, I., 'Nota in margine alla sentenza n. 303 del 2003 della Corte costituzionale: una "opinione concorrente"', *Il Corriere giuridico. Mensile di attualità, critica, opinione*, 2004, p. 1568-1572.

Mastrangelo 2009
Mastrangelo, D., 'La cultura del procedimento e il suo declino', in: D. Mastrangelo (ed.), *L'alta velocità nell'amministrazione*, Rome: Aracne 2009, p. 9-21.

Mastrodomenico 2009
Mastrodomenico, E., 'Il tempo nell'aettività autoritativa e in quella consensuale della P.A.', in: D. Mastrangelo (ed.), *L'alta velocità nell'amministrazione*, Rome: Aracne 2009, p. 39-55.

Masucci 1993
Masucci, A., *L'atto amministrativo informatico. Primi lineamenti di una ricostruzione*, Napoli: Jovene 1993.

Masucci 2000
Masucci, A., *Il documento amministrativo informatico*, Sant'Arcangelo Romagna: Maggioli 2000.

Mattarella 2010
Mattarella, B.G., 'Administrative Law in Italy: An Historical Sketch', *Rivista trimestrale di diritto pubblico*, 2010, p. 1009-1053.

Meoli 2003
Meoli, C., 'La protezione civile', in: S. Cassese (ed.), *Trattato di diritto amministrativo. Diritto amministrativo generale*, Milano: Giuffré 2003, p. 2145-2183.

Merusi 2004
Merusi, F., 'Il diritto privato della pubblica amministrazione alla luce degli studi di Salvatore Romano', *Diritto amministrativo*, 2004, p. 649-659.

Merusi 2010
Merusi, F, 'Per il ventennale della legge sulprocedimento amministrativo', *Rivista trimestrale di diritto pubblico*, 2010, p. 939-951.

Mezzotero 2009
Mezzotero, A., L'ufficio del commissario delegato ex art. 5 L. n. 225 del 1992: natura giuridica ed ambito dei poteri straordinari riguardo la procedura negoziata senza previa pubblicazione di un bando di gara', *Giurisprudenza di merito. Rivista bimestrale di giurisprudenza dei giudici di merito*, 2009, p. 2242-2272.

Mirate 2011
Mirate, S., 'Termini processuali e ragionevole durata del processo', in: R. Caranta (ed.), *Il nuovo processo amministrativo*, Torino: Zanichelli 2011, p. 865-891.

Pajno 1994
Pajno, A., 'Gli artt. 19 e 20 della l.n. 241 prima e dopo la l. 24 dicembre 1993, n. 537', *Diritto processuale amministrativo*, 1994, p. 22-69.

Parisio, Gambato Spisani & Pagliari 2011
Parisio, V., Gambato Spisani, F. & Pagliari, G., 'I riti speciali', in. R. Caranta (ed.), *Il nuovo processo amministrativo*, Torino: Zanichelli 2011, p. 663-742.

Pizzorusso1992
Pizzorusso, A., 'Garanzia costituzionale dell'azione', *Digesto (discipline privatistiche) sez. civile*, 1992, p. 607-614.

Poto 2007
Poto, M., 'Autorità amministrative indipendenti e partecipazione al procedimento amministrativo', *Responsabilità civile e previdenza*, 2007, p. 1139-1148.

Protto 2002
Protto, M., 'La L. Obiettivo: arriva il General Contractor e dilaga la «super DIA»', *Urbanistica e appalti*, 2002, p. 12-17.

Protto & Bellavista 2011
Protto, M. & Bellavista, M., 'La giurisdizione in generale', in: R. Caranta (ed.), *Il nuovo processo amministrativo*, Torino: Zanichelli 2011, p. 113-172.

Ramajoli 2011
Ramajoli, M., 'Le tipologie delle sentenze del giudice amministrativo', in: R. Caranta (ed.), *Il nuovo processo amministrativo*, Torino: Zanichelli 2011, p. 572-628.

Rega 2011
Rega, F., 'La giurisdizione del giudice ordinario', in: R. Caranta (ed.), *Il nuovo processo amministrativo*, Torino: Zanichelli 2011, p. 56-71.

Salvia 2006
Salvia, F., 'Il diritto amministrativo e l'emergenza derivante da cause e fattori interni all'Amministrazione', in: *Il diritto dell'emergenza, Annuario AIPDA 2005*, Milano: Giuffré 2006, p. 103-137.

Sandulli 2001
Sandulli, M.A., 'Semplificazione e garanzia', in: V. Molaschi & C. Videtta (eds.), *Scritti in onore di E. Casetta*, Naples: Jovene 2001, 585-602.

Sandulli 2003
Sandulli, A., 'Il procedimento', in: S. Cassese (ed.), *Trattato di diritto amministrativo. Diritto amministrativo generale*, Milano: Giuffrè 2003, p. 1035-1341.

Santoro 2015
Santoro, P., *Manuale di contabilità e finanza pubblica*, Rimini: Maggioli 2015.

Satta 2010
Satta, F., 'Contraddittorio e partecipazione nel procedimento amministrativo', *Diritto amministrativo*, 2010, p. 299-311.

Savino 2003
Savino, M., 'Le riforme amministrative', in: S. Cassese (ed.), *Trattato di diritto amministrativo. Diritto amministrativo generale*, Milano: Giuffré 2003, p. 2169-2305.

Scharf 1999
Scharf, F.W., *Governing in Europe. Effective and Democratic*, Oxford: Oxford University Press 1999.

Schneider 2007
Schneider, J-P., 'The Public-Private Law Divide in Germany', in: M. Ruffert (ed.), *The Transformation of Administrative Law in Europe. La mutation du droit administratif en Europe*, München: Sellier 2007, p. 85-99.

Sciullo 2011
Sciullo, G., 'La Conferenza di servizi come meccanismo di decisione', *Giornale di diritto amministrativo*, 2011, p. 1138-1147.

Scoca 2007
Scoca, F.G., 'Il "costo" del processo tra misura di et seq.icienza e ostacolo all'accesso', *Diritto processuale amministrativo*, 2014, p. 1414-1433.

Scognamiglio 2007
Scognamiglio, A., 'La decisione anticipata nel merito del ricorso: il processo amministrativo tra et seq.icienza e garanzia delle parti', *Diritto processuale amministrativo*, 2007, p. 122-155.

Tedeschini & Ferrelli 2010
Tedeschini, F. & Ferrelli, N., *Il Governo dell'emergenza*, Napoli: Jovene 2010.

Trimarchi Banfi 2004
Trimarchi Banfi, F., 'Il diritto privato dell'amministrazione pubblica', *Diritto amministrativo*, 2004, p. 661-689.

Vannucci & Della Porta 2007
Vannucci, A. & Della Porta, D., 'Corruption and Anti-corruption. The political Defeat of Clean Hands in Italy', *Western European Politics*, 2007, p. 830-853.

Verbruggen 2009
Verbruggen, P., 'Does Co-Regulation Strengthen EU Legitimacy?', *European Law Journal*, 2009, p. 425-441.

Vetro 2003
Vetro, F., 'La realizzazione delle infrastrutture e degli insediamenti produttivi strategici e di interesse nazionale', *Le Nuove leggi civili commentate*, 2003, p. 901-1125.

Olivier Dubos

QUALITY AND SPEED IN ADMINISTRATIVE DECISION-MAKING: A FRENCH CASE STUDY

> 'A very extensive machinery was requisite before the government could know everything and manage everything at Paris. The amount of documents filed was enormous, and the slowness with which public business was transacted such that I have been unable to discover any case in which a village obtained permission to raise its church steeple or repair its presbytery in less than a year. Generally speaking, two or three years elapsed before such petitions were granted'.[1]

This excerpt from French historian de Tocqueville reflects that administrative processes are naturally slow. How fast time passes is subjective, especially for those who rely on the administration's proper functioning. It is certainly not easy to determine what exactly constitutes an efficient and diligent administration from a theoretical perspective. Legitimate expectations of the citizens who are subject to an administrative act should obviously be taken into consideration but so should the essential requirements of the administrative action: one must not forget that it is in everybody's interest that the governance of a country runs well.

It is immediately apparent, as Cluzel[2] has shown, that there is an inherent and ambiguous relationship between the need for quality in administrative decision-making and speed in the procedure. Speed is obviously an actual component in the quality of a decision (in terms of receiving a quick decision), but it may also have the opposite effect. While speed can be measured, the quality of an act cannot as it is highly subjective or at the very least rather ambiguous. The term may be used as a superlative - and so we may speak in terms of a 'quality' procedure, which implies 'high quality', just as we may describe a product. It is also possible to speak of 'the qualities' of the procedure, meaning its characteristics. These two aspects are interrelated: if the procedure is of (good) *quality*, it is because it has certain *qualities* (characteristics). Furthermore, through requirements such as the right of defence and consultation procedures, it is possible to note guarantees of the good quality of the act itself.

The way in which the administration is evolving at present probably, at least in appearance, favours the view of those dependent on the administration as

1 De Tocqueville 1856.
2 Cluzel 2006, p. 373 *et seq.*

individuals more than as a community, and therefore it favours speed. It is true that until the 1970s one could have had the impression that the administration worked in the best interests of the State, or even for itself. This evolution is obviously linked to the crisis of the Welfare State, or even of public authorities in general.

This crisis has two aspects. First of all, it has objective origins. In the 1970s, it seemed that France could no longer efficiently ensure the cohesion of political society. The second aspect was primarily an ideological crisis. The State's driving role in building a political society was called into question by the neo-liberalism movement that began in the US.[3] So, this second aspect is a change in values, that is to say the collective belief in the functions and the modalities of State action. The new public management that was derived from neo-liberalism certainly led to a modernization of the ways in which public administration operates, strengthening its efficiency and its speed.

However, as new public management relies mainly on detailed indicators, it is not always the case that it helps improve the quality of administrative acts. Indeed, it is in no way guaranteed that metaphorically thinking of the administration as a company and the citizen as a consumer is in the interests of every actor. In this regard, the 'general review of public policies' (*Révision générale des politiques publiques*, or RGPP), instigated under the presidency of Nicolas Sarkozy and that has been carried on under the status of 'modernization of public action' (*Modernisation de l'Action Publique*, or MAP) essentially aims to make budgetary savings without any real concern for the quality of the administrative action.

The French administration has certainly not escaped the idea that speed contributes to an attempt to improve the quality of the administrative action. The entry into force, on 1 January 2016, of the Code on Relations between the Public and the Administration (*Code des relations entre le public et l'administration*, or CRPA) did not amend the secondary nature of quality and speed in the administrative action, and neither factor (that is, speed or quality) is mentioned under Article L 100-2, which sets out the fundamental principles that are binding on the French administration.[4]

It should also be noted that EU law and international law have had only a limited impact on this development. The quality requirement is present in EU rules regarding services of general economic interest but the requirement concerns the provision of the service and not the act itself.[5]

The speed of the administrative action should be seen within a specific context where the enactment of administrative acts is concerned. One of the main differences between the legislative power and the executive power is that the former is rarely legally bound to act whereas the latter almost always is. Although the legislative power is not a primary power, unlike the constitutionally authorized

3 For an account of this conquest of neo-liberal ideas in the United States, see Krugman 2008.

4 Art. L. 100-2 CRPA: 'The administration acts in the general interest and respects the principle of equality. It is bound by the duty of neutrality and of respect for the principle of secularism. It complies with the principle of equality and guarantees impartial treatment for all'.

5 Directive 2009/72/EC of the European Parliament and of the Council of 13 July 2009 concerning common rules for the internal market in electricity and repealing Directive 2003/54/EC [2009] OJ L 211/55, Art. 3.

bodies, it is free to pass one law or another as long as it upholds the Constitution. The Constitution never imposes a specific action and so the legislative power can always choose not to act. Furthermore, there is no specific legal action that can be taken against the legislature, at least not under French constitutional law, when it fails to act. The legislature is only bound to act when it transposes EU Directives.

The executive power, on the other hand, must take all necessary measures to enforce the law. It may be free in how it acts but it is never free not to act. The only situation in which it is free not to act is for autonomous regulations which do not involve enforcing a law. The question remains as to when the executive power must act. It is in fact never completely free to choose when to do so. When it exercises regulatory power, it is always bound to act within a reasonable time period.[6] Under French law, fixed time limits laid down in the legislative act are not compulsory: these are timeframes set down for guidance purposes, ignorance or unawareness of which does not per se constitute unlawfulness.

Furthermore, through the mechanism of implicit decisions, it is still possible to compel the administration to adopt an act; silence for a certain period of time leads either to a decision to accept or a decision to reject. Thus, as regards unilateral acts, French administrative law has a certain number of processes that ensure that the administration takes action without delay.

Finally, it has to be recalled that, as regards this issue and the theory of unilateral acts in general, French administrative law draws no consequences from the distinction between regulatory acts and individual acts.

This contribution will first examine how speed is part of a French concept of public administration (section 1). The development of administrative acts is traced chronologically, enabling an examination of the extent to which procedural requirements have an impact on both the speed and quality of the procedure, and the way in which the two often contradictory requirements are traded off (section 2). Next there will be an examination of how the passing of time leads to an obligation to enact an administrative act (section 3), and how, with the implicit decision mechanism, the passage of time can give rise to an administrative act (section 4). Lastly, we will gauge the impact of the judicial system on the time taken to adopt a final decision (section 5).

1. Speed and the French Concept of Public Administration

Speed is rarely seen as important in the French administration. In terms of administrative organization, it is only a secondary objective (1.1). Furthermore, from a strictly legal point of view, speed has not been established as a distinctive rule - it is more of a latent requirement (1.2).

6 Section 2.1.

1.1. *A 'Secondary' Objective*

The fact that speed is only a 'secondary' objective of administration action has been shown by Cluzel.[7] The French administration still closely resembles Max Weber's model of administration, as it favours a hierarchical approach and submission to the rule of law. This model is certainly not in itself contrary to the objective of doing things quickly, but as the administration was given new tasks and grew, this model proved to be sluggish. It could be reactive under the liberal State of the 19th century, as it was limited mainly to dealing with public order and used primarily general acts. However, it was a cumbersome factor in the context of the welfare state: the actions of the administration rested increasingly on individual acts and public services. The hierarchy and the explicit or implicit procedures to which it gave rise were such as to slow down the decision-making process. The expansion of the administration's activities and the resulting financial impact also slowed down the decision-making process. At the same time, from the 1950s onwards and even before the advent of the new public management, the rule of law was no longer the only context for administrative action: efficiency became a fully-fledged imperative. The administration therefore had to be more responsive: that was the condition for the success of its involvement in the economic and social spheres.

There was therefore tension between the Weberian model of administration inherited from the 19th century and the expansion of the State's functions in the 20th century. The arrival of the neo-liberal State did not change anything - quite the opposite. Certainly, the administration acts less through the direct provision of services but it is still omnipresent in economic and social fields through regulation. The notion of regulation certainly goes against the hierarchical Weberian model, as is shown by the development of independent administrative authorities in France.[8] However, compared with other administrative systems, the agency phenomenon is rather limited. Nonetheless, it is not just the traditional bureaucratic model that has made speed a secondary objective. In such a structure, speed is not in opposition to the idea of the quality of the administrative decision-making process, but it is obviously not a primary concern.

There are many factors that slow things down. The more contemporary objectives of democratization and transparency, which have been developing in France since the 1970s, are not fully compatible with swift administrative action.

Firstly, reasons did not previously have to be stated for all administrative acts but since Law 79-587 of 11 July 1979 (the 1979 Law),[9] the administration must state its reasons at least for unfavourable individual acts.[10] Having to give reasons increases the timeframe to make an administrative decision. Law 78-753 of 17 July 1978 (the 1978 Law),[11] often referred to as 'the freedom of access to administrative documents' law also added on time. The right of access to administrative documents is, as established under Article 1 of the 1978 Law, open to any individual

7 Cluzel 2006, p. 374.
8 Section 1.2.
9 Loi n° 79-587 du 11 juillet 1979.
10 Section 2.1.
11 Loi n° 78-753 du 17 juillet 1978.

or legal entity, irrespective of the person's nationality. Applicants do not have to specify the reasons for their request or prove that they have the right to act, nor are they required to prove that the document requested concerns him. However, the development of technology has made it easier to electronically access administrative documents without overloading the administration.

Citizen involvement also adds to the time taken to make decisions because of the imposition of new procedural requirements. First of all, several organizations must be consulted in order to take into consideration all relevant interests. In this respect it is significant that an order was made on 1 July 2004 to simplify how administrative commissions were appointed and operated as well as to reduce the number of commissions. Indeed, it was a matter of limiting the role of consultative administration and rationalizing its operation. Then the Decree of 28 November 1983 (now repealed)[12] and the Law of 12 April 2000 (the 2000 Law)[13] on citizens' rights in their dealings with the administration made it mandatory for the party involved to be heard before an individual decision was taken, for which reasons must be stated in accordance with the 1979 Law.

Lastly, 'participative democracy', the consultation of citizens before making a decision, also slows things down. This right to participation was introduced in France by Law 83-630 of 12 July 1983 (the 1983 Law)[14] on the democratization of public inquiries. Since the constitutional review of 2005, the consultation requirement is enshrined in the Charter for the Environment, which is part of the French Constitution.[15] EU law and the Aarhus Convention[16] have also strengthened the right to participation. All projects to which Article L. 123-2 of the Environmental Code (*Code de l'environnement*) refers are subject to public consultation.[17] It is

12 Décret n° 83-1025 du 28 novembre 1983.

13 Loi n° 2000-321 du 12 avril 2000.

14 Loi n° 83-630 du 27 juillet 1983.

15 Const., Art. 7: 'Everyone has the right, in the conditions and to the extent provided for by law, to have access to information pertaining to the environment in the possession of public bodies and to participate in the public decision-taking process likely to affect the environment'.

16 Convention on Access to Information, Public Participation in Decision-Making and Access to Justice in Environmental Matters, 2161 UNTS 447; 38 ILM 517 (1999).

17 Art. L. 123-2 C. env.:
'I. — Are the subject of a public inquiry which is submitted to the requirements of this prior chapter of their authorization, approval or adoption:
1° Projects of works or improvements made by public and private persons that must include an impact study under Art. L.122-1 except:
— projects for the creation of a development zone;
— temporary or low-importance projects of which a list is established by a decree of the *Conseil d'Etat*;
2° Plans, schemes, programmes and other planning documents subject to an environmental evaluation under Art. L.122-4 to L. 122-11 of the present Code or Articles L.121-10 to L.121-15 of the Urban Planning Code, for which a public inquiry is required under current legislation.
3° Projects for the creation of a national park, and a marine park, projects for a national park or for a regional natural park, registration process, ranking of the sights and of the wildlife parks and defining their scope of protection mentioned in Book III of the present code.
→

obligatory for environmental decisions and is often used, particularly by local authorities, as a way of making decisions legitimate.[18] In spite of these many factors, the French administration does not disregard the importance of speed but considers it to be a rather latent requirement.

1.2. *A Latent Requirement*

Speed seems to be first and foremost an organizational requirement: speeding up the time taken by the administration is not unusual for certain 'amendments to the administrative architecture'.[19] Task forces were developed in the 1960s, and one of the main reasons was to improve responsiveness. This is shown by Pisani's definition in 1966:

> 'The task force is adapted to a problem, a time and a place. It is localised and it is specific (...). It requires programmes developed over several years, a command and budget unit. It is simple, it has a taste for delegating, it is realistic, moving, it goes towards the event, it is involved in life, it does not wait for an initiative, it solicits'.[20]

These task forces, probably modelled on the DATAR (inter-ministerial delegation for territorial development) broke away from Weber's model of administration, but corresponded to an interventionist State. This quest for efficiency in administrative action therefore took the shape of independent administrative authorities or regulation agencies. They were developed either indirectly or directly under the influence of the EU, not with the aim of making administrative action quicker,[21] but to contribute to it. These independent administrative authorities or regulation agencies are rather simplified structures which are in no way subject to the

4° The other documents of town planning and the decision regarding the works, development, plans, schemes and programmes submitted by the particular disposals that are applicable to them in a public survey under the conditions of the present chapter.
II. — Where a project, a plan or a programme that is mentioned under paragraph I is subject to administrative authorisation, this authorisation can only come from an explicit decision.
III. — The works carried out to prevent a serious and imminent danger are excluded from the scope of this chapter.
Also, in order to take into consideration the needs of national defence, work, construction of military facilities and installations defined by the conditions laid down by decree.
IV. — The decision made at the conclusion of a public inquiry held as per the conditions under the present chapter is not unlawful owing to the fact that it ought to have been held as per the conditions defined by the Expropriation Code'.

18 We can see that locally it is used informally as local authorities hardly ever use the option to hold a referendum offered by the French Local Government Code (Art. LO 1112-1 *et seq.* CGCT).

19 Chevallier 2000, p. 489 *et seq.*

20 Pisani 1956, p. 315 *et seq.*

21 The main objective of creating regulation agencies is indeed to ensure the neutrality of the state when it intervenes in the market in the case where there still is an operator through national companies, e.g. energy or telecommunication. When the state is no longer an operator in the market, it does not have the legal obligation regarding the EU to create such regulation agencies. It can be a regulator without taking the risk of being in a conflict of interest. For example, see Directive 2009/72/EC.

hierarchical weight of a ministry that often extends the decision-making process and makes it longer.

Lastly, it may be considered that devolution, like decentralization, helps speed up administrative action because it is 'closer to the people'. Devolution allows prefects (*préfets*), who represent central government throughout the French Republic, to take a leading role in administrative action. This avoids the decision 'going up' to Paris and being made by the ministries. Since the Decree of 15 January 1997,[22] prefects now have authority for 'all individual administrative decisions falling within the jurisdiction of civil State administrations'. This principle of subsidiarity in the administrative action of the State is certainly one factor of acceleration in the decision-making process.[23]

It should also be taken into consideration that decentralization allows local authorities to be granted powers that once belonged to the State. Article 72 of the Constitution contains a paragraph that was introduced by the constitutional review of 28 March 2003 and which states that 'local authorities should make decisions for all the powers that can best be exercised at their level'.[24] Although the wording of this provision is not very satisfactory as it seems to grant powers and, at the same time, determine which out of the State and local authorities will exert this power, it introduced the principle of subsidiarity into the French Constitution. In theory, proximity in this case makes it possible to speed up the administrative action, but there is scepticism as to whether it works in practice. Local authorities often lack resources, especially the *communes*, while the larger ones may have problems with excessive bureaucracy. Speed is a requirement in the administration's action, and not just in administrative organization. However, speed is still mainly a rhetorical requirement.

Firstly, speeding up decision-making is often an idea emanating from central authorities. Thus, a Circular dated 26 July 1995 on the preparation and implementation of the reform of the French State and public services (the 1995 Circular), considered 'speed' as one of the new principles that the French administration should adopt, together with traditional principles of neutrality, equality and continuity.[25] Since then, the objective of doing things quickly has hardly been mentioned in any of the debate surrounding the reform of the State or as part of the general review of public policies. However, the 1995 Circular led to the Marianne Charter (*charte Marianne*), followed by the Marianne Standard (*référentiel Marianne*), which contained 19 commitments on the attitude of public services in the way they treat the public. It is a seal of approval that is awarded after external assessment. Four out of the 19 commitments relate to making administrative action quicker:

> '10 - We will deal with your letter within a maximum of 15 working days.
> 11 - We will deal with your emails within a maximum of 5 working days.
> 12 - We will answer your telephone calls in less than five rings and deal with them there and then.

22 Décret n° 97-34 du 15 janvier 1997.

23 Le Roux 2012, p. 9, 18.

24 Const., Art. 72.

25 Circulaire du 26 juillet 1995, JORF n° 174 du 28 juillet 1995, p. 11217.

13 - We will reply within 15 working days to all your suggestions and claims on the upholding of our commitments.'[26]

These are obviously ethical and managerial commitments but are not binding legal rules. Furthermore, French law does not have a provision that is similar to Article 41 of the CFR (which requires the administration to act within a reasonable time limit).

Indeed, speed features under French law as an aspect of the quality of administrative action: but this observation cannot be generalized. In social services for example, personalized guidance is required, and the digitalization of proceedings, a factor in speeding up the decision-making process undermines the quality of the service.

2. Formal and Procedural Requirements: Quality versus Speed?

A number of formal or procedural requirements such as the obligation to state reasons (2.1) or the obligation to consult and the right of defence (2.2) slow down the decision-making process. Others such as the single authorization mechanism tend to speed it up (2.3). It cannot be ignored that urgency or, more generally, circumstances ease the administration's formal and procedural obligations (2.4).

2.1. *The Obligation to State Reasons*

As stated above, under French law there is no obligation in theory to state reasons for administrative acts. However, since the 1979 Law obliging the administration to give reasons for administrative acts,[27] a fairly large number of individual administrative acts have become subject to this requirement. These provisions are now codified under Article L 211-2 of the *Code des relations entre le public et l'administration*:

'Natural or legal persons have the right to be informed without delay of the reasons for unfavourable individual administrative decisions that concern them. To this end, reasons must be stated for decisions that:

1. Restrict the exercise of civil liberties or, generally, constitute a police measure;
2. Impose a penalty;
3. Render the granting of an authorization subject to restrictive conditions or impose constraints;
4. Withdraw or abrogate a decision establishing rights;
5. Impose a time period, foreclosure or deprivation;
6. Refuse an advantage, the award of which constitutes a right for those persons who meet the legal conditions for securing the same;
7. Refuse authorization, except where the disclosure of said reasons could be of such a nature as to breach confidentiality or an interest protected under the provisions of sub-paragraphs a to f of Article L. 311-5, paragraph 2;

26 <www.modernisation.gouv.fr/sites/default/files/fichiers-attaches/referentiel_marianne_vf_juin_2013.pdf>.

27 Loi n° 79-587 du 11 juillet 1979.

> 8. Reject an administrative appeal, the presentation of which is compulsory prior to any judicial appeal pursuant to a legislative or regulatory provision'.

Article L 211-3 states, moreover, that 'reasons must also be stated for individual administrative acts which deviate from the general rules set down by law or regulations'. Regulatory acts are therefore exempted from the obligation to state reasons. As regards implicit decisions, Article L 232-4, paragraph 2 states:

> 'At the request of the interested party, made within the timeframe of the judicial appeal, the reasons for any implicit decision to reject [an application or request] shall be disclosed to said party within one month following said request. In such cases, the timeframe of the judicial appeal against said decision shall be extended until a period of two months has elapsed following the date on which said reasons shall have been disclosed to said party'.

Owing to uncertainties as to the scope of the obligation to state reasons, circulars have been issued in order to draw up the list of decisions to which it applies.[28]

The obligation to state reasons is first and foremost useful to the administration itself in that it serves as a kind of 'self-review'. Next, it allows the court to have full knowledge of the reasons for the act. Lastly, as regards private individuals, it reflects both an administrative democracy and a transparency requirement. From a judicial perspective, 'knowledge of the reasons for a decision allows the interested parties to assess properly whether there are grounds for them to bring an objection or a judicial appeal'.[29] Consequently, the obligation to state reasons, whilst preventing pointless judicial proceedings, also appears to be an essential factor in access to justice. It is thus a mark of the quality of an administrative act; however, in adding to the administration's workload, it runs the risk of slowing down the issuing of administrative acts. Furthermore, the French administrative courts do not simply review the existence of the reasons for an act, but also their very quality; they sanction the inadequacy of the reasons stated, especially where these are standardized.

2.2. *Procedural Obligations*

Procedural obligations improve the quality of the decision itself because it is compulsory for authors of administrative acts to hear the intended addressee (right of defence), to consult a commission or, more generally, the wider public. French law allows the administrative authorities, beyond procedural requirements, to decide freely to proceed with a consultation except where this would infringe the impartiality principle.[30] Legislation may provide for such optional consultations. For example, Article L 1112-15 of the Local Government Code (*Code général des collectivités territoriales*, or CGCT) provides:

28 Circulaire du 28 septembre 1987, JORF n° 0243 du 20 octobre 1987.
29 Chapus 2001, n° 1318.
30 CE 19 mai 1993, *Waendendries*, *Rec.* p. 158.

'Voters in each territorial community may be consulted on the decisions that the authorities in said community plan to take in order to settle matters that fall within the remit of the latter. The consultation may be limited to voters in one section of the community, for those matters specifically concerning that section of the community'.

Under Article L 121-1 of the *Code des relations entre le public et l'administration*:

'With the exception of those cases where a decision is made on an application, individual decisions for which reasons must be stated pursuant to Article L. 211-2, together with those decisions which, while not mentioned under the terms of this Article, affect individuals, are subject to compliance with a preliminary adversarial procedure'.

There are therefore many acts subject to compliance with the right of defence.

Consultation is also another widespread procedural requirement under French administrative law: administrative authorities must, prior to issuing an act, consult a body whose opinion is not binding.[31] The vast majority of consultative bodies are collegial, but there may also be single authorities. The composition and the method employed for appointing such collegial bodies can vary. They may be bodies composed of civil servants, public service users or experts. Members are most often appointed, but may be elected, particularly in the administration of national education or social security.[32] These consultative bodies may therefore be a form of representative administrative democracy. In order to ensure that their involvement does not excessively extend the duration of administrative procedures, they may be bound to decide within a limited timeframe. For example, Article R 133-14 of the *Code des relations entre le public et l'administration provides*:

'Where an administrative commission, whatever its denomination, must compulsorily be consulted on a draft law or regulatory decree or ministerial order, its opinion is deemed to have been given in the absence of an express opinion issued by the same within a period of five weeks from the date on which the referral is made to said commission'.

With a view to reducing the role played by these commissions, Law 2011-525 of 17 May 2011 (the 2011 Law)[33] on simplifying and improving the law made provision for them to be replaced with consultations open to all via the internet. The objective of the 2011 Law was not, however, to speed up the decision-making process.

French law is cognisant of the trend towards smart regulation and participatory administrative democracy. Article L 132-1 of the *Code des relations entre le public et l'administration*, for example, provides:

'Where the administration is bound to proceed with the consultation of a consultative commission prior to issuing a regulatory act, it may decide to hold an open consultation serving to gather, via a website, comments from the persons concerned. This open consultation shall be substituted for a mandatory consultation pursuant to a

31 Where assent procedures are concerned, it is a question of competence: the body which hands down the opinion is then deemed to be the co-author of the act.

32 Le Clainche 2011, p. 39.

33 Loi n° 2011-525 du 17 mai 2011.

> legislative or regulatory provision. The consultative commissions whose opinion must be gathered pursuant to a legislative or regulatory provision may provide their comments in the context of the consultation provided under the present Article. All consultations of independent administrative authorities provided by law and regulations, assent procedures, and those concerning the exercise of a civil liberty, the guarantee of a constitutional requirement, reflecting an authority to make proposals or implementing the participatory principle, shall remain mandatory'.

Under Articles R 132-8 and R 132-10 of the same Code, the State and its public administrative establishments may also resort to such consultations where they adopt a regulatory act. The time factor is taken into consideration only to ensure that the general public has 'a reasonable timeframe in which to participate'.[34] Public participation therefore prevails over the speed of the decision.

Another more limited and more established way of involving the general public takes the form of a public inquiry. There are three separate schemes governing public inquiries: public inquiries governed by the Expropriation Code (*Code de l'expropriation*); public inquiries governed by the Environmental Code; and public inquiries governed by the CRPA.

Public enquiries governed by the Expropriation Code are not only those public inquiries that are conducted prior to the last act of the expropriation procedure (*a déclaration d'utilité publique*) provided under Article L 110-1 of the Expropriation Code, but also where a law provides for the applicability of the Expropriation Code as a public utility code.[35] Article R 11-4 of the Expropriation Code provides for a minimum timeframe of 15 days for the duration of the public inquiry but does not, however, make any provision as to a maximum duration.

Public inquiries provided by the Environmental Code[36] relate in particular to projects within the scope of Directive 2001/42/EC.[37] The deadline for the public inquiry is set at 30 days and may be extended by 30 days by the officer in charge of the inquiry.[38]

Public inquiries governed by the CRPA are those inquiries that are not governed by the two previous codes.[39] These are, for example, public inquiries relative to changes to the territorial boundaries of municipalities provided under Article L 2112-2 of the Local Government Code, or relative to the transfer of private roads open to traffic in the communal public domain provided under Article L 318-3 of the Urban Planning Code (*Code de l'urbanisme*). Article R 134-10 of the CRPA

34 Art. L. 131-1 CRPA: 'Where the administration decides, aside from those cases governed by legislative or regulatory provisions, to involve the general public in the conception of a reform of the drafting of a bill or an act, it shall make public the modalities of said procedure, make available to the persons concerned all useful information, provide a reasonable timeframe within which to participate and ensure that the results or outcomes envisaged are made public at an appropriate time'.

35 For example, inquiries under Art. L. 322-6 C. urb. on re-parcelling.

36 Art. L. 122-4 C. env.

37 Directive 2001/42/EC of the European Parliament and of the Council of 27 June 2001 on the assessment of the effects of certain plans and programmes on the environment [2001] OJ L 197/30.

38 Art. L. 123-9 C. env.

39 Art. L. 134-1 CRPA.

provides that the duration of the inquiry must be 15 days as a minimum and makes no provision for a maximum duration. However, Article R 134-27 of the CRPA provides that the investigating commissioner (*commissaire enquêteur*) has a maximum of one month in which to draft the report.

Lastly, it should be noted that ignorance of procedural obligations does not automatically entail the annulment of an act. Article 70 of the 2011 Law simplifying and improving the quality of the law provides:

> 'Where the administrative authority, prior to making a decision, proceeds with the consultation of an organisation, only those irregularities likely to have had some influence on the decision made in light of the opinion given may, where applicable, be raised against the decision'.

For its part, the Council of State (*Conseil d'Etat*) considered:

> 'These provisions state, as regards irregularities arising over the course of the consultation of an organisation, a rule inspired by the principle according to which, while administrative acts must be adopted in the forms and in accordance with the procedures provided by law and regulations, an irregularity or flaw affecting the conduct of a preliminary administrative procedure, be it on a mandatory or optional basis, shall only render unlawful the decision made where it emerges from the file that it was likely to have, in that instance, an influence on the decision taken or that it deprived the interested parties of a guarantee'.

There are certain procedural flaws which deprive the addressee of the act of a constitutional guarantee, such as respect for the right of defence; any failure or flaw automatically results in the annulment of the act even where it would have no influence on the content of the act. However, as regards other procedural obligations, it falls to the courts to conduct an examination *in concreto* of any flaw or defect in the consultation process.

2.3. *The Single Authorization Mechanism*

In environmental law or urban planning law, some projects are subject to a combination of authorization schemes. In order to simplify the various administrative procedures to which businesses are subject, the French legislature instituted a single authorization mechanism that applies to establishments classified for environmental protection and facilities that have an impact on water quality.[40] Under Article L 511-1 of the Environmental Code, the following are considered as establishments classified for environmental protection:

> 'Factories, workshops, depots, work sites and, in general, to all facilities operated or owned by any public or private person or entity, which might present hazards or drawbacks for the convenience of the neighbourhood, or for public health and safety,

40 This provision was initially put in place on an experimental basis in 2014 in a number of French regions, then generalized by Law n. 2015-990 of 6 August 2015 for growth, activity and equality of economic opportunity and Law n. 2015-992 of 17 August 2015 on energy transition for green growth (Loi n° 2015-990 du 6 août 2015; Loi n° 2015-992 du 17 août 2015).

> or for agriculture, or for the protection of nature and the environment, or for the conservation of sites and monuments or elements of the archaeological heritage'.

The second category of facility designates, under Article L 214-1 of the same Code:

> 'Installations not appearing in the nomenclature of classified facilities, structures, works and activities carried out for non-domestic purposes by any person or body, public or private, and resulting in the drawing of surface or underground water, whether returned or not, or in a change in the level or method of flow of water or discharges, the destruction of spawning grounds, zones for the growth or feeding of pisciculture fauna, runoff, direct or indirect discharges or deposits, chronic or periodic, even if these are not pollutants'.

The applicant must thus submit a single application to the administration in a dossier which includes various authorization schemes. It is thus possible to secure simultaneously, in addition to authorization for the facility itself, a clearing permit, a derogation to the ban on harming protected species and habitats, planning permission and, in relation to the construction of wind turbines, the permit provided under the Energy Code (*Code de l'énergie*). According to Planchet, this offers a number of benefits:

> '[it] simplifies the procedures incumbent on the project manager, who benefits from a 'one-stop-shop' and has only one contact point, being the department prefect, the competent authority. The administration may have an overall view of the operation and grasp all of its economic and environmental aspects. The inquiry is fast-tracked as the various departments concerned review the application simultaneously, the aim being to make inquiries in under 10 months. The process is secure. Its conduct is no longer subject to a multitude of successive agreements but depends on the final authorisation. The implementation decrees have bolstered these advantages by preventing the repeated submission of materials, by providing for a preliminary examination stage, which may result in a refusal with written reasons before the investigation stage, instituting a strict calculation of the timeframes for the inquiry inspired by that applicable to planning applications, or even leaving the task of establishing the procedures for organising State services for handling applications to the prefect'.[41]

2.4. *Exceptional Circumstances and Urgency*

Procedural obligations may be attenuated or even set aside in the event of exceptional circumstances or urgency. Exceptional circumstances correspond to a period of unrest such as a natural disaster, insurrection, a general strike or terrorist attacks. In such a scenario, the administrative authorities are no longer bound to observe formal and procedural obligations incumbent upon them under normal circumstances.[42]

Emergencies apply outside periods of unrest, and may result either in the waiver of procedural and formal obligations - including the right of defence[43] - or

41 Planchet 2015, p. 2193.

42 CE 3 mai 1946, *Dame veuve Goguet*, *Rec.*, p. 126.

43 Art. L. 121-2 CRPA.

reduce the timeframes usually granted to consultative bodies to issue an opinion.[44] As regards stating reasons, Article L 211-6 of the CRPA provides:

> 'Where absolute emergency has prevented the statement of reasons for a decision, the lack of reasons does not render said decision unlawful. However, should the interested party make an application for the same, within the timeframe of a judicial appeal, the authority that made the decision shall disclose the reasons for said decision within one month'.

3. The Passing of Time and the Obligation to Enact an Administrative Act

Even though the administration mostly acts as a result of compliance with a higher rule, it is rarely obliged to act within a set time period (3.2), and must in principle only act within a reasonable time period (3.1).

3.1. The Obligation to Act Within a Reasonable Time Period

The administration's obligation to act within a reasonable time period is mainly important in enacting regulations. Indeed, as regards individual administrative acts, the implicit decision mechanism allows citizens to ensure that an administrative act is enacted. The most pertinent case is that of implementing decrees[45] for laws.

According to the *Conseil d'Etat's* case law 'exercising regulatory power involves not only the right but also the obligation to take measures that are necessary to enforce the law within a reasonable time period'.[46] It is a constitutional obligation. Thus, if the regulatory authority refuses to take measures to enforce the law after this reasonable time period, an action may be brought before an administrative court to declare the refusal unlawful;[47] the court may issue an injunction against the regulatory authority with a penalty payment, ordering it to enact the implementing decree.[48] Above all, this failure to act is considered to constitute negligence for which the administration could be held liable.[49] This obligation to act within a reasonable time period requires, in the case of a new law, the adoption of various regulatory texts.[50]

The situation is exactly the same in cases where the legislature itself sets the time periods during which the government must pass the implementing decrees for laws. Case law in fact considers that such deadlines are not obligatory but rather

44 Art. L. 133-14 CRPA regarding consultations prior to the issuing of a regulatory decree or ministerial order.
45 The term decree (*décret*) refers, in French law, to regulatory acts issued by the Prime Minister or the President for the direct purposes of implementing laws. Other regulatory acts issued by other administrative authorities, e.g. ministries, prefects or local authorities, are referred to as orders (*arrêtés*).
46 CE 28 juillet 2000, *Association France Nature Environnement, Recueil Lebon*, p. 590.
47 CE 13 juillet 1962, *Kevers-Pascalis, Recueil Lebon*, p. 475.
48 CE 26 juillet 1996, *Association Lyonnaise des locataires, Recueil Lebon*, p. 293.
49 CE 27 novembre 1964, *Ministre des Finances* c/ *Dame veuve Renard, Recueil Lebon*, p. 590.
50 CE 28 juin 2002, *M. Villemain*, p. 586.

serve as a guideline. Thus the decree passed after the deadline is not considered to be unlawful.[51] According to Sellier,

> 'This ignorance of the legislative time limit is paradoxically justified by the concern for guaranteeing that the intentions of the legislature are respected. To consider that once the scheduled deadline has passed the implementing decree for a law can no longer legally be enacted would allow the government to paralyse the intentions of the legislature as, without an implementing decree, the law itself will not be enforced'.[52]

This paradoxical situation derives from the way in which French administrative law is structured, and more specifically from how the courts control the administration through actions to declare an administrative act unlawful but which cannot directly compel the administration to issue an act. The only way to do that is to use the implicit decision mechanism.

Thus, regardless of whether the law stipulates the time periods for passing implementing decrees, the obligation only arises after a reasonable time period has passed, the length of which is in fact determined by the administrative courts.[53] The standard reasonable time period to enact implementing decrees is about a year.[54] In order to allow a longer time period, the *Conseil d'Etat* takes into account circumstances such as a change in government or even the extent of the legislative reform.[55]

3.2. *The Obligation to Act Within a Set Time Period*

The administration is only obliged to act within a set time period in specific situations. Firstly, there are very important deadlines for the drafting of an act. It is not therefore the enactment of the act itself that is restricted by a deadline, but the formalities required for the enactment. Therefore, it is about combining the speed of the enactment with the quality of the administrative act resulting from those formalities. Thus, a consultative body may have a certain deadline within which to issue an opinion.[56] When it is provided that the people shall participate in the administrative decision-making process, deadlines are also very important and are set down in the laws or in the specific rules that govern the relevant area.[57] For individual acts, the party involved must also be allowed enough time to reply so as to ensure that their right of defence is respected. This deadline may be set by the law itself or left to the discretion of the administration, but should be sufficient for the party concerned to have time to prepare their response.[58]

Secondly, there are situations where the enactment of an act itself must take place within a set time. This is especially the case where a deadline is provided by

51 CE 7 avril 1933, *Caisse régionale de crédit agricole du Sud-Est, Recueil Lebon*, p. 437.
52 Seiller 2013, n° 178.
53 CE 13 juillet 1962, *Kevers-Pascalis*, p. 475.
54 De Barolet 1997, p. 909.
55 Seiller 2013, n° 182.
56 Section 2.2.
57 Section 2.2.
58 Frier 2014.

law. For example, for orders under Article 38 of the Constitution, the government can only act within the time period set by the enabling law. By comparison, when the administration exercises its pre-emption right, it is restricted to a two-month deadline under Article L 213-2 of the Urban Planning Code. After that, the pre-emption right is lost.[59] Equally, Article L 121-2 of the Expropriation Code provides that 'the act declaring public utility or the decision to refuse to declare the same shall be issued at the latest one year following the conclusion of the preliminary inquiry'. It is a matter of making a decision depending on the circumstances identified during the investigation, which may very well change over time. The obligation to act may also be immediate, as in the fight against pollution. Under Article L 223-1 of the Environmental Code,

> '[w]hen the alert thresholds are reached or are likely to be reached, the prefect immediately informs the public in accordance with the terms and conditions set out in Section 2 of Chapter 1 of the present Title and takes measures to limit the scale and the effects of peak pollution levels on the population'.

The obligation to issue an administrative act within a set time period may also arise from a court decision. When a claim is brought against an act before the administrative courts, the court may declare a refusal to carry out an act to be unlawful. To ensure that its decision is effective, the court can compel the administration to make a new decision within a set timeframe.[60] This injunction can include a penalty payment.[61] Finally, in order to ensure that court monetary orders are enforced, Article L 911-9 of the Administrative Justice Code provides that

> 'When the State has been ordered to pay a certain sum of money in a decision that has the authority of a final court judgment, which determines the amount of that sum, the said sum must be processed for payment within a period of two months as from the date on which notice is given of the court's decision [...] If the payment is not processed within the time limits mentioned in the foregoing paragraphs, the accounting officer to whom the expense has been allocated must make the payment, at the creditor's request and upon presentation of the court decision.'

Today the French administrative courts use the penalty payment without hesitation.

4. The Passing of Time and the Implicit Enactment of an Administrative Act

On this issue, French law has undergone a number of changes, particularly so in recent years (4.1). The implicit decision mechanism has therefore been amended (4.2).

59 CE 13 mai 1996, *Commune de Franconville-la-Garenne*, p. 178.
60 Art. L. 911-1 and 911-2 C. just. adm.
61 Art. L. 911-3 C. just. adm.

4.1. *Developments in French Law*

The implicit decision is typical of the structure of French administrative law, which takes an objective view of the principle of legality. An administrative act can only be challenged before an administrative court by an action to declare the act unlawful. For the action to be admissible, an administrative act must have been made previously. Thus, if the administration fails to act, the citizen is totally helpless and a victim of a miscarriage of justice insofar as there is no action for failure to act in the French legal system. The implicit decision mechanism serves to compel the administration to take a position so that the matter may be brought before the administrative courts. This may result in an individual act or a regulation. Since the Decree of 2 November 1864,[62] there is the principle whereby silence on the part of the administration for over four months is deemed to correspond to an implicit decision of rejection. This principle, however, originally only applied to situations where a ministry had to decide on an appeal against a decision issued by a subordinate authority. The Law of 17 July 1900 has generalized this principle.[63]

After the Second World War, in order to make administrative action more efficient, the implicit decision of acceptance was developed.[64] It has since evolved quite anarchically[65] as it seems to be a way of making the administration more productive and therefore shortening the time taken to make a decision. The Law of 12 April 2000 (the 2000 Law)[66] on the rights of citizens and their relationship with the administration, however, has made the process more organized. Article 21 of the same law maintains the principle whereby silence is deemed to be a rejection; however, it reduces the deadline to make a decision from four to two months. The law also states that it is possible, by decree and having consulted the *Conseil d'Etat*, to set up systems of implicit decisions of acceptance; these are also created within two months from the application.[67] In giving the government alone this power (by means of a decree) and by involving the *Conseil d'Etat*, the legislature intended to prevent the proliferation of implicit decisions of acceptance.

The quest for efficiency in public action led the legislature to overturning a century-old principle, under which silence on the part of the administration would be equivalent to a rejection. Law 2013-1005 empowering the Government to simplify the relations between the administration and the citizens established the principle whereby silence on the part of the administration for a period of two months is deemed equivalent to a decision of acceptance.[68] This outcome is now codified under Article L 321-1 of the CRPA. In reality, however, this change is misleading.

62 Décret imperial du 2 novembre 1864.
63 Loi du 13 juillet 1900.
64 This technique already existed in the 19th century, see Cluzel 2006, p. 380.
65 In 2000, more than 400 cases of implicit decisions of acceptance were recorded, see Amoudry 1998-1999, p. 150.
66 Loi n° 2000-321 du 12 avril 2000.
67 *Ibid.*, Art. 22.
68 Loi n° 2013-1005 du 12 novembre 2013.

While Article L 321-1 sets down the new principle, that 'silence kept for two months on the part of the administration on an application is equivalent to a decision of acceptance', Article D 321-1 of the same law nevertheless stipulates:

> 'The list of procedures for which silence on an application is equivalent to a decision of acceptance is published on a website falling within the remit of the Prime Minister. It mentions the authority to which applications must be addressed, together with the timeframe at the end of which acceptance is secured'.

This, therefore, means that the principle is not applicable *a priori* to a procedure unless the latter is expressly mentioned in the list provided under Article D 321-1, however, the list is provided for information purposes only. It is therefore not genuinely a 'principle'. On the other hand, the 'exceptions' to this principle are expressed in broad terms. Under Article L 231-4:

> 'By derogation to Article L 231-1, silence on the part of the administration is equivalent to a decision of rejection:
> 1. Where the application does not relate to the adoption of a decision presenting the character of an individual decision;
> 2. Where the application is not part of a procedure provided by law or regulations or presents the character of a claim or administrative appeal;
> 3. If the application presents a financial character except, in social security matters, in the cases provided by decree;
> 4. In those cases, stipulated by decree of the *Conseil d'Etat*, where implicit acceptance would not be compatible with compliance of France international and European commitments, the protection of national security, the protection of freedoms and constitutional principles, and the safeguarding of public order;
> 5. In relations between the administration and its officials'.

Article L 213-5 adds that 'having regard to the purpose of certain decisions or on grounds of proper administration, the application of Article L 231-1 may be precluded by a decree of the *Conseil d'Etat* and of the Council of Ministers'. We can therefore see that the scope of this pseudo-exception, unlike that of the principle itself, is not set out restrictively. While the changes made to the rule of law are not obvious, the fact remains that French law broadly recognizes the mechanism of implicit decisions of acceptance. This is shown by the length of the list provided under Article D 321-1.[69] For its part, the mechanism of implicit decision of rejection retains considerable importance in all relevant fields and in compelling the administration to issue a regulatory act. If the administration is obliged to enact a regulation, a citizen may force the administration to act. This may arise from a legal text, as we have seen with implementing decrees for laws, or a factual situation. For instance, in order to maintain public order, which is the duty of administrative authorities, it is possible to penalize the administrative authority for its failure to act.[70]

69 Application de l'article 21 de la loi n° 2000-321 du 12 avril 2000, <www.legifrance.gouv.fr/Droit-francais/Silence-vaut-accord-SVA>.

70 CE 14 décembre 1959, *Doublet*, p. 540.

4.2. *The Implicit Decisions Scheme*

The mechanism of implicit decisions of acceptance is not without its dangers. These dangers arise not so much from the fact that silence may lead to an administrative decision as from the nature and more precisely the effects of a decision made when the administration fails to act. Indeed, whereas implicit rejections rarely create a right, the same cannot be said for implicit decisions of acceptance. This difference is taken into account in the various aspects of the scheme applicable to implicit decisions.

As regards their formation, the *Code des relations entre l'administration entre et le public* protects the addressees of a decision, providing under Article L 114-2 that 'where an application is addressed to an administration that does not have competence, the latter will transmit the application to the competent authority and advise the interested party of the same'. However, Article L 114-3 makes the distinction between implicit decisions of rejection and implicit decisions of acceptance:

> 'The timeframe at the end of which an implicit decision of rejection is likely to arise runs from the date on which the application was received by the administration to which said application was initially made. The timeframe at the end of which an implicit decision of acceptance is likely to arise only runs from the date on which the application was received by the competent administration'.

Similarly, if the application does not contain all of the required supporting documents, for implicit decisions of acceptance, Article L 114-5, paragraph 2 provides that 'the timeframe mentioned under Article L 114-3, at the end of which, in the absence of an express decision, the application is deemed to be accepted only runs from the date on which the required supporting documents and information are received'. As regards implicit decisions of rejection, the timeframe is simply suspended:

> 'The timeframe mentioned under the same Article, at the end of which, in the absence of an express decision, the application is deemed to be rejected is suspended during the time period granted to produce the requisite supporting documents and information. However, the production of said supporting documents and information prior to the expiry of the set time period brings said suspension to an end.'[71]

Third-party rights are also taken into consideration in the rules on the enforcement of implicit decisions. If an implicit decision is not published, how can third parties become aware of it and how can it be enforced on them? This point is very important since it allows third parties to enforce their right to judicial protection. The time period in which an action against an administrative act must be brought only runs from the moment on which the decision is published. Article L 232-2 of the CRPA provides:

71 Art. L. 114-5 CRPA.

> 'In the event that the requested decision may be acquired implicitly and must be subject to a publicity requirement with regard to third parties where said decision is express, the application is published by the administration, electronically where applicable, indicating the date on which it will be deemed accepted if no express decision is issued'.

In addition, as regards urban planning applications, Article R 424-15 of the Urban Planning Code requires the beneficiary to display an excerpt from the permission on the work site. This publicity serves to guarantee third-party rights and the rights of beneficiaries. Third parties are thus informed of the act and may challenge it. For beneficiaries, publicity is also a guarantee because the time period to bring court action begins from the date on which the act was adequately publicized. If implicit decisions are not publicized, they can be challenged without there being a deadline for third parties. The implicit decision thus becomes a trap for those for whom it has been made.

5. Judicial Proceedings Against Administrative Acts: Quality v. Speed?

The preliminary administrative appeals (5.1) and judicial proceedings (5.2) provided under French law are likely either to slow down or accelerate the decision-making process. While the key quality of an administrative act is its lawfulness, speed obviously remains a factor in the quality of the decision-making process. Lastly, it should be noted that, particularly in the urban planning sphere, French law contains a number of derogations intended to provide a framework for access to justice, thus preventing challenges from being brought all too easily against administrative decisions adopted in that sphere (5.3).

5.1. *Preliminary Administrative Appeals*

Preliminary administrative appeals have an ambivalent relationship with time: they suspend the time limits for bringing a judicial action and therefore extend the time period during which the administrative act is not considered final. At the same time, however, by preventing litigation, they avoid the uncertainties linked to the definitive character of the act during proceedings before the court.

Under French administrative law, administrative appeals are not compulsory in principle, but there are many scenarios in which administrative appeals must be brought to the attention of the administrative courts. For example, it is considered possible to apply for an interim suspension order (*référé suspension*) even before the administration has responded to the preliminary administrative appeal;[72] the urgency of the situation prevails over the mandatory nature of the preliminary administrative appeal.

Mandatory appeals exist in various areas of administrative action, and especially regarding taxation matters.[73] Administrative appeals may take various

72 CE Sect. 12 octobre 2001, *Société des produits Roche, Rec.*, p. 463.

73 Truchet 2014.

forms: they may be an informal appeal, an appeal to a higher administrative authority, or a supervisory application. The French administration only rarely appoints a commission specifically tasked with hearing administrative appeals; there is such a commission for disputes concerning the personal situation of military personnel.[74]

5.2. *Judicial Proceedings*

As explained by Backes and Jansen,[75] the organization and nature of the various remedies against administrative acts have an impact on the process for adopting administrative acts and the speed of the decision-making process. The French model for the judicial review of administrative acts - based on actions for annulment on grounds of *ultra vires* which result in the annulment of administrative acts found to be unlawful - leads to the administration being compelled to instigate a new procedure without there being any guarantee as to the adoption of a lawful act. French administrative proceedings have evolved over the last 20 years, becoming more efficient in providing justice for individuals and not simply subjecting the administration to the law.

Urgent proceedings were reformed, particularly by Law 2000-597 of 30 June 2000 on urgent applications before administrative courts,[76] which established the *référé-suspension*. Under Article L 521-1 of the Administrative Justice Code:

> 'When an application is made to have an administrative decision, including a rejection, set aside or revised, the urgent applications judge to whom the case has been referred may order the decision, or some of its effects, to be suspended or executed when the urgent nature of the case justifies such a course of action, and when a submission has been made that is sufficient to create a serious doubt regarding the legality of the decision, at the current stage of the proceedings'.

Such proceedings are likely to have an impact on the adoption procedure for administrative acts: indeed, it could be imagined that, faced with a suspensory injunction, the administration could withdraw the act and, where possible, adopt another lawful one rather than wait for a consideration of the merits of the case. There are currently no statistics that would serve to verify the truth of such a hypothesis. In the environmental sphere, specific provision is made under Article L 122-12 of the Environmental Code for a special injunction which is also of such a nature as to push the administration to adopt the act lawfully without waiting for the administrative court decision on the merits of the case. The Article provides:

> 'Where an application made before the administrative court against a decision to approve a plan, diagram, programme or other planning document covered by Article L 122-4,paragraphs I and II, is based on the lack of any environmental assessment, the urgent applications judge, hearing an application to suspend the contested decision,

74 Décret n° 2001-407 du 7 mai 2001.
75 Cf. in this book, chapter on the Netherlands.
76 Loi n° 2000-597 du 30 juin 2000.

shall grant said application as soon as the lack of assessment has been noted by the court'.

Unlike the suspensory injunction provided under Article L 521-1 of the Administrative Justice Code, there can be no doubt as to the unlawful nature of the act; the only rational position left to the administration is to resume the procedure for adopting the act without waiting for any decision on the merits of the case.

Ordinary proceedings have also undergone significant developments over the last 20 years, and these are likely to have an influence on the speed of administrative procedures. Law 95-125 of 8 February 1995[77] on the organization of the courts and civil, criminal and administrative procedure conferred on the administrative courts a power of injunction serving to ensure the effectiveness of the annulment decisions that they hand down. In those scenarios where the administration has non-discretionary powers, Article L 911-1 of the Administrative Justice Code provides:

> 'When a court decision necessarily requires a legal entity governed by public law or an entity governed by private law charged with the management of a public service to adopt an enforcement measure for a specific purpose, the said court, having heard submissions to this effect, will order the said measure, in the same decision, and, where appropriate, will specify a time limit within which the decision must be enforced.'

Where the administration has discretionary power to implement the annulment decision, Article L 911-2 provides:

> 'When a court decision necessarily requires a legal entity governed by public law or an entity governed by private law charged with the management of a public service to take a decision again, after receiving a fresh instruction, the said court, having heard submissions to this effect, will order, in the same decision, that the new decision must come into effect within a specific time limit'.

This provision is all the more effective in that the court can supplement it with a periodic penalty payment.[78] This power of injunction serves to prevent the administration from indefinitely adopting unlawful decisions. It improves not only the speed of the decision-making process, but also the quality of the decision.

In addition, actions for annulment on grounds of *ultra vires* have in recent years lost ground against full remedy proceedings i.e. actions aimed at securing a judicial decision that will replace the void administrative decision. Traditionally, full remedy proceedings have been used for acts that have a pecuniary impact, such as the administration's fiscal decisions, decisions concerning pensions, or decisions on social welfare. In environmental matters, litigation concerning facilities classified for environmental protection provides a full review under the Law of 19 December 1917 (as amended)[79] on dangerous, unhealthy or uncomfortable establishments. Insofar as the administration's power to impose penalties has expanded in recent years, the relevant litigation has gradually become a full review owing to

77 Loi n° 95-125 du 8 février 1995.
78 Art. L. 911-3 C. just. adm.
79 Loi du 19 décembre 1917.

developments in both the applicable law and the case law. Above all, the *Conseil d'Etat* considered in a leading case that appeals against penalties imposed on a citizen are full remedy proceedings.[80] This solution does not apply to penalties imposed on the administration's officials[81] or on its users.[82]

5.3. *The Specifics of the Scheme Applicable to Urban Planning*

Article L 600-1 *et seq.* of the Urban Planning Code make various specific provisions for urban planning litigation: these seek to prevent and provide a framework for frivolous or abusive litigation that results in slowing down the decision-making process and access to justice. The specifics of urban planning litigation began to develop in the 1990s, but have witnessed a marked acceleration since 2013.[83]

Firstly, a more restrictive approach is taken towards the concept of *locus standi*. The objective nature of actions for annulment on grounds of *ultra vires* rests in particular on a broad conception of the interest in bringing proceedings, where it is simply a matter of proving, as Maurice Hauriou put it, the existence of a 'rumpled' interest and not the infringement of a subjective right. The Urban Planning Code contains a series of provisions aimed at deterring applicants from bringing an action. Article L 600-1-1 provides that associations have no legal standing unless their articles of association were filed prior to the publication of the decision. This prevents the creation of an association the sole purpose of which is to challenge an urban development project. In addition, legal standing is assessed not from the date the appeal is filed, but rather the date on which the act is published. Thus a person who, in full knowledge of the facts, comes to live in an area close to a forthcoming development, the characteristics of which said person could have assessed though the details displayed at the town hall, cannot bring proceedings.[84] Furthermore, under Article L 600-1-2, a private individual or an association:

> 'has no standing to bring an appeal for annulment on grounds of *ultra vires* against a building, demolition or development permit unless the building, development or works are of such a nature as to directly affect the conditions of occupation or use of the asset owned or regularly occupied or for which they hold a sale agreement, a promise to lease or a preliminary contract mentioned under Article 261-15 of the Construction and Housing Code (*Code de la construction et de l'habitation*).'

In a complementary way, the Code also deters litigants from bringing frivolous or abusive proceedings. Where a claim goes beyond the defence of the applicant's legitimate interests, the beneficiary of the act may apply to the court for damages and interest.[85] If the applicant withdraws from the proceedings in exchange for the payment of a sum of money, they are subject to certain fiscal obligations.[86]

80 CE Ass. 16 février 2009, *Société Atom*, n° 274000.
81 CE Ass. 13 novembre 2013, *Dahan*, n° 347704.
82 CE 20 mai 2011, *Letona Biteri*, n° 326084.
83 In particular, Ordonnance n° 2013-638 du 18 juillet 2013 on urban planning litigation.
84 Art. L. 600-1-3 C. urb.
85 Art. L. 600-7 C. urb.
86 Art. L. 600-8 C. urb.

Furthermore, where usually there is no time limit on the plea of unlawfulness of a regulatory act, it is only possible to raise a similar plea within a period of six months, for instance in respect of a proposed urban development project, where a formal or procedural flaw is at issue.[87]

Secondly, the powers held by the court hearing such administrative cases have been strengthened in order to prevent scenarios in which the date for the adoption of the act is put back indefinitely. Its role is similar to that of the court hearing the full remedies proceedings. Under Article L 600-4-1:

> 'Where it annuls or orders the suspension of an act relating to urban development, the administrative court rules on all grounds of the application that it deems likely to form the basis of the annulment or suspension, on the case file as it stands'.

Moreover, where the court finds that a flaw may be rectified, it will invite the administration to do so within a specific time period.[88]

It would thus seem that French administrative law has developed fairly efficient ways of dealing with the requests made by the people. Apart from these situations, it has not developed legal techniques that can force the administration to act within a specific time period. It would appear, however, that recent years have seen the development of certain measures, particularly in urban planning law and environmental law, which aim to prevent administrative or judicial delay. Significant improvements remain to be made, and it would appear that French administrative law combines a slow administrative culture inherited from the roots of the *Ancien-Régime* and a sophisticated interpretation of the typical procedures of neoliberal bureaucracy.

87 Art. L. 600-1 C. urb.

88 Art. L. 600-5, Art. L. 600-5-1 and Art. L. 600-9 C. urb.

BIBLIOGRAPHY

Amoudry 1998-1999
Amoudry, J., *Rapport fait au nom de la commission des lois constitutionnelles, de législation, du suffrage universel, du Règlement et d'administration générale sur le projet de loi relatif aux droits des citoyens dans leurs relations avec les administrations*, Sénat, n° 248, Paris 1998-1999.

Chapus 2001
Chapus, R., *Droit administratif général*, Paris: Montchrestien 2001.

Chevallier 2000
Chevallier, J., 'L'accélération de l'action administrative', in: D. Gerard, F. Ost & M. van de Kerchove, (eds.), *L'accélération des temps juridiques*, Brussels: Publications des facultés universitaires de Saint-Louis de Bruxelles 2000, p. 489-508.

Cluzel 2006
Cluzel, L., *Le service public et l'exigence de qualité*, Paris: Dalloz 2006.

De Barolet 1997
De Barolet, F.J.L, 'CE, 3 octobre 1997', *Actualité Juridique Droit Administratif*, 1997, p. 909-911.

De Tocqueville 1856
De Tocqueville, A., *The Old Regime and the Revolution*, New York: Harper & Brothers 1856.

Frier 2014
Frier, P.L., 'Vice de procédure', in: D. de Béchillon (ed.), *Répertoire de contentieux administratif*, Paris: Dalloz 2014, Section 2, Art. 1, paras. 88-92.

Krugman 2008
Krugman, P., *L'Amerique que nous voulons*, Paris: Flammarion 2008.

Le Clainche 2011
Le Clainche, M., 'L'administration consultative, élément constitutif ou substitut de la démocratie participative', *Revue française d'administration publique*, 2011, p. 39-48.

Le Roux 2012
Le Roux, M., 'Fasc. 116: Administrations déconcentrées', in: *JurisClasseur Administratif*, 2012, para. 18.

Pisani 1956
Pisani, E., 'Administration de gestion, administration de mission', *Revue Française de Science Politique*, 1956, p. 315-330.

Planchet 2015
Planchet, P., 'Quand les droits de l'urbanisme et de l'environnement font cause commune', *Actualité Juridique Droit Administratif*, 2015, p. 2193-2199.

Seiller 2013
Seiller, B., *Droit administratif*, Paris: Flammarion 2013.

Truchet 2014
Truchet, D., 'Recours administratifs', in: D. de Béchillon (ed.), *Répertoire de contentieux administratif*, Paris: Dalloz 2014, section 3, art. 1, para. 102.

Victoria Jenkins

PLANNING FOR MAJOR INFRASTRUCTURE IN ENGLAND: FRONT-LOADING PARTICIPATION IN THE INTERESTS OF EFFICIENCY

1. Introduction

Planning for major infrastructure is considered essential to economic growth, particularly in meeting energy demands that drives this. In a time of economic crisis, as long as wealth creation remains the conventional orthodox, a fast and efficient process for national infrastructure will be a key priority.[1] Local environmental interests and community concerns are clearly vulnerable to the expediencies of the growth imperative; but planning law provides an important means of addressing the conflicts between the need for national infrastructure and the representation of local considerations. Land use planning is quintessentially a political process which restricts the rights of property owners to develop land in the public interest. Traditionally, the planning system derives its democratic mandate from the fact that decision-makers are elected members of government.[2] In line with its common law tradition, the UK adopts a discretionary system that places significant power in the hands of these decision makers, albeit subject to a process of review by the courts.[3] More recently, however, there has been increasing attention to participatory rights in planning;[4] but together, the discretionary nature of the planning system and opportunities for participation may be seen to counter efficiency aims. A problem that is seen nowhere more acutely than in the context of planning for major infrastructure.

This contribution will consider how these challenges have been met, in England, by the introduction of a new system for the planning of nationally significant infrastructure under the Planning Act 2008.[5] Under this regime, National

1 This conventional economic wisdom has been challenged among others by Jackson in his recent report. See further Jackson 2011.

2 Lord Slynn in *R (On the Application of Holding & Barnes Plc and Others)* v. *Secretary of State for the Environment, Transport and the Regions* [2002] Env. L.R. 12, para. 69.

3 Booth 2003, p. 31-43.

4 Skeffington 1969. In 1980 McAuslan considered public participation to be a central challenge to the dominant public perspective in planning: McAuslan 1980.

5 Planning is a devolved function in the devolved regions of the UK. The Scottish Parliament has primary law making powers in any area which is not specifically excluded (Scotland Act

→

Planning Policy Statements (NPPSs) are followed unless the adverse impacts of the proposed development on the local community would outweigh its benefits. The procedure allows participation on NPPSs and requires the developer to enter into a pre-application process of consultation. 'Front-loading' opportunities for participation in planning was intended to provide a means to avoid objections at a later stage and enable applications to be determined more quickly.[6] However, there has been a trade-off in the form of a reduction of participatory rights in the decision-making process on the final application. Thus, the familiar public inquiry, which has been the essential means of considering conflicting views on development in England, has been replaced by an 'examination in public' which is more narrowly focused. Furthermore, significant barriers exist to bringing a judicial review claim.

The contribution begins by considering the significance of participation in ensuring the representation of both local communities and environmental concerns. It then discusses the rationale behind the new regime before providing a detailed outline of procedures. The next section considers the experience of public participants in the process in more detail with particular reference, by way of example, to the application to build a new nuclear plant at Hinkley Point in Somerset. The contribution subsequently analyses the barriers to challenging such decisions through the courts. It concludes by considering the ways in which 'front loading' participation has impacted on the representation of local community and environmental interests and efficiency aims.

2. Planning for Major Infrastructure: Representing Community and Environmental Interests

The advent of public participation in planning decisions takes place within a wider framework of participative approaches in government decision-making which challenge traditional notions of representative democracy in the UK.[7] Participation is considered important to revitalize civil society and democracy, but also in improving the quality of government decision-making.[8] In the planning of large infrastructure projects, participation is essential in tackling the conflict between national interests in development and concerns about the negative impacts on local communities. The focus on local community concerns in democratic decision-

1998). Planning in Scotland is wholly a matter for the Scottish Government and is governed by the Town and Country Planning Act (Scotland) 1997 and the Planning etc. (Scotland) Act 2006. The National Assembly for Wales was originally given only secondary legislative powers in a defined area (Government of Wales Act 1998), but the Government of Wales Act 2006 paved the way for a referendum on primary legislative powers for the Assembly which returned a positive vote in 2011. The Assembly has a 'referred powers' model at present, although it is proposed to create a model more akin to Scotland in the current draft Wales Bill. Some projects of national significance in Wales still come within the remit of the Planning Act 2008. Significant changes were made to the local planning system under the Planning (Wales) Act 2015, but changes to the powers of the National Assembly over energy projects are also proposed in the Wales Bill. See further Williams & Jenkins 2016.

6 Office of the Deputy Prime Minister 2008

7 Oliver 2003.

8 Oliver 2003.

making may be applauded, but will not necessarily ensure the assertion of environmental interests. Indeed, the social imperatives of local communities can be at odds with concerns for environmental sustainability. Conversely, community participation may have a role in educating local people about environmental issues and actually encourage greater environmental citizenship. Thus, participation in environmental decision-making is considered to be important in eliciting values about environmental interests; contributing to problem solving in this context; and promoting environmental citizenship.[9] It can also provide a useful tool for promoting acceptance of new development, particularly where this involves technological change. This is particularly important to the planning of national significant infrastructure given that many of the proposed projects are renewable energy developments essential to national strategies for climate change.[10] Nevertheless, there is a tension between the urgency of action on climate change and the principle of public participation.[11]

Planning provides an important tool for asserting environmental interests:

> 'There are few examples of an environmental problem which lack a spatial dimension or have no connection with land use. Sometimes the linkages are all too apparent, as in the siting of nuclear installations, incinerators or even wind turbines. Often the connection needs the trained eye of a practitioner such as the design of urban forms which minimise reliance upon private motor cars [...]'.[12]

However, environmental sustainability will always need to be balanced with economic and social considerations. Thus, the creation of land use planning frameworks with the participation of local communities is considered to be key in supporting sustainable development now and for future generations.[13]

Planning decisions take place within a statutory framework for the protection of environmental interests by government organizations,[14] but also provide for representation of environmental concerns by non-governmental organizations and interested members of the community.

There are several important issues with respect to participation in any decision-making process. Who should participate? When should they be given the opportunity to do so? What methods should be used to ensure that participation is effective? And how can we ensure access to justice for those parties who are nevertheless aggrieved by the decision? There is no room here to consider the vast literature on participation;[15] thus the objective is only to identify some of the problems that emerge for individuals and groups attempting to represent local community and environmental interests in national infrastructure planning in

9 Lee & Abbot 2003, p. 80.
10 Lee *et al.* 2013, p. 33.
11 *Ibid.*
12 Miller 2001, p. 2.
13 Stallworthy 2002.
14 In England, these are Natural England which is responsible for nature conservation and the Environment Agency which deals with pollution control.
15 For a useful overview see Lee & Abbot 2003, p. 80. Particular attention is now given to the notion of deliberative democracy in this context – see, for example, in general, Fishkin 2009; and in the environmental context Steele 2001, p. 415.

England. It is also necessary to assess whether, in the environmental context, the new regime is compliant with the provisions of the Aarhus Convention (the Convention) and its elucidation in the Directives on Strategic Environmental Assessment (SEA) and Environmental Impact Assessment (EIA).[16] These now provide the framework for ensuring that decision-makers consider the likely significant environmental effects of development; and that relevant statutory bodies as well as the wider public are given the opportunity to comment.[17] The Convention provides for participation of the 'public' in environmental decision-making, but in many respects it provides good practice for any process of consultation. It is therefore also a useful reference point for evaluating the effectiveness of participatory rights for the assertion of local community interests in the planning of national infrastructure.

The Convention defines 'the public' as 'one or more natural or legal persons, and, in accordance with national legislation or practice, their associations, organizations or groups'; whilst the 'the public concerned' means 'the public affected or likely to be affected by, or having an interest in, the environmental decision-making'.[18] Thus, the Convention specifically recognizes the role of non-governmental organizations in promoting environmental protection. The Convention states that: 'Each Party shall provide for early public participation, when all options are open and effective public participation can take place'.[19]

This is logically important to any process of consultation in decision-making.[20] However, practicalities dictate that local people often only get involved in the process at the later stages when they recognize the possible negative impacts of a proposal for development on their personal or community interests. The 'public' are subsequently accused of acting in their own self-interest; often described as NIMBYISM (Not in my Backyard), meaning not wanting development in their local area, but not caring where the development otherwise takes place.[21] However, it may also be argued that it is simply the case that the benefits of participation must

16 Convention on Access to Information, Public Participation in Decision-Making and Access to Justice in Environmental Matters, 2161 UNTS 447; 38 ILM 517 (1999); Directive 2001/42/EC of the European Parliament and of the Council of 27 June 2001 on the assessment of the effects of certain plans and programmes on the environment [2001] OJ L 197/30; Council Directive 85/337/EEC of 27 June 1985 on the assessment of the effects of certain public and private projects on the environment [1985] OJ L 175/40. This was amended to comply with the Aarhus Convention by Directive 2003/35/EC of the European Parliament and of the Council of 26 May 2003 providing for public participation in respect of the drawing up of certain plans and programmes relating to the environment and amending with regard to public participation and access to justice Council Directives 85/337/EEC and 96/61/EC - Statement by the Commission [2003] OJ L 156/17.

17 Directive 85/337/EEC, Arts. 6 and 10.

18 Convention on Access to Information, Public Participation in Decision-Making and Access to Justice in Environmental Matters, 2161 UNTS 447; 38 ILM 517 (1999), Art. 2. On the significance of the role of environmental groups see further Lee & Abbot 2003, p. 80.

19 Convention on Access to Information, Public Participation in Decision-Making and Access to Justice in Environmental Matters, 2161 UNTS 447; 38 ILM 517 (1999), Art. 6(4).

20 Office of the Deputy Prime Minister 2008, p. 87-103.

21 Rydin 2011, p. 87 *et seq.*

outweigh the disadvantages for individuals before it is 'worth their while' becoming involved.[22]

The Convention is silent about the methods of participation which are left to the discretion of signatory states. Finally, the Convention provides that it should be possible to challenge a development decision on the grounds of 'substantive' and 'procedural' legality, and that 'the process should provide adequate and effective remedies ... and be fair, equitable, timely and not prohibitively expensive'.[23] There is no third party right of appeal in the planning system in England, and there are significant barriers to a judicial review claim; not least the restrictive nature of review and the costs of bringing an action. These are therefore particular concerns with regard to compliance with the Convention which will be discussed further in the context of decision-making on major infrastructure projects. The Convention clearly only operates within the context of environmental decision-making, but it has given renewed vigour to campaigners interested more generally in issues relating to access to justice.[24]

3. The Background to the Planning Act 2008

Planning in England is to a large extent a local function; with local government taking decisions in its capacity as the Local Planning Authority (LPA).[25] In the local planning process there is a presumption in favour of the locally agreed development plan 'unless material considerations indicate otherwise'.[26] This gives the LPA wide discretion in making planning decisions, but to ensure a balance of national and local concerns, national planning policy forms a 'material consideration' in all development decisions.[27]

Since the *Skeffington* report first considered the issue of direct participation in planning decisions in 1969, the public have gained rights to take part in the development plan process, to make representations on individual decisions and to attend planning meetings.[28] At present, however, they have no right to be heard at a

22 Rydin 2011, p. 87 *et seq*.

23 Convention on Access to Information, Public Participation in Decision-Making and Access to Justice in Environmental Matters, 2161 UNTS 447; 38 ILM 517 (1999), Art. 9, which has been implemented in an EU context by Art. 10a of Directive 2014/52/EU of the European Parliament and of the Council of 16 April 2014 amending Directive 2011/92/EU on the assessment of the effects of certain public and private projects on the environment Text with EEA relevance [2014] OJ L 124/1.

24 See recommendation of Lord Jackson report (Jackson 2009) that the conclusion of his report regarding the costs of judicial review should apply to all cases not just those related to environmental decision-making.

25 'An essential element of the character of a community is that it is defined by place, and there is a legitimate community interest in the control of land use. Development control is therefore for the most part justifiably a local function': Stallworthy 2002, p. 105.

26 Section 70(2) Town and Country Planning Act 1990; Section 38(6) Planning and Compulsory Purchase Act 2004.

27 'The National Planning Policy Framework', DCLG, 2012, available at: <www.gov.uk/government/publications/national-planning-policy-framework--2>.

28 These rights are derived from the Town and Country Planning Regulations (Local Development) (England) Regulations 2004 No. 2204, the Town and Country Planning (Development →

planning meeting although in the majority of cases objectors are allowed to speak by convention for three minutes.[29]

The Secretary of State (SS) retains a number of key powers in relation to development planning and decision-making;[30] which includes a power to 'call in' a planning application for his decision as he sees fit.[31] This power is usually exercised where a project is of 'more than local importance' by reason, *inter alia*, that it could have significant effects beyond the locality or give rise to substantial regional or national controversy.[32] Where an application is 'called-in' by the SS, a public inquiry is also held.

The inadequacies of this procedure in dealing with major infrastructure projects led to the introduction, on an *ad hoc* basis, of several pieces of separate legislation on different types of infrastructure, meaning, gas, electricity and highways.[33] Some attempt was made to take a more comprehensive approach in the creation of the Transport and Works Act 1992, but the position remained unsatisfactory.[34] These different pieces of legislation adopted varying approaches to decision-making, but were united in making provision for a public inquiry.[35] The public inquiry has thus emerged, historically, as the central vehicle for public participation in decision-making on larger and more controversial development in England.

Public inquiries are held by an Inspector on behalf of the SS to 'collect and collate information or to serve as a vehicle for the resolution of conflicts'- or both.[36] The use of inquiries in the planning system as a means of conflict resolution allows interested individuals to air their grievances and present evidence for their arguments. They are not, however, designed to provide a means of challenging government policy as outlined in the leading case of *Bushell*:

Management Procedure) Order 2010/2184, and the Local Government (Access to Information) Act 1985.

29 Manns 2002, p. 39-51.

30 For example, to modify part of a development plan or call it in for his decision (Section 21 Planning and Compulsory Purchase Act 2004); to hear appeals from the developer (Section 78 Town and Country Planning Act 1990); and, ultimately, to revoke or modify a planning permission (Sections 97 and 107 Town and Country Planning Act 1990).

31 Section 77 Town and Country Planning Act 1990.

32 The other considerations are that the development conflicts with national policy on important matters; raises significant architectural or urban design issues; or may involve the interests of national security or of foreign governments. This policy was outlined in answer to a parliamentary question, in 1999, as discussed in Moore & Purdue 2012.

33 The Gas Act 1965, Highways Act 1980 and Electricity Act 1989.

34 Transport and Works Act 1992.

35 Section 9 Transport and Works Act 1992 provided for a parliamentary procedure in limited cases and s11 provided for the use of a public inquiry. The Gas Act 1965 provided for the authorization of gas storage and the provisions on public inquiries were found in Schedule 2 para. 8. Sections 36-37 The Electricity Act 1989 provided for consent for electricity generating stations of more than 50 MW and overhead power lines and the provisions on public inquiries were found in Schedule 8. The Highways Act 1980 provided for the construction of new highways and the provisions on public inquiries were found in Schedule 1.

36 Wade & Forsyth 2009, p. 938 *et seq*. Ultimately, the final decisions will be taken by, or on behalf of, the SS according to national policy. Most planning inquiries operate under statutory rules but they are also subject to the common law rules of natural justice with respect to a duty to act fairly and without bias.

> 'Policy as descriptive of departmental decisions to pursue a course of conduct is a protean word and much confusion in the instant case has, in my view, been caused by a failure to define the sense in which it can properly be used to describe a topic which is unsuitable to be the subject of an investigation as to its merits at an inquiry at which only persons with local interests affected by the scheme are entitled to be represented.'[37]

However, there are often 'grey areas' between matters of policy and more local considerations that may be a valid subject of the inquiry.[38] The significance of such 'grey areas' was highlighted more recently in the case of *Hillingdon*. Lord Justice Carnwarth stated that *Bushell* should be viewed on its facts, and should not be 'read as laying down any general rule that government "policy" is automatically outside the scope of debate at a local planning inquiry [...]'.[39]

The public inquiry became much maligned by successive governments concerned about the cost and delays involved. The extent of this problem was highlighted by the oft quoted example of the fifth terminal at Heathrow which took nearly 5 years to complete and cost in the order of £70 million.[40] The cause was usually considered to be the procedure at the inquiry, the adversarial nature of which, coupled with a lack of focus on planning issues, resulted in unnecessarily protracted hearings. However, it has also been acknowledged that another key cause of delay was not the inquiry itself but the time taken between the end of the public inquiry and the decision by the Minister.[41]

On coming to power in 1997, the Labour Government took the view that:

> 'Processing major projects through the planning system has become increasingly difficult. Current procedures do not adequately address the tension between the natural justice argument that the views of all concerned should be fully aired at an inquiry, and the argument that such an all-embracing process is slow and costly and damages the economy'.[42]

The Planning and Compulsory Purchase Act 2004 subsequently defined a 'major' project for the first time as a project of national or regional importance and strengthened the powers of the SS in relation to them.[43] A series of new procedural rules were also introduced to increase efficiency at public inquiries. These included the introduction of pre-inquiry meetings and timetables; rules on the appointment of technical advisers and mediators; and a requirement for participants to register their interest in the inquiry.[44] Most importantly, cross-examination at planning

37 *Bushell* v. *SS for the Environment* [1981] A.C. 75 Lord Reid; Wade & Forsyth 2009, p. 936.
38 Wade & Forsyth 2009.
39 *R (Hillingdon LBC)* v. *Secretary of State for Transport* [2010] EWHC 626.
40 Booth 2003. Other inquiries lasting several months include the development of Stansted Airport, the Sizewell B Nuclear Power Station and Hinkley Point C Nuclear Power Station. See further O'Riordan *et al.* 1988.
41 Barker 2006, p. 76.
42 'Modernising Planning: Streamlining the Processing of Major Projects through the Planning System (consultation paper)', *Journal of Planning Law*, 1999, Jul., B120-B135.
43 Section Planning and Compulsory Purchase Act 2004.
44 Town and Country Planning (Major Infrastructure Planning Inquiries Procedure) (England) Rules 2002/1223. Some further minor amendments to the inquiry rules for major →

inquiries was curtailed in the interests of efficiency. Planning inquiries adopted the traditional adversarial approach that applies in court proceedings in the UK. Each party was entitled to legal representation to present their evidence and to cross-examine that of the opposition. However, under the new rules only the applicant, LPA and 'major participants' were allowed to cross-examine evidence. The Inspector could also refuse to hear evidence or permit cross-examination that was irrelevant or repetitious; or if it appeared that the latter would jeopardize the timetable.[45]

The new arrangements were to be monitored over a five-year period, but even as the final set of new regulations were passed, a further critical review of the planning system was commissioned by the Government. The aim of the Barker Review was to consider the role of the planning system in economic development.[46] It concluded that a new independent commission should be created to take decisions on national infrastructure within a clear framework of national policy.[47] The subsequent White Paper identified the key challenges for the planning of major infrastructure as:

- Meeting the Challenge of Climate Change
- Supporting Sustainable Economic Development
- Increasing the Supply of Housing
- Protecting the Enhancing the Environment and Natural Resources.
- Improving Local and National Infrastructure.
- Maintaining the Security of Energy Supply.[48]

The White Paper proposed a new framework for decision-making on national infrastructure in line with the recommendations of the Barker Review.[49] The subsequent legislation in the form of the Planning Act 2008 came into force only shortly before its architects were superseded by the Coalition Government in the UK.[50] The Coalition Government subsequently introduced a number of amendments to the original regime for the planning of national infrastructure. The most significant was the transfer of power under the regime from an independent body to the SS.[51] The

development were also introduced. In addition to the above, these made provision for holding inquiries in concurrent sessions; introduced measures to improve pre-inquiry meeting and inquiry timetables; and, gave 'major participants' a right to appear at the inquiry but introduced a requirement that they provide pre-inquiry statements including identification of areas of common ground. Town and Country Planning (Major Infrastructure Planning Inquiries Procedure) (England) Rules 2005/2115.

45 Town and Country Planning (Major Infrastructure Planning Inquiries Procedure) (England) Rules 2005/2115.

46 Barker 2006, p. 76.

47 The report was published alongside the equally significant conclusions of the Stern Review on the economic impacts of Climate Change; Stern 2006.

48 HMG, Planning for a Sustainable Future. White Paper Cm 7120, 2007.

49 *Ibid.*, p. 20-21.

50 The Coalition Government entered into power in the UK, in May 2010, following over a decade of rule by a Labour Government in the UK. The Coalition was between the Conservatives who had the most votes in Parliament and the Liberal Democrats.

51 Localism Act 2011.

Growth and Infrastructure Act 2013 also included powers to allow the SS to direct that certain business or commercial development projects, in England, may be treated as nationally significant infrastructure and subject to decision-making by him/her rather than the Local Planning Authority.[52] This created an important change in the nature of the system of infrastructure planning in England which had previously focused on energy and transport projects. However, the implications of this provision are reduced by the requirement for a direction from the SS in response to a request by the developer on an individual development proposal.[53] Following a rethink on wind energy policy, the current Conservative Government is now in the process of removing wind energy projects from the regime and returning them to LPA control.[54]

4. The Planning Act 2008: An Outline

The Planning Act 2008 created a new form of authorization for nationally significant infrastructure projects (NSIPs) in the fields of energy, transport, water, waste water and NSIPs waste.[55] These are defined by detailed thresholds, e.g., with respect to the generating capacity of energy developments.[56] The new authorization is referred to as a Development Consent Order (DCO) as it includes not just planning permission for the project but associated development consents.[57] This is important in streamlining the process of development but falls short of providing a one-stop shop for planning and environmental permissions. It is for the applicant to decide whether to include something that could be considered as associated development in an application for development consent or whether to apply for consent for it via other

52 Section 26 Growth and Infrastructure Act 2013. The types of project were set out in The Infrastructure Planning (Business or Commercial Projects) Regulations 2013 (SI 3221). They are:
1. Office use.
2. Research and development of products or processes.
3. An industrial process or processes.
4. Storage or distribution of goods.
5. Conferences.
6. Exhibitions.
7. Sport.
8. Leisure.
9. Tourism.
And the winning and working of minerals. The first such project was brought within the regime on 9 May 2014 and involved a mixed-use development including a theme park on the north Kent coast: Walker 2014.

53 *Ibid.*

54 The determination of onshore wind farm applications over 50 MW has been removed from the jurisdiction of the SS under Section 36 Electricity Act 1989 (which carries with it deemed planning permission) and from the nationally significant infrastructure development consent regime under the Planning Act 2008; The Onshore Wind Generating Stations (Exemption) (England and Wales) Order 2016 (S.I. 2016/21) ('the Exemption Order'); The Infrastructure Planning (Onshore Wind Generating Stations) Order 2016 No. 306.

55 Section 15 Planning Act 2008.

56 Sections 14-30 Planning Act 2008.

57 Section 31 Planning Act 2008.

routes.[58] The SS decides on a case-by-case basis whether or not development should be treated as associated development.[59] However, a DCO can only remove the requirement to obtain certain consents if the relevant consenting body agrees, such as Natural England (the nature conservation agency for England) or the Environment Agency.[60] The Government is proposing to streamline the process further by withdrawing the need for this consent in relation to ten different types of non-planning consent. Despite overall support for the proposal, concerns have been raised about the potential adverse impact on the quality of decision-making and inconsistency.[61] A suggestion that the need for prior approval of statutory agencies in all cases should be removed, was rejected by the Government, nor do they propose to streamline consents with the environmental permitting regime.

The regime created a new framework of NPPSs which govern decision-making.[62] The SS has a general duty to ensure that the NPPSs contribute to the sustainable development and they are also subject to sustainability appraisal.[63] The NPPSs can identify the amount, size or type of development that is appropriate nationally - and even suitable locations.[64] To ensure they have a democratic mandate, the NPPSs must be formally passed by Parliament.[65] However, there is

58 'Planning Act 2008: Guidance on associated development applications for major infrastructure projects', DCLG, 2013, para 8, <www.gov.uk/government/uploads/system/uploads/attachment_data/file/192681/Planning_Act_2008_-_Guidance_on_associated_development_applications_for_major_infrastructure_projects.pdf>. Examples of associated development specific to on-shore generating stations would include: off-site fuel storage; overhead/underground lines; substations; and waste storage facilities.

59 *Ibid.*, para. 5.

60 Planning Act 2008. The relevant list of consents is set out in the Infrastructure Planning (Interested Parties and Miscellaneous Prescribed Provisions) Regulations 2015, No. 462.

61 The Government consulted on this proposal in the summer of 2014 and 77% of respondees were generally in agreement. The Government intends to press ahead with this proposal. It will remove three consents concerning discharge for works purposes and trade effluent from the section 150 during this Parliament, with European Protected Species Licence to follow early in the next Parliament. The remaining six consents will be streamlined between 2015 and 2017.

62 Section 5 Planning Act 2008. The Act covers sixteen different types of projects.

63 Section 5(3) Planning Act 2008 – including in any process of amendment (Section 6(6) Planning Act 2008). The SS has a duty to exercise his functions in this respect with reference to the objective of contributing to sustainable development; in particular, having regard to the desirability of mitigating and adapting to climate change and achieving good design (Section 10 Planning Act 2008). The implications with regard to Directive 2001/42/EC are outlined below; Sheate, Eales & Vaizgelaite 2010.

64 Section 5 Planning Act 2008. The NPPS on Nuclear Power, for example, includes locational information; 'National Policy Statement for Nuclear Power Generation', Department of Energy and Climate Change (EN-6), 2011.

65 Section 130 Localism Act 2011. A draft NPPS or amendment to an existing NPPS must be laid before Parliament and can only be designated if the House of Commons resolves within 21 sitting days that it should be proceeded with, or that period ends without the House of Commons resolving that it should not be proceeded with. Originally, the NPPS were laid before Parliament and the SS had a duty to outline the Government's response to any resolution of the Houses of Parliament or any recommendation of a Parliamentary Committee. This could include a recommendation to debate a policy before either House of Parliament.

also statutory provision for consultation on these documents. The SS has a duty to carry out 'such consultation and publicity as he thinks appropriate' and 'with such persons and such descriptions of persons as may be prescribed'.[66] In deciding what is appropriate, the SS must consider the views of relevant local authorities.[67] The SS must consider the responses to the process of consultation in deciding whether to proceed with the NPPS.[68] The opportunities for consultation at this early stage in the decision-making process is highly significant because the relevant NPPS must be followed unless the adverse impacts of the proposed development on the local community would outweigh its benefits.[69] However, the only means of challenging an NPPS is by way of judicial review and within six weeks.[70]

An independent Infrastructure Planning Commission (IPC) was originally created to take decisions under the new system. Its members were drawn from a range of fields such as planning, engineering and business. However, this was abolished by the Coalition Government and as of 1st April 2012 the process has been administered by the Planning Inspectorate. The Planning Inspectorate makes a recommendation to the SS who is ultimately responsible for decisions. This change was considered important to ensure the democratic legitimacy of the decision-making process, but there are still opportunities for direct participation. The consultation process begins before the initial application. The developer must consult with statutory bodies as prescribed; local authorities whose boundaries fall within the land; and, people with an interest in the land.[71] Most projects decided under the Planning Act 2008 will have the potential to create significant effects on the environment; thus all applications for development consent under the Planning Act 2008, before the pre-application consultation process begins, the developer must provide an environmental statement or ask for a screening opinion.[72] The local authority is not only consulted but must be invited to submit a local impact report, the content of which is left to the discretion of the local authority.[73] The local interest is also represented by Parish Councils, which form the lowest tier of local government in England.[74] Nevertheless, the developer also has a duty to consult directly with local people and must prepare a statement setting out how he/she proposes to consult with the 'local community' about the proposed application. The 'local community' is defined geographically as those within the vicinity of the land.[75] In deciding whether to accept an application, the Planning Inspectorate must consider

66 Section 7 Planning Act 2008.
67 Section 8 Planning Act 2008.
68 Section 7 Planning Act 2008.
69 Section 104 Planning Act 2008.
70 Section 113 Planning Act 2008.
71 Sections 42-44 Planning Act 2008.
72 Infrastructure Planning (EIA) Regulations 2009 SI 2263.
73 Section 60 Planning Act 2008.
74 Infrastructure Planning (Applications: Prescribed Forms and Procedure) Regulations 2009/2264. Parish Councils vary in size and function but generally represent smaller communities in the local authority area and maintain and provide facilities for them, such as parks, public toilets, cemeteries, community halls and cycle and footpaths. For further details on Parish Councils see Clayden 2009.
75 Section 47 Planning Act 2008.

the adequacy of this process of consultation which the developer must report on.[76] Thus, there is some external verification of what would otherwise be an entirely developer-led initiative on consultation.

The introduction of an early opportunity to participate in the process of decision-making on nationally significant infrastructure has been accompanied by a significant reduction in opportunities to make representations at the later stages in the process. An application for development consent is always subject to some sort of public examination which is carried out by the Planning Inspectorate as an Examining Authority,[77] but the public examination is an investigatory process and the majority of evidence will be provided in writing.[78] The Examining Authority may decide that it is necessary to include consideration of oral representations in relation to specific issues;[79] and interested parties, including the local authority and anyone that has made a representation on the proposal, may request an 'open floor hearing'.[80] Nevertheless, the open floor hearing differs from the traditional public inquiry in that it is intended to adopt an inquisitorial rather than adversarial approach:

> 'The Examining Authority, ...will probe, test and assess the evidence through direct questioning of persons making oral representations. Normally parties will be invited to summarise their case, made in their relevant or written representations, and then be questioned on the evidence they have put forward to support their case. While truth-seeking, the Examining Authority should seek to set an approach which is not aggressively adversarial [...]'.[81]

Cross-examination of evidence is only allowed by specific direction of the Examining Authority and those entitled to appear at the hearing have no automatic right to call witnesses. This approach places the Examining Authority very much in

76 Section 55 Planning Act 2008.

77 The provisions of the Act were originally supplemented by the Infrastructure Planning (Examination Procedure) Rules 2010 and initially: 'Planning Act 2008: Guidance for the Examination of Applications for Development Consent for Nationally Significant Infrastructure Projects', DCLG, 2012, <www.gov.uk/government/uploads/system/uploads/attachment_data/file/8369/2130206.pdf>. This guidance was replaced by 'Planning Act 2008: Guidance for the Examination of Applications for Development Consent', DCLG, 2015, <www.gov.uk/government/uploads/system/uploads/attachment_data/file/485064/Making_changes_guidance_to_Development_Consent_Orders.pdf>.

78 *Ibid.*, para. 71.

79 Section 91 Planning Act 2008. This is to ensure adequate examination of the issue or that an interested party has a fair chance to put their case.

80 Section 93 Planning Act 2008; Infrastructure Planning (Interested Parties) Regulations 2010/102; Infrastructure Planning (Interested Parties and Miscellaneous Prescribed Provisions) Regulations 2015/462.

81 'Planning Act 2008: Guidance for the Examination of Applications for Development Consent', DCLG, 2015, para. 96.

control of the process and the emphasis is on ensuring efficiency.[82] To this end the examination is also completed according to a statutory timetable.[83]

The Examining Authority provides a report of its recommendations to the SS within 3 months of the public examination and the SS then has a further 3 months to make the final decision.[84] For most projects this will be the end of the process, but in some instances the development proposal may be subject to a 'special parliamentary procedure'. This is the case, for example, in the event that the project involves the compulsory acquisition of certain property; the land is owned by a local authority and/or statutory undertaker land; and, at least one such landowner had objected to the application. This further level of scrutiny is very contentious given the rigorous procedures outlined above. It appears to defeat the efficiency aims of the new process of planning for national infrastructure as proposals subject to this procedure encounter considerable delay.[85] In addition, it prioritizes local government and national authority interests over national imperatives as well as local environmental and community interests. Nevertheless, the Government has refused to abolish the procedure.[86] The only means of challenging a decision on major infrastructure, albeit to refuse or grant development consent, is by way of judicial review and within six weeks.[87] This time limit initially contrasted with the rule that judicial review cases be brought 'promptly' and no later than 3 months. However, changes to the Civil Procedure Rules have meant that since April 1st 2013 there has been a 6-week time limit for all judicial review cases involving planning decisions.[88]

5. The Experience of Public Participation in Planning for Nationally Significant Infrastructure

The Planning Act 2008 has now been in force for a number of years and during this time more than 50 projects have been awarded development consent.[89] This section will consider the experience of those asserting participatory rights at the different stages within the process in more detail.

82 A preliminary meeting is held with the applicant and other 'interested parties', to discuss how the application should be examined. However, the Act is clear that the Examining Authority is to decide how to consider the application. Sections 87-88 Planning Act 2008.

83 Section 98 Planning Act 2008.

84 Sections 98 and 107 Planning Act 2008 respectively.

85 The Rookery South energy from waste project was the first to gain development consent from the SS under the Planning Act 2008. However, it was also subject to the 'special parliamentary procedure' which caused a delay of a further sixteen months.

86 Instead the Localism Act 2011 circumvented the procedure to some degree and the Growth and Infrastructure Act 2013 narrowed this even further.

87 Section 118 Planning Act 2008.

88 Civil Procedure Rules 54.5(5).

89 By February 2016 a total of 50 DCOs had been granted across England and Wales. 62% were energy projects and 32% were transport projects. They are displayed in map form in the following tweet from the Planning Inspectorate: <https://twitter.com/PINSgov/status/697782105468706816/photo/1>.

5.1. *National Planning Policy Statements (NPPSs)*

The traditional discretionary approach to planning decisions in the UK has been altered in the context of nationally significant infrastructure by the pre-eminence of NPPSs. Thus, it is important to ensure participation in the development of these statements. Participation on the NPPS is directed largely towards ensuring representation of the public interest in matters of national interest; including economic and social as well as environmental concerns. There are a number of statutory consultees, including the key environmental agencies for England - the Environment Agency and Natural England[90] and local authorities; but there is also provision for the direct representation of the views of the public. This provides the first step in front-loading participation in the process of decision-making. The duty to consult on NPPSs leaves the SS much discretion, meaning to carry out 'such consultation and publicity as he thinks appropriate' and 'with such persons and such descriptions of persons as may be prescribed'.[91] Public participation on the NPPS related to nuclear power is particularly important because, as outlined above, these go beyond statements of policy to provide details of the siting of development. Special attention will therefore be given to the process of planning for nuclear power in the discussion that follows.

Before considering the process of public consultation on NPPS in more detail, it is important to note that the Planning Act 2008, also includes, as outlined above, a statutory duty to carry out a sustainability appraisal. There has been some debate as to whether these statements should be the subject of formal environmental assessment under the SEA Directive. The SEA Directive applies to plans and programmes whereas these are statements of policy; but it has been argued that those NPPSs that include locational information should be viewed as plans or programmes rather than policies.[92] The Aarhus Convention itself anyway extends to policies and executive regulations and/or generally applicable legally binding normative instruments.[93] The Convention refers to the importance of policy consultation with non-governmental organizations (NGOs).[94] However, the duty under the Planning Act 2008 to carry out a sustainability appraisal of the NPPS does not provide for public consultation.[95]

Seven draft NPPSs were published in 2009 on nuclear power, energy projects and ports. In addition to the usual consultation procedures, six national events were held in England.[96] A further ten local events were held with the communities in the

90 See further Infrastructure Planning (National Policy Statement Consultation) Regulations 2009, No. 1302.

91 Section 7 Planning Act 2008.

92 Sheate, Eales & Vaizgelaite 2010.

93 Convention on Access to Information, Public Participation in Decision-Making and Access to Justice in Environmental Matters, 2161 UNTS 447; 38 ILM 517 (1999), Arts. 7 and 8.

94 *Ibid.*, Art. 2.

95 Section 5(3) Planning Act 2008.

96 These involved a presentation on the NPPS followed by a one-hour question and answer session.

vicinity of the ten potential locations for new nuclear power stations.[97] The purpose of these meetings was clearly explained as helping the public understand the NPPS and have an input in the drafting process; and not to debate the underlying energy policy of the NPPS. The meetings on the nuclear NPPS were also explained as providing an opportunity to consider whether, having met the Government's criteria, the particular site designated was indeed suitable. One of the key sites designated for nuclear development was Hinkley Point C. The application was made by EDF energy, a French company in which the national government have an 80 percent share. The Hinkley Point C nuclear power station has undoubtedly been one of the most controversial projects decided under the Planning Act 2008, given that it will involve the construction of the first new nuclear power station in the UK for a generation. On the other hand, the area is not unfamiliar to nuclear power because, as the name suggests, it is the third facility to be built here. Many local people have grown up with and work in the nuclear industry but the project was not without controversy.[98]

At the consultation in Hinkley on the NPPS for Nuclear Energy specific locational issues were discussed such as, the suitability of transport links for construction of the site and the levels of radioactivity in local waters; but concerns were also raised about wider policy issues such as nuclear waste disposal and evidence of health issues associated with nuclear energy.[99] A particular concern was that, given the Government's estimation that all ten power stations would be needed to meet future energy demands, there would be considerable pressure to accept any applications on these sites - thus the development at Hinkley Point C was effectively a *fait accompli*. This problem was compounded in the case of Hinkley Point C, because the development was proposed in an area with existing nuclear power plants.[100]

The NPPSs on energy were subsequently laid before the Select Committee on Energy and Climate Change.[101] The concerns raised at the Hinkley Point C meeting with regard to the national imperative for ten nuclear power stations were re-iterated by the Select Committee on Energy and Climate Change; which also voiced more general criticisms of the way in which the consultation process had been carried out. In particular, the short nature of the consultation process before the proposals reached the Committee.[102] It was the Committee's view that the Government had not gone far enough in engaging the public and recommended that the Government 'learns from this experience for future NPPS and considers more innovative ways, particularly with regard to greenfield sites, in which it can engage

97 These events were advertised in the local press for two weeks prior to the meeting and leaflets were distributed to anyone within a six-mile radius of the nuclear power station sites.

98 BBC News, Hinkley Point: Weekend of Protest Planned BBC News, 6 October 2012, available at: <www.bbc.co.uk/news/uk-england-somerset-19855910>.

99 Transcript of the public meeting in respect of the Hinkley nuclear power station, available at: <http://webarchive.nationalarchives.gov.uk/20100430153934>; <www.energynpsconsultation.decc.gov.uk/home/involvement/>.

100 *Ibid.*

101 'The Proposals for National Policy on Energy. Third Report of Session 2009-2010 Vol 1 HC231', House of Commons Energy and Climate Change Committee.

102 *Ibid.*

the public in these important documents'.[103] There were around 3.000 responses to the official consultation document which highlighted a number of concerns about the consultation process itself: that the draft documents were too long; that not enough time was given to respond to them; that the material was too technical; that the publicity and awareness raising of the consultation events was not sufficient; and, that the process did not engage with the public and local communities with the meetings not well attended.[104] Although the experience of consultation on the first raft of NPPSs was therefore quite unsatisfactory, many of the time pressures were created by the desire to complete the process before the General Election.[105] On coming to power the Coalition Government resolved to revise the existing NPPS, but the consultation process for this was even less effective.

Under the Coalition government the potentially suitable sites for nuclear power station development were updated - with more sites considered and three sites removed from the list. It was also made clear that it was necessary to list all eight sites in the NPPS, but that this did not necessarily mean that a station was needed at all of the sites.[106] The process of revising the NPPS was subject only to a standard process of consultation, i.e., comments were simply requested online, by e-mail or post;[107] despite the recommendations of the Select Committee.[108] The legal framework makes no distinction between the requirement for consultation for new NPPSs and amendments to them, but the discretion left to the SS in carrying out the consultative process means that this consultation was still sufficient. There were also significant delays in publishing a number of NPPSs which left important gaps in the framework for decision-making for some time.[109]

Given the fact that consultation on NPPSs cannot be used as a means of debating government policy on the issues underlying the relevant development, it is important that government ensures that non-governmental organizations and the public are made more aware of the necessity of taking part in wider consultations, for example, on energy policy. The more established non-governmental organizations are already clearly cognisant of this fact and the courts have been prepared to support them in ensuring a fair consultation process on such matters;[110] but there is

103 *Ibid.*, recommendation 28. A particular problem was experienced with the meeting at Hartlepool and Hinkley point and one other location which were not subject to prior advertisement because they were held in November Therefore, Government officials returned to these locations at a later date to address a public meeting. 'The Government Response to the Consultation on the Draft National Policy Statements for Energy Infrastructure', Department of Energy and Climate Change, 2010.

104 *Ibid.*

105 The deadline for the process was therefore set for the 6 May 2010.

106 'The Government Response to the Consultation on the Draft National Policy Statements for Energy Infrastructure', Department of Energy and Climate Change, 2010, p. 16.

107 'The Proposals for National Policy on Energy. Third Report of Session 2009-2010, Vol. 1, HC231', House of Commons Energy and Climate Change Committee.

108 The Government Response to the Consultation on the Draft National Policy Statements for Energy Infrastructure', Department of Energy and Climate Change, 2010, p. 16.

109 NPPS on hazardous waste, water supply, airports or national networks (including both road and rail).

110 *R (Hillingdon LBC)* v. *Secretary of State for Transport* [2010] EWHC 626.

certainly more that could be done to directly engage society in policy making.[111] It has also been argued that the fact that there is limited scope to take account of dissenting views during consultation on the NPPS, and in light of a strong policy in favour of development, participation at later stages in the process is focussed on finding a way to 'deal with the public concerns without dismissing them completely or classifying them as unimportant, and yet still allowing the development to proceed'.[112] This assertion will be considered in the context of planning for nuclear energy in the discussion that follows.

5.2. *Pre-application Consultation*

The second key aspect of 'front-loading' participation is in the pre-application consultation. Local authorities have a significant role at this stage. They assist the developer in creating a Statement of Community Consultation, act as a statutory consultee and are invited to provide a local impact report.[113] In addition, Parish Councils are consulted to ensure representation of narrower community interests.[114] These councils were first formed at the end of the 19th century to adopt local civic duties. They provide representation at a level closer to the 'community', but their coverage is not comprehensive and in modern times they have enjoyed few significant powers.[115] Although, as outlined above, some commentators have applauded the 'hard-wiring' of local government representation within the Planning Act 2008, neither this or consideration of the views of Parish can substitute for direct public participation.[116]

Pre-application consultation with the public is the responsibility of the developer. The duty is actually to consult with the 'local community' rather than the public, which is geographically defined as 'people living within the vicinity of the development'.[117] The original guidance stated that:

> 'The Act uses the broad term 'vicinity' to allow for the fact that projects will vary greatly in their size and impact on people nearby - consultation for long, linear schemes will necessarily be different from that for a new power station'.[118]

In the case of Hinkley Point C Nuclear Power Station, the most intensive consultation was undertaken with the public within five miles of the primary site and half a mile of the associated development.[119]

111 See, for example, Scheer & Hoppner 2010.

112 Rydin, Lee & Lock 2015, p. 139.

113 Sections 42-44 Planning Act 2008.

114 Infrastructure Planning (Prescribed Forms and Procedures) Regulations 2009, No. 2264, Art. 3. For a discussion of the different notions of 'local'; Layard 2012, p. 551-576.

115 Jones 2010.

116 Kelly 2008, p. 1-12.

117 Section 42 Planning Act 2008.

118 'Planning Act 2008: Guidance on pre-application consultation', DCLG, 2009, para. 52.

119 'Hinkley Point C Development Consent Order Application Consultation Report: Executive Summary', EDF Energy, 2011, <http://infrastructure.planningportal.gov.uk>. This can be contrasted with one of the first projects, the Rookery South energy from waste generating station in Bedfordshire, where the greatest consultation effort, in the form of direct mailing, →

With regard to the nature of the 'local community' and methods of participation the most recent guidance states that:

> '[...] an inclusive approach is needed to ensure that different groups have the opportunity to participate and are not disadvantaged in the process. Applicants should use a range of methods and techniques to ensure that they access all sections of the community in question'.[120]

This moves some distance from the definition of 'community' by reference to 'vicinity'. A number of methods of consultation were suggested in the original guidance in reaching out to the wider community, including local exhibitions; drop in sessions; workshops; telephone advice line; citizen panels; internet; and the media. Several examples of these were used in the Hinkley Point C development. Nevertheless, there are many difficulties facing developers in framing an effective consultation process with little guidance as to how to negotiate this process other than to draw upon the expertise of the local authority.[121] Ultimately, the developer has a great deal of discretion in framing the consultation process subject to the requirement that the report of this process is considered sufficient by the Examining Authority.[122] The introduction of tighter parameters would perhaps assist the developer in providing some assurance as to its acceptability by the Examining Authority.

Environmental interests are also an important consideration in pre-application consultation and the planning of national infrastructure has significantly altered the notion of an 'early and effective' opportunity to comment on environmental information in this context. Ordinarily, in the planning process in England, the public are only consulted on the environmental statement once it is published. However, in the case of nationally significant infrastructure the developer must state whether the proposal falls within the scope of the Directive, and if so, how the applicant intends to publicize and consult on preliminary environmental information.[123] The statutory environment agencies - the Environment Agency and Natural England - as well as non-governmental organizations and the public will also have an opportunity to comment on environmental issues associated with the project as part of the pre-application consultation.[124] This goes some way to addressing concerns about the application of the EIA Directive in England that:

> 'Notwithstanding the promulgation of provisions on participation in the EU Directives on EIA and SEA, these instruments describe a passive public, receiving a narrow

was employed within a five km radius of the site: The Proposed Rookery South (Resource Recovery Facility). Consultation Report, 2010, EDF Energy, <http://infrastructure.planningportal.gov.uk>.

120 'Planning Act 2008: Guidance on pre-application consultation', DCLG, 2009, para. 54.

121 *Ibid.*

122 Section 55 Planning Act 2008.

123 Infrastructure Planning (Environmental Impact Assessment) Regulations 2009, Regulation 9.

124 Infrastructure Planning (Prescribed Forms and Procedures) Regulations 2009, No. 2264, Art. 3 and Schedule 1. The requirements to consult on the preliminary environmental information can be found in the Infrastructure Planning (Environmental Impact Assessment) Regulations 2009, Regulation 11.

> category of information (the developer's environmental statement) and being consulted upon this rather than shaping the process through active participation [...]'.[125]

However, an essential problem with the process of pre-application consultation is that it is the responsibility of the developer. In the context of EIA, a developer-led system has been identified as a key concern with the process given that 'The responsibility to produce an environmental statement also confers considerable freedom upon the developer to present a project in a particular way and to shape responses to it'.[126] There is, of course, the safeguard that acceptance of the application is dependent on a satisfactory report of this process; but this does not deter from the fundamental problem of a development bias in the system.[127]

5.3. *The Examination in Public*

The purpose of the Examination in Public (EiP) is to provide the Examining Authority with evidence relating to the local impacts of the development proposal to be weighed against the provisions of the NPPS on this type of development. The central difference between the public inquiry and the public examination is that the latter does not always have to involve an oral hearing, but where such a hearing is held it will adopt an inquisitorial rather than an adversarial approach. There are strict rules governing the EiP on issues such as, pre-inquiry meetings and the appointment of technical advisers and the process is subject to a statutory time limit of six months. In adopting an inquisitorial approach the Examining Authority is also placed clearly in control of proceedings.[128] The emphasis at the hearings is clearly on increasing efficiency and the original guidance stated that:

> 'The Examining Authority is expected to make use of its powers of control over the conduct of hearings to ensure that they are carried out as efficiently as possible, whilst remaining fair to all parties and thorough in their examination of evidence'.[129]

The legislation also includes provision for the Examining Authority to refuse to hear evidence which, in his/her view, *inter alia*, relates to the merits of policy set out in a NPPS to ensure a focus on local issues.[130] Furthermore, interested parties must clearly identify themselves and make a submission prior to the hearing which must 'contain sufficient information to enable the SS to understand which aspects of the

125 Holder 2001, p. 191.
126 Holder 2001, p. 289.
127 'Planning Act 2008: Guidance on associated development applications for major infrastructure projects', DCLG, 2015.
128 Rule 14 Infrastructure Planning (Examination Procedure) Rules 2010/103; Section 98(1) Planning Act 2008 respectively.
129 'Planning Act 2008: Guidance on associated development applications for major infrastructure projects', DCLG, 2015.
130 The list also includes irrelevant, vexatious or frivolous; or relates to compensation for compulsory acquisition of land or of an interest in or over land: Section 94 Planning Act 2008.

application the person supports or objects to, and the reasons why'.[131] Thus, any representations on national policy issues can also be filtered out at this stage.[132]

The experience of the EiP on the Hinkley Point C application is illustrative of the fact that despite the new approach many of the problems associated with public inquiries continue to plague the EiP. There were a series of both specific issue and open floor hearings on this development, but the examination was completed within the statutory period of six months. At the first open floor hearing the interested parties, that had made prior submissions, were allowed three minutes, or thereabouts, to make their representations.[133] The Examining Authority noted from the pre-submissions that several interested parties proposed to make representations on policy matters, but they were nevertheless allowed to speak. Indeed, within the first ninety minutes of the hearing there had been a number of individual representations on issues such as evacuation in the case of a nuclear incident; the suitability of EDF to build and run the plant; and, health concerns associated with the plant. These were all issues of national policy or matters for the Office of the Nuclear Regulator.[134] Some comments were also made about the quality of the participatory process and response of the developer to local concerns; which again, although important, were not relevant to this forum. The main concerns raised that were of relevance to the Examining Authority related to transport and traffic issues, of which there were a great many.[135] This raises the problem of the repetition of evidence which was apparent both within the open floor hearing and between this and specific issue hearings.

This evidence suggests that those making representations continue to be confused about the remit of the Inspector in taking decisions on infrastructure projects. However, several individuals voiced a desire to make their representations, notwithstanding the knowledge that this would not be considered relevant by the Inspector.[136] This kind of forum may well have some value as a mechanism for allowing the public to air their grievances about a project, but it does not serve the key purposes of participation in terms of providing legitimacy within the process or increasing the quality of government decisions. In the long term it is probable that those people involved will leave deeply unsatisfied with their experience of participation. Nevertheless, the experience at the EiP on the Hinkley Point C application also adds weight to the suggestion that the focus on NPPS in decision-

131 'Planning Act 2008: Guidance on associated development applications for major infrastructure projects', DCLG, 2015, para. 23.

132 'Hinkley Point C New Nuclear Power Station', NNB Generation Company Limited, <https://infrastructure.planninginspectorate.gov.uk/projects/south-west/hinkley-point-c-new-nuclear-power-station/?ipcsection=hearings>.

133 This convention is widespread in local planning. Manns & Wood 2002, p. 39-51.

134 'Hinkley Point C New Nuclear Power Station', NNB Generation Company Limited, <https://infrastructure.planninginspectorate.gov.uk/projects/south-west/hinkley-point-c-new-nuclear-power-station/?ipcsection=hearings>.

135 *Ibid*. In this instance, although traffic was a relevant concern one individual also wanted to discuss alternative roads proposals which, as the Inspector pointed, could not be considered by him as he could only make a recommendation on the existing proposal.

136 *Ibid*.

making which strongly support development means there is little room to influence the proposal during the consultation process.[137]

6. Access to Justice in Planning for Nationally Significant Infrastructure

In addition to an early and effective opportunity to participate in environmental decision-making, the Aarhus Convention considers access to justice as essential in environmental decision-making. However, in advance of any significant experience of planning for NSIPs it was predicted, given the restricted rights to present evidence in the EiP, that there would be an increase in judicial review cases.[138] In fact, by March 2014, 25 per cent of decisions have been subject to judicial review in the Administrative Court, but all of them had been appealed to the Court of Appeal.[139] With reference to the development consent for Hinkley Point C, two challenges in judicial review were launched in the same week in 2013. These cases demonstrate the difficulties in establishing grounds for judicial review in England which is strictly procedural. The first challenge was made by Greenpeace on the grounds that the Government had not acted in accordance with its own policy on nuclear energy regarding the disposal of waste. This was, however, later dropped on the basis that it was a 'lost cause'.[140] The second case was brought by the Irish National Trust (An Taisce)[141] on the grounds that, under the provisions of the EIA Directive, the government should have consulted the Irish people before the application was made, because the project was 'likely to have significant effects' on the environment in Ireland.[142] Having carried out a screening process the UK government had concluded that no such assessment was necessary because the risk of nuclear accident was extremely remote. The Court of Appeal agreed concluding that to find otherwise would be to adopt a 'zero risk' approach to the likelihood of environmental effects which would frustrate the purpose of the Directive.[143]

The lack of substantive review in judicial review cases was one of the criticisms of access to justice in the UK made by the Aarhus Compliance Committee, in 2008. Other relevant issues were the restrictive time limits for judicial review and prohibitively expensive costs of judicial review proceedings.[144] As outlined above, the time limit for judicial review in planning cases of any kind is 6 weeks. This is

137 Rydin, Lee & Lock 2015, p. 143.

138 Maurici 2009, p. 446-451.

139 'All Planning Act Judicial Review Decisions Appealed', Local Government Lawyer, 3 March 2014, <www.localgovernmentlawyer.co.uk/index.php?option=com_content&view=article&id=17607%3Aall-planning-act-judicial-review-decisions-appealed&catid=182%3Aangus-walkers-planning-blog&Itemid=111>.

140 Independent 2013.

141 *R (on the application of An Taisce (National Trust For Ireland))* v. *Secretary of State for Energy and Climate Change* [2014] EWCA.

142 Directive 2014/52/EU, Art. 7; implemented by Art. 24 of the Infrastructure Planning (Environmental Impact Assessment) Regulations 2009.

143 Independent 2013.

144 United Nations Economic and Social Council Report of the Compliance Committee: Findings and recommendations with regard to the Communication ACCC/C/2008/33.

not, however, particularly restrictive in comparison to other European countries and an applicant is only required to provide outline arguments at the permission stage rather than detailed grounds for review. Article 9 of the Aarhus Convention states that it should be possible to challenge a development decision on the grounds of 'substantive' or 'procedural' legality. The Aarhus Compliance Committee expressed concern that although in the UK it is possible to challenge substantive legality in narrow respects;[145] this was not sufficient to meet the standards for review required under the Convention.[146] Indeed, the test of Wednesbury unreasonableness has long been criticized in this respect;[147] but courts in England have, however, become more accustomed to application of the proportionality principle, following the incorporation of the European Convention on Human Rights in the Human Rights Act 1998. The Committee would not go so far as to rule that UK was non-compliant with Article 9 because reflection on the 'proportionality principle' could provide an adequate standard of review in cases within the scope of the Aarhus Convention, given the implementation of these provisions in Article 10 of the EIA Directive.[148] Nevertheless, the introduction of a stronger merits review in judicial review further to EU law, in England, is certainly not uncontroversial and would be 'a constitutional innovation that requires much more attention'.[149]

By far the most contentious issue raised by the Aarhus Compliance Committee was the issue of costs. Judicial review costs are notoriously expensive given, in particular, the general rule in litigation that the loser pays the winner's costs, but:

> 'A strong argument can be made for departing from the ordinary costs rules in the public law context. A public law costs regime should promote access to justice and facilitate scrutiny of executive action, in the public interest'.[150]

Thus, the judiciary have discretion in judicial review proceedings to issue a Protective Costs Order (PCO) in cases of general public importance.[151] However, such orders will only be applied in a minority of cases and the lack of a PCO can

145 It is possible to challenge, *inter alia*, material error of fact; error of law; regard to irrelevant considerations and failure to have regard to relevant considerations; jurisdictional error; and on the grounds of Wednesbury unreasonableness.

146 United Nations Economic and Social Council Report of the Compliance Committee: Findings and recommendations with regard to the Communication ACCC/C/2008/33.

147 '[...] something so absurd that no sensible person could ever dream that it lay within the powers of the authority [...]', *Associated Provincial Picture Houses Ltd.* v. *Wednesbury Corporation* [1948] 1 KB 223.

148 Ryall also argues that: 'The principle of effective judicial protection, as elaborated in the case law of the EU, provides a strong legal basis on which to build an argument for a more intensive approach to judicial review on the part of the national courts where EU law rights are at issue...'; Ryall 2009, p. 63.

149 Lee & Abbot 2003, p. 80.

150 Steele 2012, p. 249-265.

151 *R (on the application of Corner House Research)* v. *Director of the Serious Fraud Office* [2009] 1 A.C. 756. This is outlined as follows: the public interest requires that those issues are resolved; the applicant has no private interest in the outcome of the case; having regard to the financial resources of the application and respondent and to the likely costs it is fair to make the order; and if order is not made the applicant will probably discontinue proceedings and will be acting reasonably in doing so.

undermine issues of standing.[152] Article 9 of the Convention provides that the procedure for review of environmental decisions should not be 'prohibitively expensive'. Historically, the UK Government has argued that the requirement of the Convention in relation to costs applies only to court fees,[153] but, in 2008, the Aarhus Complaints Committee found the UK Government to be in contravention of the Convention with respect to costs, despite the introduction of PCOs given their discretionary nature.[154]

The European Court of Justice (ECJ) similarly ruled that Article 10a of the EIA Directive applied to all costs of the case; and subsequently found that the use of PCOs failed to meet the requirements of the Directive because of the requirement of public interest and their discretionary nature.[155]

A report by Lord Justice Jackson, in January 2010, on the wider issue of cost rules for civil litigation subsequently concluded that the easiest way of complying with the Aarhus convention, was to ensure that all claimants in judicial review cases should not normally be at risk from paying the costs of the other side. This is referred to as Qualified Cost-Shifting (QCS) and would mean that if the defendant lost it would have to pay the claimants costs, but a losing claimant would only pay a winning defendant's costs where – and to the extent that – in all the circumstances it is reasonable for them to do so.[156] The government failed to take up the recommendations of the Jackson report,[157] but instead introduced new rules from 1st April 2013 to the effect that in 'Aarhus Convention claims' a PCO will restrict a claimant's liability to pay the defendants costs to £5.000 for individuals and £10.000 for organizations.[158] This is a reciprocal cost cap because conversely if the defendant loses he/she has to pay the costs of the claimant only to a cap of £35.000.[159] In the

152 *Coedbach Action Team Ltd* v. *SS for Energy and Climate Change* [2010] EWCA Civ 1494, para. 13. It was agreed that the judge was entitled to hold that the issues of the application of a PCO and standing stood or fell together because the applicant had indicated that they could not proceed without a PCO.

153 'Aarhus Convention Implementation Report', DEFRA, 2008.

154 Ryall 2009, p. 63.

155 Case C-427/07 *Commission of the European Communities* v. *Ireland*, EU:C:2009:457; Case C-530/11 *European Commission* v. *United Kingdom of Great Britain and Northern Ireland*, EU:C:2014:67.

156 Jackson 2009.

157 Indeed, the Coalition Government is concerned about the increasing numbers of judicial review cases, which has risen from 160 in 1975 to around 11,000 by 2011. Although by far the majority are asylum and immigration cases, a substantial number also relate to planning: 'Reform of Judicial Review' *JPEL*, 2013, p. 270. This has led, *inter alia*, to the introduction of a reduction in the time limits in planning cases to six weeks.

158 Civil Procedure Rule 45.41 – 45.44. An Aarhus Convention claim is defined as 'a claim for judicial review of a decision, act or omission all or part of which is subject to the provisions of the [Convention on Access to Information, Public Participation in Decision-Making and Access to Justice in Environmental Matters, 2161 UNTS 447; 38 ILM 517 (1999)], including a claim which proceeds on the basis that the decision, act or omission, or part of it, is so subject'. Rule 45.41. The Implementation Guide indicates that the definition of 'environmentally-related' should be 'as broad in scope as possible', directing us to Art. 2(3) of the Convention which simply refers, without further definition, to 'environmental matters'.

159 *Ibid.*

recent case of Venn, the Court of Appeal found that planning law and policy were both valid matters in this respect noting that:[160]

> 'National legislation may address the issue of environmental protection in different ways. The UK has a sophisticated Town and Country Planning system, and Parliament has chosen to implement much of the UK's environmental protection through that system'.

The decision was made with reference to local planning decisions, but this logic should apply equally to decisions on nationally significant infrastructure. The law on costs in judicial review is now the subject of new provisions in the Criminal Justice and Courts Act 2015 which are yet to be brought into force; but are not anyway expected to affect cases of 'environmental judicial review.[161] This discussion has centred around costs orders, but it should not be forgotten that this is not the only consideration in ensuring effective access to justice, as perhaps most pertinent is the provision of legal aid.[162]

7. Conclusion

Nationally significant infrastructure in England is now subject to a separate system of planning that is designed to increase efficiency in the light of the imperative of economic growth. In order to streamline the process, these projects can now gain associated development consents alongside planning permission; although the regime falls short of a one-stop shop for planning and environmental permitting. The clear steer in decision-making provided by NPPSs should also alleviate some of the delays in the process. The original regime also aimed to increase efficiency by creating an independent decision-making body in the form of the IPC, but this was abolished by the incoming Coalition Government as undemocratic.[163] Decisions are now taken by the SS and, it is argued, that local government representation is 'hardwired' into the process.[164] However, successive governments have remained committed to ensuring a process of direct participation within the decision-making process.

The regime focuses on pre-application consultation in order to provide an 'early and effective opportunity' for participation which is a key requirement of the Aarhus Convention. However, this 'front-loading' of participation has been used as justification for restricting participatory rights at later stages in the process. The EiP

160 *Venn* v. *Secretary of State for Communities and Local Government* [2014] EWCA Civ 1539.

161 Sections 88 - 90 Criminal Justice and Courts Act 2015. These provisions will provide a legislative base for cost capping orders in cases in the 'public interest' and where, in the absence of the order, the applicant for judicial review would otherwise withdraw the application or cease to participate in the proceedings (and it would be reasonable for the applicant to do so) (Section 88). There is also provision for the Lord Chancellor to make alternative arrangements in cases of 'environmental judicial review' (Section 90).

162 The extension of which was supported in the Sullivan Review. The Working Group on Access to Environmental Justice 2008.

163 Localism Act 2011.

164 Section 42 Planning Act 2008.

provides less room for oral consideration of public evidence than the traditional public inquiry and thus it is doubtful that it will have the same benefits, as encapsulated by the (late) Royal Commission on Environmental Pollution in the following terms:

> 'Public inquiries, for all their limitations, have brought together diverse participants in a visible and relatively open forum and provided vital opportunities for argument, new ideas, and crucial scrutiny. It has often taken a serious of challenges to individual projects to bring about change in general policies or underlying assumptions'.[165]

Given the truncation of rights to participate at this stage in the process access to justice is very important. The English system has UK has attracted much controversy, particularly with respect to costs, but significant changes have been made to comply with EU law.

Front-loading participation has resulted in some efficiency gains with statutory targets for the EiP and SS decision-making, but delay is still evident in the length of time taken in pre-application consultation which in the case of Hinkley Point C, for example, was a total of three years. Other important sources of delay relate to the special parliamentary procedure;[166] and judicial review, particularly where there is an appeal to the Court of Appeal. Perhaps most significantly, funding issues will be paramount. In the case of Hinkley Point C, despite the grant of development consent, in March 2013, building still had yet to start in February 2016 because the developer, EDF Energy, was struggling to secure financing for the project despite signing a deal with the China Nuclear Power Corporation, in October 2015, to provide one third of the cost.[167]

Whilst, problems remain in ensuring that nationally significant infrastructure projects are brought to fruition within a reasonable time period, the processes for public participation are also problematic. The legitimacy of the pre-application consultation process will rest on the clarity with which the aims of the participation are framed and communicated to those involved; yet the consultative processes in the early stages of national infrastructure planning are prescribed by the SS or developer which may well lead to bias in favour of development.[168] Furthermore, in practice, individuals and community groups will require advice and support, financially and otherwise, at every stage of consultation in the decision-making process. This has traditionally been provided by Planning Aid whose funding in England nearly doubled when the Act was introduced. However, since the inception of neighbourhood planning under the Localism Act 2011 attention has

165 Royal Commission on Environmental Pollution, '23rd Report, Environmental Planning (Cm 5459)', 2002, para. 5.11.

166 Such as the Rookery South project. The Rookery South energy from waste project was the first to gain development consent from the SS under the Planning Act 2008. However, it was also subject to the 'special parliamentary procedure' which caused a delay of a further sixteen months, <www.planningportal.co.uk>; Elvin, 2012, p. 163-171.

167 Decision on New Nuclear Plant 'Delayed' 27 January 2016 <www.bbc.co.uk/news/business-35415187> and the Telegraph 2015.

168 Section 42 Planning Act 2008.

turned to support for locally based projects under this regime.[169] Most importantly, it is arguable that the decision-making according to NPPSs with a strong bias in favour of development means there is little room anyway for those participating in the planning process to influence the final outcome.[170]

169 News Briefing, 'Government confirms extended funding for Planning Aid England', 5 July 2012; Royal Town Planning Institute, <www.rtpi.org.uk>. New funding and aid for neighbourhood plans 6 November 2014, <www.planningportal.gov.uk/general/news/stories/2014/november14/061114/061114_2>.

170 Rydin, Lee & Lock 2015, p. 139.

BIBLIOGRAPHY

Barker 2006
Barker, K., *Barker Review of Land Use Planning. Final Report – Recommendations*, Norwich: HMSO 2006, available at: <www.gov.uk/government/uploads/system/uploads/attachment_data/file/228605/0118404857.pdf>.

Booth 2003
Booth, P., 'Planning by Consent', in: B. Cullingworth (ed.), *British Planning: 50 Years of Urban and Regional Policy*, London: Routledge 2003, p. 31-43.

Clayden 2009
Clayden, P., *The Parish Councillors Guide: The Law and Practice of Parish, Town and Community Councils in England and Wales*, Kent: Shaw 2009.

Elvin 2012
Elvin, D., 'Major Infrastructure Projects: Where are we Now?, *Environmental Law and Management*, 2012, p. 163-171.

Fishkin 2009
Fishkin, J., *When the Public Speak: Deliberative Democracy and Public Consultation*, Oxford: Oxford University Press 2009.

Holder 2001
Holder, J., *Environmental Assessment: the Regulation of Decision-Making*, Oxford: Oxford University Press 2001.

Holder & Lee 2007
Holder, J. & Lee, M., *Environmental Protection Policy and Law – Text and Materials*, Cambridge: Cambridge University Press 2007.

Independent 2013
Independent, 'Greenpeace Abandons Hinkley Point Lost Cause', 26 October 2013.

Jackson 2009
Jackson J., *Review of Civil Litigation Costs: Final Report*, Norwich: HMSO 2009.

Jackson 2011
Jackson, T., *Prosperity without Growth: Economics for a Finite Planet*, London: Routlegde 2011.

Jones 2010
Jones, I., *Community and Town Councils Survey 2010: Findings Report*, Cardiff: Welsh Assembly Government 2010.

Kelly 2008
Kelly B., 'The Planning Bill: Implications of the Proposals for a New Regime for Major Infrastructure for Democracy and Delivery', *Journal of Planning Law*, 2008, p. 1-12.

Layard 2012
Layard, A., 'Law and Localism: the Case of Multiple Occupancy Housing', *Legal Studies*, 2012, p. 551-576.

Lee & Abbot 2003
Lee, M. & Abbot, C., 'The Usual Suspects? Public Participation Under the Aarhus Convention', *Modern Law Review*, 2003, p. 80-108.

Lee et al. 2013
Lee, M., Armeni, C., De Cendra, J., Chaytor, S., Lock, S., Maslin, M., Redgwell, C. & Rydin, Y., 'Public Participation and Climate Change Infrastructure', *Journal of Environmental Law*, 2013, p. 33-62.

Manns & Wood 2002
Manns, S. & Wood, C., 'Public Representations at Development Control Planning Committees', *Public Policy and Administration*, 2002, p. 39-51.

Maurici 2009
Maurici, J., 'Judicial Review under the Planning Act 2008', *Journal of Planning Law*, 2009, p. 446-451.

McAuslan 1980
McAuslan, P., *The Ideologies of Planning Law*, Oxford: Oxford University Press 1980.

Miller 2001
Miller, C., 'The Environmental Roles of Town and Country Planning', in: C. Miller (ed.), *Planning and Environmental Protection*, Oxford: Hart Publishing 2001, p. 1-18.

Moore & Purdue 2012
Moore, V. & Purdue, M., *A Practical Approach to Planning Law*, Oxford: Oxford University Press 2012.

Office of the Deputy Prime Minister 2008
Office of the Deputy Prime Minister, 'Community Involvement in Planning: The Government's Objectives', in: Evans, R. 'Planning and the People Problem', *Journal of Planning Law*, 2008, 13 Supp. (Delivery or Democracy?), p. 87-103.

Oliver 2003
Oliver, D., *Constitutional Reform in the* UK, Oxford: Oxford University Press 2003.

O'Riordan et al. 1988
O'Riordan, T., Kemp, R. & Purdue, M., *Sizewell, B: An Anatomy of the Inquiry*, London: Macmillan 1988.

Ryall 2009
Ryall, A., *Effective Judicial Protection and the Environmental Impact Assessment Directive in Ireland*, Oxford: Hart Publishing 2009.

Rydin 2011
Rydin, Y., *The Purpose of Planning: Creating Sustainable Towns and Cities*, Bristol: The Policy Press 2011.

Rydin, Lee & Lock 2015
Rydin, Y., Lee, M. & Lock, S.J., 'Public Engagement in Decision-Making on Major Wind Energy Projects', *Journal of Environmental Law*, 2015, p. 139-150.

Scheer & Hoppner 2010
Scheer, A. & Hoppner, C., 'The Public Consultation to the United Kingdom Climate Change Act 2008', *Climate Policy*, 2010, p. 261-276.

Sheate et al. 2010
Sheate, W., Eales, R. & Vaizgelaite, I., *Appraisals of Sustainability and the New National Policy Statements: Opportunities Missed and Challenges to Come*, RSPB, WWF and Collingwood Environmental Planning 2010.

Skeffington 1969
Skeffington, A., *Report of the Committee on Public Participation in Planning*, Norwich: HMSO 1969.

Stallworthy 2002
Stallworthy, M., *Sustainability, Land Use and Environment*, London: Routledge 2002.

Steele 2012
Steele, I., 'Judicial Review in an Age of Austerity: Costs and Funding', *Judicial Review*, 2012, p. 249-265.

Steele 2001
Steele. J., 'Participation and Deliberation in Environmental Law: A Problem Solving Approach', *Oxford Journal of Legal Studies*, 2001, p. 415-442.

Stern 2006
Stern, N., *Stern Review on the Economics of Climate Change*, Norwich: HMSO 2006.

The Telegraph 2015
The Telegraph, 'Hinkley Point New Nuclear Power Plant: the Story so Far', 12 October 2015.

Wade & Forsyth 2009
Wade, H. & Forsyth, C., *Administrative Law*, Oxford: Oxford University Press 2009.

Walker 2014
Walker, A., *550: First Business or Commercial Project to Use Planning Act Regime*, Bircham Dyson Bell: 2014, available at: <www.bdb-law.co.uk/blogs/planning-act-2008/550-first-business-or-commercial-project-to-use-planning-act-regime/#sthash.byFkAL6T.dpuf>.

Williams & Jenkins 2016
Williams, H. & Jenkins, V., 'The Planning (Wales) Act 2015: a Case Study in Evidence-Based Planning Reform under Devolution', *Journal of Planning and Environmental Law*, 2016, p. 637-652.

Working Group on Access to Environmental Justice 2008
Working Group on Access to Environmental Justice, *Ensuring Access to Environmental Justice in England and Wales: Report of the Working Group on Access to Environmental Justice*, 2008, available at: <www.wwf.org.uk/filelibrary/pdf/justice_report_08.pdf>.

Lena Gipperth

QUALITY AND SPEED IN JUDICIAL PROCEDURES AND ADMINISTRATIVE DECISION-MAKING: ENVIRONMENTAL PERMITS IN SWEDEN

1. Introduction

Environmental legislation and its implementation through administrative decision-making and judicial procedures has had a key role in addressing many environmental problems in Sweden. The reduction of industrial pollution particularly from point sources (that is, identifiable pollution sources) is to a great extent attributed to the enforcement of the Environmental Protection Act (*Miljöskyddslag*) 1969.[1] This Act introduced a general permit system in which the issue of permits was conditional on the applicant using the best available technology. The result is that industry has managed to cut 99 percent of emissions since the 1960s due to new and rebuilt plants using the latest techniques.[2]

The Environmental Protection Act was followed by a number of new laws in the 1970s that aimed at further protection for human health and the environment.[3] This meant a patchwork development of environmental legislation as several overlapping duties and procedures were laid out, and this affected both the quality and speed of administrative decision-making in the field. In the late 1980s the government appointed a state commission to analyse the possibility of merging some of this environmental legislation to make regulation less complicated, to centralize its organization and to have a more efficient and seamless permit system.

In 1999 the Environmental Code (*Miljöbalk*) was enacted.[4] It replaced 16 environmental laws and created a more comprehensive regulatory system. The overarching objective of the Code is to promote sustainable development that will ensure a healthy and sound environment for current and future generations. In principle the Code applies to all activities within Swedish territory that may harm the environment or human health. All such activities must be carried out in compliance with general rules of conduct (chapter 2 of the Code) but might also

1 Miljöskyddslag (SFS 1969:387).
2 Bergquis 2007.
3 *Inter alia*, the Health Act (Hälsoskyddslag (SFS 1982:1080)), the Chemicals Act (Lag om hälso- och miljöfarliga varor (SFS 1973:329)) and the Waste Act (Renhållningslag (SFS 1979:596)).
4 Miljöbalk (SFS 1998:808).

need to be carried out in accordance with special rules of conduct depending on the type of activity (chapter 9-15 of the Code). The general rules of conduct require precautionary measures to be taken, such choosing a location which is likely to cause as little harm as possible to the environment and public health, or using as little energy and raw materials as possible.[5]

The Code established five regional environmental courts with the main tasks of: (i) issuing permits; (ii) hearing appeals on administrative decisions taken by any of 290 municipalities and 12 County Administration Boards (CABs) which issue permits and enforcement orders); and iii) hearing claims for compensation in relation to damage caused by certain activities. The aim of establishing environmental courts was to simplify, coordinate and streamline administrative proceedings and judicial review.[6]

This reform of the previous administrative framework and the involvement of the environmental courts has developed further. Since May 2011 the courts have been transformed into Land and Environment Courts (LECs) and their area of competence has been extended to include property law cases as well as appeals of decisions taken under the Planning and Building Act (*Plan- och bygglag*).[7] This transformation makes it possible to hear appeals on expansion of activities that require both a permit for environmental hazardous activities and a building permit at the same time and by the same authority, thus speeding up the process. These courts are linked to the general court system and consist of a panel of one judge, one environmental technical advisor, and two lay expert members. Many decisions taken by the LECs can be appealed before the LEC of Appeal and in some cases the Supreme Court. With the aim of further shortening the administrative decision-making process for decisions in the field of environmental and planning law, the court structure will be simplified in 2016 specifically with respect to appeals relating to local plans.[8]

The development of environmental law over the last 40 years has contributed to decreasing emissions from many of the main Swedish point sources in an astounding way.[9] On the other hand it has also contributed to the development of a rather complex and comprehensive administrative procedure and legal framework in this field, of which the Confederation of Swedish Enterprises (*Svenskt Näringsliv*) is very critical.[10] Although there are administrative procedures in a wide range of areas affecting the Swedish society and particularly its industry (labour law, intellectual property law, tax law etc.), the area of environmental and planning law is illustrative of its great importance and it is an object of intense debate in the

5 *Ibid.*

6 Miljöbalk (Prop. 1997/98:45).

7 Plan- och bygglag (SFS 2010:900).

8 En kortare instanskedja för detaljplaner och områdesbestämmelser (Prop. 2015/16:55).

9 Bernes & Lundgren 2009, p. 304.

10 The Confederation of Swedish Enterprise (*Svenskt Näringsliv*) has clearly and for a long time expressed their opinion that it takes way too much time to get a permit: Dahl & Gutiérrez-Aranda 2012, and initiated an assessment on office turnaround times, published in 2011; Skår 2010.

public arena.[11] In particular the permit process is seen as a barrier for Swedish industry when competing on a European and international market, according to the Confederation of Swedish Enterprise.[12]

Now that the context of administrative decision-making in Swedish environmental law has been laid out, this contribution will: (i) analyse the Swedish permit system regulated by the Environmental Code[13] and Planning and Building Act[14] (2010); (ii) the administrative decision-making procedures to issue environmental and building permits; and (iii) its ability to produce decisions of high quality and speed by reference to official reports; and finally (iv) how speed in the procedure and quality in decision-making is influenced by legal requirements.

2. The Demand for Permits

The need to obtain a permit before carrying out activities that affect the environment is primarily regulated in the Environmental Code[15] and governmental ordinances. Currently there are about 6,300 activities for which permits are compulsory.[16] Several EU directives, such as the Industrial Emissions Directive,[17] have direct influence on what activities require permits and in addition, in Sweden permits are also required for a range of other activities. The Planning and Building Act sets out that a permit is required if the activity concerns a new or altered building.[18]

According to the Environmental Code there are two main permit procedures: (i) a judicial procedure where permits are issued by courts; and (ii) an administrative procedure where permits are issued by administrative authorities.[19] An administrative decision can be appealed before a court and the procedure will then be a mixed judicial/administrative one (figure 1). The Environmental Code lists several situations and activities for which a permit is needed. Two of the most common situations when a permit is mandatory are when starting or conducting some of the large 'environmentally hazardous activities' or a 'water operation'.[20] However, it is common to see a project or an activity as both an environmental hazardous activity and a water operation, and therefore in need of several permits. This holds true for example for ports and industries in need of pumping water from a water body. If the activity will potentially have a significant effect on a Natura

11 According to the Confederation of Swedish Enterprise (*Svenskt Näringsliv*), 38% of the country's workforce is employed in establishments required to apply the Environmental Code: Carlsson 2013.

12 Examples on the debate: Pehrson & Linderstam 2013; Mellwing 2013.

13 Miljöbalk (SFS 1998:808).

14 Plan- och bygglag (SFS 2010:900).

15 Miljöbalk (SFS 1998:808).

16 Magnusson 2016.

17 Directive 2010/75/EU of the European Parliament and of the Council of 24 November 2010 on industrial emissions (integrated pollution prevention and control) [2010] OJ L 334/17.

18 Plan- och bygglag (SFS 2010:900).

19 Miljöbalk (SFS 1998:808).

20 Environmentally Hazardous Activities are regulated in chapter 9 of the Environmental Code (Miljöbalk (SFS 1998:808, 9 kap.) and water operations in chapter 11 (Miljöbalk (SFS 1998:808, 11 kap.).

2000 area (the Habitats Directive),[21] another permit will be required.[22] As long as permits are required by the Environmental Code, it is usually possible to conduct the examination of all permits jointly.[23] But if an activity, in addition to a permit required by the Environmental Code, is also required to get a building permit according to the Planning and Building Act,[24] the cases will be dealt with separately. This situation often occurs when expanding an activity with a building. If an environmental court issues a permit under the Environmental Code,[25] there is no guarantee that the local authority will issue a permit under the Planning and Building Act.[26]

Environmentally Hazardous Activities

An 'environmentally hazardous activity' is a concept that was introduced by the Environmental Protection Act[27] and is a type of activity that is now regulated by the Environmental Code.[28] In order to explicitly assess environmentally hazardous activities against the risk of causing detriment and harm, the government has decided that some activities must have a permit or that local authorities must be notified of them. In the governmental Ordinance of Environmentally Hazardous Activities and the Protection of Public Health, activities are classified as:

(i) requiring a permit issued by a LEC;
(ii) requiring a permit issued by a CAB; and
(iii) requiring notification of an act to a local administration (an appointed municipal board).[29]

Since 2012, the number of CABs assessing and issuing permits has decreased from 21 to 12. The reform aimed at promoting a faster and fairer procedure for the whole country.[30] For some small scale environmental hazardous activities (such as for new water closets and geothermal heating pumps), applications for a permit are to be made at the local municipal board, and not to LEC and CAB.[31]

21 Council Directive 92/43/EEC of 21 May 1992 on the conservation of natural habitats and of wild fauna and flora [1992] OJ L 206/7.
22 Miljöbalk (SFS 1998:808), 7 kap., § 28a.
23 *Ibid.*
24 Plan- och bygglag (SFS 2010:900).
25 Miljöbalk (SFS 1998:808).
26 Plan- och bygglag (SFS 2010:900).
27 Miljöskyddslag (SFS 1969:387).
28 'Environmentally hazardous activity' is defined (Miljöbalk (SFS 1998:808), 9 kap., § 1) as:
1. the discharge of wastewater, solid matter or gas from land, buildings or structures onto land or into water areas or groundwater; or
2. any use of land, buildings or structures that entails a risk of detriment to human health or the environment due to discharges or emissions other than those referred to in point 1 or to pollution of land, air, water areas or groundwater; or
3. any use of land, buildings or structures that may cause a detriment to the surroundings due to noise, vibration, light, ionizing or non-ionizing radiation or similar impact.
29 Förordning om miljöfarlig verksamhet och hälsoskydd (SFS 1998:899).
30 Förordning om miljöprövningsdelegationer (SFS 2011:1237).
31 Förordning om miljöfarlig verksamhet och hälsoskydd (SFS 1998:899).

Permits and notifications are also required for changes in an activity, such as an extension or expansion of an existing activity, but since 2013 only if the change itself or together with earlier changes may cause nuisance of significance to human health or the environment.[32] The court or the CABs can order that the entire activity be re-examined, including any part of it that has not directly changed. For activities that do not need a permit (classified as 'C' or 'lacking classification'), there can always be a voluntary application for a permit. Although often regarded as a long and expensive process, there are also clear advantages to having a permit: it provides legal certainty and protection against new requirements from enforcement agencies.

The process of notifying a local administration is quicker and easier than a proposal for a permit, but does not give any legal certainty. If an activity has no permit, the local administration has the jurisdiction to take enforcement measures by ordering precautionary measures or prohibiting the activity or even order a permit application be made, either in connection with the notification or later in the process.[33]

For some of the largest activities that have the greatest environmental impact, a permit from the LEC is not sufficient: approval from the central Swedish government on the planned location is needed.[34] Although the legal requirements still need to be complied with, this procedure allows for a more political rather than strict judicial assessment, since the rule of location is rather vague and gives room for discretion. This governmental approval is a part of the permit process and the LEC will then continue the process of determining the conditions for the permit. If the government refuses to approve the location, the LEC must reject the application for a permit. The governmental decision cannot be appealed other than on a strict formal basis. The demand for a special governmental approval of the location does not necessarily delay the process, since the choice of site will not later be an issue for appeal.

Water operations

Sweden has an old tradition of regulating water operations, such as those relating to dams and hydropower plants.[35] The earlier Water Act[36] was to a large extent

32 Miljöprövningsförordning (SFS 2013:251).

33 Miljöbalk (SFS 1998:808), 26 kap., § 9 gives the supervision authority the right to order enforcement of the rules of conduct and other requirements of the Code.

34 Miljöbalk (SFS 1998:808), 17 kap.

35 Water operations are defined in the Environmental Code (Miljöbalk (SFS 1998:808), 11 kap., § 2) as:
1. the construction, alteration, repair and removal of dams or other water structures in water areas, filling and piling in water areas, the removal of water from or digging, blasting and cleansing in water areas, as well as other measures in water areas whose purpose is to change the depth or position of the water;
2. the diversion of groundwater and the erection of structures for this purpose;
3. recharging in order to increase the volume of groundwater, as well as the erection of structures and other measures for this purpose; and
4. measures undertaken to drain land, except for the purpose of diverting wastewater or measures to lower or empty a water area or to provide protection against water where the →

transposed into the Environmental Code,[37] but also into a new law that made special provision for water operations.[38] The rules in the Environmental Code, although based on the tradition of older laws, are placed in a whole new legal context because they are to be interpreted to promote a sustainable development.[39] Except the general rules of conduct (chapter 2) mentioned above, there are also additional rules of conduct that are to be applied for specific activities. An example is the requirement to show that the total benefits of water operations are higher than the total costs for the public and individuals. Water operations generally require a permit and only as an exception will a notification suffice. Apart from the general rules, there are special procedural rules in order to also consider private claims for economic compensation (an issue which does not require mandatory consideration when examining environmentally hazardous activities).

Figure 1. Main part of the Swedish permit regime for environmental hazardous activities and water operations, as regulated in the Environmental Code[40]

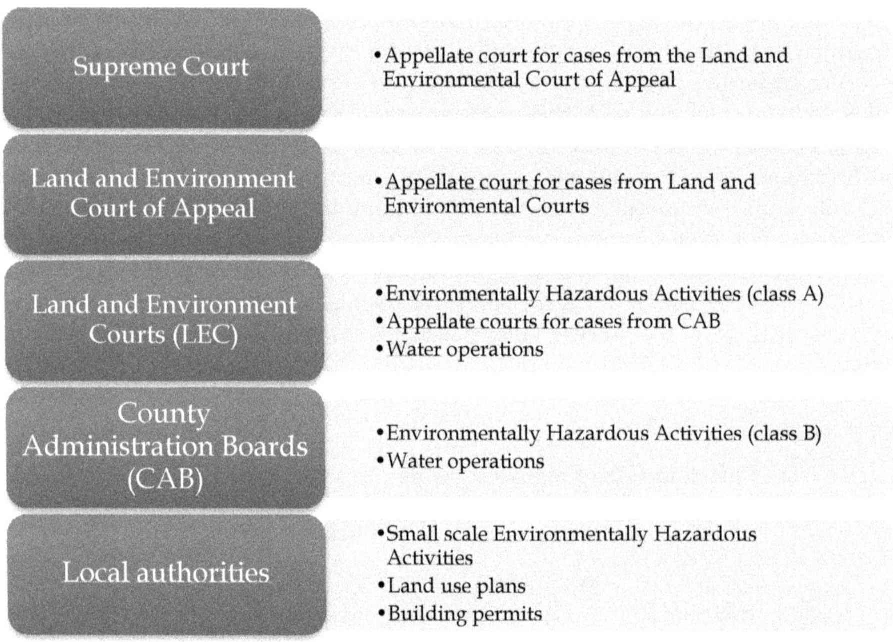

purpose is to increase permanently the suitability of a property for a certain purpose (land drainage).

36 Lag med särskilda bestämmelser om vattenverksamhet (SFS 1998:812).

37 Miljöbalk (SFS 1998:808).

38 Lag med särskilda bestämmelser om vattenverksamhet (SFS 1998:812).

39 Miljöbalk (SFS 1998:808), 1 kap., § 1.

40 Miljöbalk (SFS 1998:808).

Planning and Building Act

Swedish environmental legislation has been highly influenced by EU environmental law over the last 20 years. The planning legislation applied in parallel to the Environmental Code[41] has on the contrary developed without such influences and is based on the freedom for local municipalities to decide upon future land use.

The Swedish land use planning system is based on decisions on future land use, taken by 290 local municipal boards. The local authorities also issue building permits. There are links between the Planning and Building Act[42] and the Environmental Code[43] on how to balance common interests of land, particularly areas of national interest. However, generally the power to decide on land use is in the hands of the local authority. The balancing act between exploitation and conservation is thus more of a political decision than a judicial one, though there are loose rules that guide decisions. The inability of the government and national authorities to directly control local planning matters causes problems when implementing EU directives that require specific results, such as the Air Quality Directive,[44] the Water Framework Directive[45] and the Marine Strategy Framework Directive.[46] If a standard is exceeded, the local authority must take action, but has no jurisdiction to rule over other municipalities. For example, if an air quality standard is exceeded because of heavy traffic, the local authority in this town will not be able to prevent the building of a new shopping mall in a neighbouring municipality, even if it has been proven to cause more traffic and emissions into their area. The regional CAB is required to re-examine all land use plans, but in reality it has never prevented this situation. There is very strong political support for municipalities to have this planning jurisdiction and so it is difficult for the Parliament to limit their power despite it having the formal power to do so.

Swedish planning legislation is focused on promoting a sustainable use of land, while environmental legislation focuses on protection of the environment and human health. To further integrate the planning legislation with the environmental legislation, a new Planning and Building Act was enacted and entered into force in May 2011.[47] The extent of integration has been rather modest. The most important integration that has occurred is that there is a more unified appeal system. Local authorities' decisions on plans and building permits will onwards also be heard at appeal before the LECs (see figure 1). The relatively generous right to appeal against

41 *Ibid.*
42 Plan- och bygglag (SFS 2010:900).
43 Miljöbalk (SFS 1998:808).
44 Directive 2008/50/EC of the European Parliament and of the Council of 21 May 2008 on ambient air quality and cleaner air for Europe [2008] OJ L 152/1.
45 Directive 2000/60/EC of the European Parliament and of the Council of 23 October 2000 establishing a framework for Community action in the field of water policy [2000] OJ L 327/1.
46 Directive 2008/56/EC of the European Parliament and of the Council of 17 June 2008 establishing a framework for community action in the field of marine environmental policy (Marine Strategy Framework Directive) [2008] OJ L 164/19.
47 Plan- och bygglag (SFS 2010:900).

local planning decisions often prolongs the process of obtaining building permits.[48] Many activities require both a building permit[49] and a permit under the Environmental Code,[50] and many months (sometimes several years) can pass before proposals for permits are finally decided on.

The lengthy process of obtaining permits for windmills has long been seen as contradictory to the policy of promoting the development of wind energy. In an attempt to speed up the process, the requirement for a permit was removed in 2009 by the Planning and Building Act,[51] on the condition that a permit is needed for the windmill under the Environmental Code.[52] To obtain such a permit, the local municipality needs to actively approve the windmill. However, this has made the process even slower. It has been reported that municipalities are reluctant to give such approval and many also demand compensation for giving this approval.[53]

3. Procedure for Getting a Permit

In Sweden, the EIA is an integrated part of the permit system (see figure 2) and thus assessed by the authority or court providing the permit. Prior to applying for a permit, there is a need for consultation with concerned authorities and private parties (Art. 4, chapter 6 of the Environmental Code).[54] The application must include an EIA report, meeting the criteria set out in Article 7, chapter 6 of the Code, and, *inter alia*, a protocol from the consultation. After reviewing the application from a formal perspective the application is sent out to concerned authorities and private parties that are given a possibility to state their opinions about or suggestions concerning the proposed operations or changes thereof. The court or the CAB often finds the need to order the applicant to complement the original proposal with such information they deem necessary (Art. 2 of chapter 22 of the Environmental Code).[55] If the applicant does not follow the order, the application might be rejected. An incomplete application might in the long run be very costly for the applicant.

An open hearing is usually held by the courts and sometimes also by the CAB. When the case is sufficiently assessed, a decision is taken. The acceptance of the EIA is a decision within the final decision of the proposal (Art. 9 of chapter 6 of the Environmental Code).[56] If approved, the permit is issued with conditions. Stakeholders with the right to appeal can do so within three weeks beginning from the day of the decision, and do not risk any costs by doing so.

48 Anyone affected by the plan who has also participated in the planning process by giving his or her opinion has the right to appeal to 1) the CAB; and 2) the LEC; and 3) after special assessment, to the LEC of Appeal (Plan- och bygglag (SFS 2010:900), 13 kap., § 11).

49 Plan- och bygglag (SFS 2010:900).

50 Miljöbalk (SFS 1998:808).

51 Plan- och bygglag (SFS 2010:900).

52 Miljöbalk (SFS 1998:808).

53 Kaliber 2013.

54 Miljöbalk (SFS 1998:808), 6 kap., § 4.

55 *Ibid.*, 22 kap., § 2.

56 *Ibid.*, 6 kap., § 9.

It is important to note that in the procedure to obtain permits, both the Environmental Code[57] and the Planning and Building Act[58] set out the basic presumption that courts and authorities are responsible for assessing whether there is sufficient information for a comprehensive review of the effects of the proposed activity. The applicant is responsible for providing sufficient information and for the costs of doing so. Although the court or the authority is guiding the applicant to some degree during the permit process, many applicants still have a lawyer. Whether the absence of a lawyer slows down the process of obtaining a permit has not been analysed.

Figure 2: The procedure for getting a permit (environmentally hazardous activity)

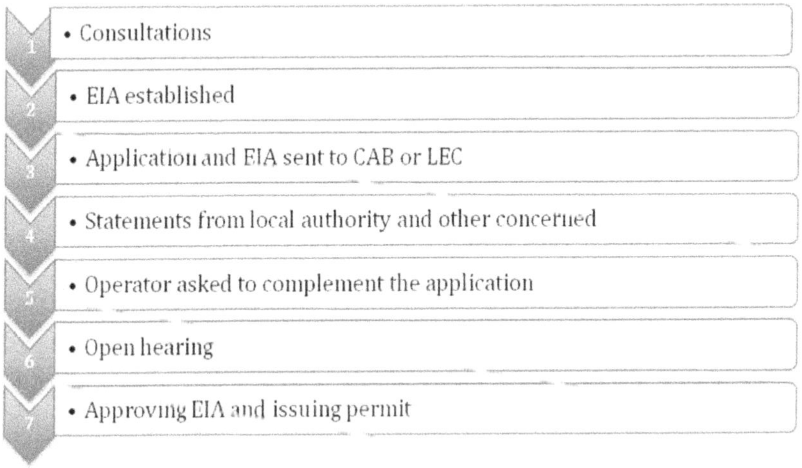

4. How Long Does it Take to Get a Permit?

There are few examples of comprehensive surveys and analyses of the speed and quality of decision-making concerning environmental or building permits. The reports available do not show any homogenous trends. In a report dated from 2008, the Environmental Protection Agency (EPA) compiled figures from 2004-2007 of how long it took to get a permit from a regional CAB.[59] Several changes in the Environmental Code[60] came into force during this same period aiming at speeding up the process, but on average the procedural time decreased from 67 to 61 weeks (9%). In a study initiated by the Confederation of Swedish Enterprise published in 2010 (*Ramböll*-study I), the average procedural times for CABs to decide on an application for a permit (for environmentally hazardous activities classified as B-activities) was 56 weeks, but increased by 30 percent, from 46 weeks in 2007 to 61

57 *Ibid.*
58 Plan- och bygglag (SFS 2010:900).
59 Wikström, Nyström & Malmberg 2008.
60 Miljöbalk (SFS 1998:808).

weeks in 2010.[61] During the same time, the number of proposals increased from 483 to 513 per year. The difference in these two studies is explained by the methods used and the fact that the study done by EPA did not include applications for sand or stone pits that take less time than average to handle. In February 2016, the Confederation of Swedish Enterprises presented a new study by Ramböll on the procedural times for CABs and LECs to decide on permits, during the period from 2011-2014 (*Ramböll*-study II).[62] This study shows that the procedural time taken by CABs in general increased by 10 from 56 to 66 weeks, although the number of applications have decreased from 435 (2011) to 401 (2014). The trend with fewer applications is explained in the report as resultant of the general economic decline.[63]

It is important to note that there are clear differences in procedural time between the different CABs and between different types of activities. According to the *Ramböll*-study I, it varied between 42 weeks on average for sand and stone pits and similar activities to 103 weeks for shooting ranges.[64] While the procedural time between 2004 and 2007 according to the EPA study decreased in 13 of 21 counties, it increased in eight counties.[65] According to the *Ramböll*-study I, the average procedural time varied with 29 weeks on average for the CAB in the county of Västerbotten to 106 weeks for the CAB in the county Södermanland.[66] During the period 2011-2014 the amount of CAB-issued permits had decreased from 21 to 12, but the study still showed a clear difference between different CAB procedural times. While the county of Uppland took 87 weeks on average to come to a decision, the CAB in Västerbotten took 36 weeks.[67]

A relevant issue to further analyse is how long it takes in different parts of the process, such as from when the application is submitted to when the decision is taken, and how long each actor takes in his or her role during this process. Of the total 56 weeks in the *Ramböll*-study I, (2007-2010) the CAB used on average 11 weeks; the consulted authorities 22 weeks; and the applicant 23 weeks to responding to requests about the application.[68] From 2011-2014 the total time had increased on average by 10 weeks and that was only as an effect of the extra 10 weeks that the applicants had to respond to requests. The time taken by consulted authorities and CABs has not changed.[69]

61 Skår 2010. According to the same study, the average procedural time for environmentally hazardous activities, classified as A-activities and examined by the LECs, was 60 weeks.
62 Skår 2016.
63 Skår 2016.
64 Skår 2010.
65 Wikström, Nyström & Malmberg 2008.
66 Skår 2010.
67 Skår 2016, p. 22.
68 Skår 2010.
69 Skår 2016.

Figure 3: Average procedural time for application to CABs to start or adjust environmentally hazardous activities during the period 2007-2010 compared to the period 2011-2014

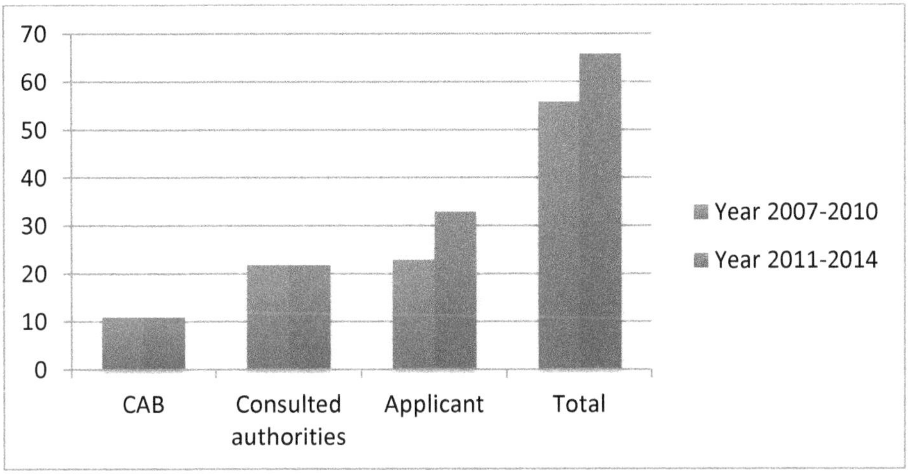

As the procedural time for CABs to handle an application increased, the time for deciding by the LECs on applications regarding an environmentally hazardous activity decreased from 60 weeks during the period 2007-2010 to 52 weeks during the period 2011-2014. The time taken by the consulted authorities and the courts has increased slightly (on average one week each) between the two time periods. The time used by the applicants has, however, decreased by eight weeks, a clear difference compared to the time applicants take in cases handled by the CABs.

The procedural time for deciding on application to the LECs for a permit for water operations does not follow the same trend as for applications for environmentally hazardous activities. Instead, these procedures increased by 13 weeks on average, from 40 weeks during the period 2007-2010 to 53 weeks during the period 2011-2014. The time applicants took decreased by two weeks during this period, while the time for consulting authorities increased by two weeks and the time spent by the courts increased by 10 weeks.

The figures presented above do not include the time spent before the proposal has been submitted. A study from 2008 of the total procedural time it takes to put up a windmill - beginning with consultation all the way to a final decision - showed that the CAB takes on average 10-18 months to issue a decision. If appealed, the case takes about 6-12 months at each court. The estimated time relates to normal cases without any extreme difficulties. There are, however, cases that have taken more than 10 years, explained by many rounds of appeals.[70] Windmill cases are an illustrative example as the application for a permit mostly concerns a new activity. It is an activity with mostly known effects and is not technically complicated.

The amount of appeals of decisions taken by a CAB has increased every year from 2011-2014. The total time in the LEC for handling appealed cases has,

70 Wind power station on land producing more than 25 MW or in water producing more than 1 MW (Prövning av vindkraft, (SOU 2008:86), p. 103, 163, 345.

however, decreased during the same period, from 36 weeks in average during 2007-2010 to 32 weeks in average during 2011-2014.

The procedural time can be translated into costs, and the resources spent by courts and CABs is in accordance with the *Ramböll*-study I, that is, on average (i) 23 working days for proposals for class-A activities; (ii) 18 working days for proposals for class B-activities; and (iii) 13 working days for proposals for water operations. The resources spent by the applicant are estimated to be 1.4 annual manpower for A-classed activities, and 0.4 annual manpower for B-classed activities and water operations.[71] There are no similar figures for the period 2011-2014.

5. Why Does it Take so Long to Get a Permit?

As shown above, the total procedural time differs a lot between the type of activities, authorities and courts as well as different stages of the process. Obviously there are many reasons for the difficulty in speeding up the permit process.[72] Reasons for the differences in procedural time can, according to staff working at CABs and LECs, be explained by the differences in the complexity of cases, the quality of the proposal, the consulting authorities' speed to reply, the localization of, and the extent of the proposed activity.[73]

To some extent the delay in decision-making goes back to the working environment at the CABs and LECs. Lack of sufficient resources and a heavy workload are to be highlighted. As seen above, the working culture of the consulted authorities can be another reason for delay. In high pressure situations they ask for extended time to respond to the application or any other matter for which they are asked to respond. Difficulties in recruiting competent personnel might add to the pressure for authorities. The decrease in time taken during some parts of the process in LECs is explained by strategic work by the courts, such as by defining new routines but also by the applicants' will and capacity to formulate applications of good quality.

Interesting to note is also the fact that the speed of the process is not solely linked to the speed of authorities and courts. Insufficient EIAs or proposals and a need for courts and CABs to ask the applicant to add information to the proposal, as well as the operators' own requests for a prolonged time to respond to demands on statements, additional information and so on, might often be a sign of lack of competence of operators and consulting firms. As shown in the *Ramböll*-studies, the time spent by the applicants to add to the proposal varies over time and between different types of cases. The time applicants used for adding to the application or responding to questions from consulted authorities in CAB cases regarding environmentally hazardous activities increased quite dramatically (10 weeks on average between the periods). At the same time applicants in court spent much less time adding to their application. One explanation presented in the *Ramböll*-study II is a decrease in quality of the applications to the CAB during recent years.[74] It is,

71 Skår 2010.

72 Many of the reasons are described in Wikström, Nyström & Malmberg 2008.

73 Skår 2016.

74 Skår 2016.

however, important to realise the complexity of many operations and the difficulty to foresee all types of objections put up by authorities and other concerned.

6. Reforming the Permit Regime

Immediately after the Environmental Code came into force, a governmental committee was assigned to review and further develop the Code.[75] The Commission for the Environmental Code (*Miljöbalkskommittén*) worked between 1999 and 2005 and proposed changes in the Code aiming at better efficiency and a more comprehensive regulation for the different types of activities. These proposals have to a large extent been implemented by the legislators and mostly been aimed at easing the possibility for business to expand. Procedural requirements, such as that concerning the EIA consultation, have been changed in order to speed up the process to implement new projects. Many types of operations no longer need a permit or notification to the local authority and may thus commence their activity, but still need to comply with the general rules of conduct in the Code. After a reform of the permit system (2008) only about 4,650 operations needed a permit and only 18,750 need to notify a local authority.

From 2007-2009 a new national commission was given the task by the government to suggest how the permit system could become more efficient and harmonized. In 2009, this commission presented a proposal for a new system, integrating property courts and environmental courts and getting a more comprehensive permit system. The reform came into force in May 2011 and thereafter mainly regional CABs and local authorities have issued permits, and courts are mainly a forum for appeals. Permits for environmentally hazardous activities, class A (see above section 2) and water operations will, however, still be examined by LECs.

Another result of the reforms was a changed procedure to build and start a wind power plant. Despite the political will to promote the development of wind energy, the process to obtain a permit was very complicated and often slow. In 2009, the Parliament decided on several alleviations in the permit requirements.[76] These changes were clearly in line with the governments' general objective to decrease the administrative costs for business related to national rules by 25 percent until the year 2010.[77] The reform did not, however, have the desired effect. In fact, the time to get a permit for a windmill according to the Environmental Code[78] is estimated to have doubled.[79] There is also an indication that municipalities negotiate with wind energy business and ask for economic compensation to give an approval.[80]

A conclusion drawn in the *Ramböll*-study I was that the amount of permit cases in courts and CABs are likely to increase because of the implementation of the

75 Miljöbalk (SFS 1998:808).
76 Prövning av vindkraft (Prop. 2008/09:146).
77 Regelförenklingsarbetet 2006-2010 (Skr. 2009/10:226).
78 Miljöbalk (SFS 1998:808).
79 Andersson 2010.
80 Kaliber 2013.

Industrial Emissions Directive[81] and the Water Framework Directive,[82] as well as a positive economic development.[83] These changes would draw increased resources for the authorities as well as for applicants. In the *Ramböll*-study II it is clear that a small increase of applicants to the courts can be seen, but applications to CABs are decreasing.[84]

7. What Can be Done to Increase Speed and Quality?

Since the Environmental Code was enacted in 1998,[85] industry representatives, farmers and other stakeholders have required an easier and quicker process for getting permits. The debate has focused on speeding up the process and the issue of quality has been fairly absent. The major changes in the Environmental Code[86] have also aimed at making it easier for operators to get a permit. Still, the processes for getting permits do not seem to have been dramatically shortened and the complaints from the industry have continued.[87] So what more can be done to shorten the process? Some of the suggestions presented in the EPA report from 2008 are still valid:

(i) make it easier to disregard inadequate proposals for permits;
(ii) use general requirements instead of individual permits;
(iii) give more resources to CABs;
(iv) provide better information to operators, particularly during the EIA consultation about what is required from an EIA and a proposal;
(v) enhance further cooperation between CABs;
(vi) provide more education of staff at authorities, consultancies and operators.

In an official report of the Swedish Government 2015,[88] a proposal was made to introduce a new authority with a mission to issue all the main permits required by the Environmental Code.[89] The response from consulted authorities on the proposed changes has varied, but many of the CABs opposed this proposal, as they did not share the view of benefits from assembling the examination of permits.[90] They argued that this change would rather be negative for the quality of the decisions, as the competence and the supervisory tasks will spread out to different authorities. However, the development towards a more uniform organization for examining permits according to the Environmental Code[91] and the Planning and Building Act[92]

81 Directive 2010/75/EU.
82 Directive 2000/60/EC.
83 Skår 2010.
84 Skår 2016.
85 Miljöbalk (SFS 1998:808).
86 *Ibid.*
87 Stenberg 2013; Karlsson 2012.
88 Vägar till ett effektivare miljöarbete (SOU 2015:43).
89 Miljöbalk (SFS 1998:808).
90 Response from the County Administration Board in Stockholm County: Bosson & Strid 2015.
91 Miljöbalk (SFS 1998:808).
92 Plan- och bygglag (SFS 2010:900).

has at least so far led to a smoother organization but also to a more efficient use of resources, both economic and in terms of knowledge. It is, however, doubtful that it is possible to speed up the process without affecting the quality. A more holistic and ambitious environmental policy within the EU will push industry and other actors to have knowledge and relate their operations not only to single substances but also to ecosystem functions. Unless Member States provide strong support, the burden of obtaining information will fall on the operators and will have to be examined by state administrations and courts. One common view among actors and authorities is the lack of knowledge or resources to get knowledge, either by recruiting new personnel or by educating the existing staff. Improving the level of competence is seen as a way to shorten the process of getting permits. Finally, it is also worth pointing out the benefits of decision-making processes taking time, particularly in the primary stages, in order to avoid detriment and damage, leading to high costs for the operators in the future.

BIBLIOGRAPHY

Andersson 2010
Andersson, W., '16 kap. 4 § Miljöbalken - vad hände sen?', Energy Agency 2010.

Bergquist 2007
Bergquist, A-K., 'Guld och Gröna Skogar. Miljöanpassningen av Rönnskärsverken 1960-2000', Umeå Studies in Economic History 2007.

Bernes & Lundgren 2009
Bernes, C. & Lundgren, L.J., *Bruk och missbruk av naturens resurser: en svensk miljöhistoria*, Stockholm: Naturvårdsverket 2009, p. 304.

Bosson & Strid 2015
Bosson, M. & Strid, J., 'Yttrande över remiss om betänkandet 'Vägar till ett effektivare miljöarbete' SOU 2015:43', Länstyrellsen Stockholm, 2015, available at: <www.lansstyrelsen.se/Stockholm/SiteCollectionDocuments/Sv/om-lansstyrelsen/remisser/2015/101-23920-2015.pdf>.

Carlsson 2013 niet 2011
Carlsson, A., 'Jag köper inte Svenskt Näringslivs utredning', *Svenskt Näringsliv*, 5 July 2013, available at: <www.svensktnaringsliv.se/fragor/almedalen2013/jag-koper-inte-svenskt-naringslivs-utredning_197085.html>.

Dahl & Gutiérrez-Aranda 2012
Dahl, S. & Gutiérrez-Aranda, G., 'Långa handläggningstider äventyrar miljöinvesteringar', *Svenskt Näringsliv*, 23 May 2012, available at: <www.svensktnaringsliv.se/fragor/miljo-energi-klimat/langa-handlaggningstider-aventyrar-miljoinvesteringar_562787.html>

Kaliber 2013
Kaliber, Sveriges Radio 'Veto med en prislapp', 13 February 2013, available at: <http://sverigesradio.se/sida/avsnitt/152810?programid=1316>.

Karlsson 2012
Karlsson, S., 'Långa miljöprövningar bromsar investeringar, *Svenskt Näringsliv*, 23 November 2012, available at: <www.svensktnaringsliv.se/regioner/falun/langa-miljoprovningar-bromsar-investeringar_176173.html>.

Magnusson 2016
Magnusson, M., *Vägledning om miljörapportering*, Stockholm: Naturvårdsverket 2016, available at: <www.naturvardsverket.se/Stod-i-miljoarbetet/Vagledningar/Egenkontroll-miljorapportering/Miljorapportering/>.

Mellwing 2013
Mellwing, D., 'Miljöbalken - Sveriges krångligaste lag', *Entreprenör*, 2013, available at: <www.entreprenor.se/nyheter/miljobalken-sveriges-krangligaste-lag_501798.html>.

Pehrson & Linderstam 2013
Pehrson, P. & Linderstam, S., 'Gruvor sinkas av långa handläggningstider', *Dagens Samhälle*, 2013, available at <www.dagenssamhalle.se/debatt/gruvor-sinkas-av-langa-handlaeggningstider-4890>.

Skår 2010
Skår, N., *Undersökning av genomförandetider och framtida resursbehov för projekt med miljöpåverkan*, Stockholm: Ramböll Management Consulting & Svenskt Näringsliv 2010.

Skår 2016
Skår, N., *Ledtider vid tillståndsprövning av verksamheter med miljöpåverkan*, Stockholm: Ramböll Management Consulting & Svenskt Näringsliv 2016.

Stenberg 2013
Stenberg, J., 'Oförutsägbara miljöprocesser riskerar stoppa gruvboom', *Entreprenör*, 18 June 2013, available at: <www.entreprenor.se/nyheter/oforutsagbara-miljoprocesser-riskerar-stoppa-gruvboom_501802.html>.

Wikström, Nyström & Malmberg 2008
Wikström, D., Nyström, E. & Malmberg, H., *Rapport 5880. Handläggningstider för miljöprövning enligt miljöbalken. Redovisning av ett regeringsuppdrag om handläggningstider för tillståndsärenden som beslutas av miljöprövningsdelegationerna*, Stockholm: Naturvårdsverket 2008.

Chris Backes
Sander Jansen

FASTER AND BETTER!? DECISION-MAKING IN THE NETHERLANDS

1. Introduction

Over the last decade, faster (and better) decision-making has been a hot topic in discussions about the improvement of administrative law and government policy in the Netherlands. Whilst administrative lawyers were proud of the coming into force of the first General Administrative Law Act (GALA) in 1994,[1] politicians had a more critical view on the functioning and effectiveness of the law governing the administration. They felt that their plans and actions were hampered by complex laws, by judges who over-scrutinized and were much too critical and by citizens who objected to plans devised by the administration much too often. There was a feeling that 'almost nothing can be done any more' because of difficult procedures, detailed rules and intensive but ineffective judicial review: this culminated in a report in 1997 of a 'taskforce reducing juridification of the public administration', the so-called 'taskforce Van Kemenade'.[2] The report was commented on by many who argued that the analysis and argumentation was partial.[3] Nevertheless it had a great impact, sparking a broad discussion about the functioning of administrative law, especially of the procedural rules and judicial review.

The next triggers for the discussion on speeding up decision-making were the EU environmental directives, especially the directive on air quality standards (Directive 1996/61/EC).[4] In 2005 stringent binding quality standards for particulate matter and NOx came into force. The air quality in many parts of Europe (Italy, France, Belgium, UK, Germany, the Netherlands) did not comply with these standards. As a consequence, Dutch judges prohibited any activity that would cause a little extra pollution of the air quality in places where the quality standards were not met, which at that time was nearly everywhere in the Netherlands. New housing areas, motorways, football stadiums and industrial sites could not be built.

1 Algemene wet bestuursrecht (Awb).
2 Werkgroep Van Kemenade 1997.
3 For example, Neerhof, Schlössels & De Werd 1997, p. 1254-1266; De Waard 1998, p. 60-66.
4 Council Directive 96/61/EC of 24 September 1996 concerning integrated pollution prevention and control [1996] OJ L 257/26.

The interesting thing was that this only happened in the Netherlands and not in any of the other countries which did not meet the air quality standards.[5]

Consequently the Council for Environment and Infrastructure[6] explored why there were huge differences between the Netherlands and other countries. They identified a whole range of factors. One is that the Netherlands is a small country with an extremely dense population, is highly active (in housing, traffic, industry, and has extremely intensive agricultural output) in a very small space, and is exposed to pollution from neighbouring countries. Other factors which are more relevant from our point of view are a very low threshold to start judicial review proceedings and the speedy delivery of (last instance) court decisions. To illustrate this, within a period of six years, German courts dealt with 110 procedures initiated by environmental NGOs. In the same period, Dutch courts decided (on average) around 600 claims brought by NGOs each year. Taking the size and population of both countries into account this is about 200 times as many. Moreover, about 50 percent of the claims of Dutch NGOs were successful whilst only about 25 percent were successful in Germany.[7] Another important factor is that judges seem to (have to) apply the relevant EU law quite strictly, mainly due to the very strict interpretation and transposition of EU directives by the Dutch legislator. In combination these factors seemed to explain that EU law, especially certain environmental law directives, had a much bigger impact on the Netherlands than on other countries. The decisions allowing all kinds of projects with environmental effects like new housing areas, motorways or industrial installations were quashed and investments were blocked or extremely delayed.

Another report which was crucial for the discussion to speed up decision-making was delivered in the same year (2008) by an *ad hoc* commission: the Commission on Accelerating Decision-making on Infrastructural Projects (*Commissie Versnelling Besluitvorming Infrastructurele Projecten*), well known by the name of its chair as the *Elverding* Committee. This commission carried out a thorough analysis of the time which was needed for the planning of 120 infrastructural projects such as roads or railways and the reasons for delay. In its report the commission found that planning procedures for infrastructural works take on average 12 years.

The reasons for such long-lasting procedures are manifold. According to the report, the main delaying factors are to be found at the political level. Competences are very much scattered and partly due to Dutch culture, authorities consult each other intensively and often. When a political agreement is finally made after years of consideration, the budget is often no longer available. Having taken such a political decision, it then has to be brought into practice and the official planning procedures have to be applied. Within the time period needed to do so, authorities can often change their mind and tend to disagree with what was concluded, partly due to electoral changes in their political composition. Furthermore, participation of

5 Backes, Van Nieuwerburgh & Koelemeijer 2005, p. 157-164.

6 This council (VROM-*Raad*) is an independent body which advises the Dutch government on request and on its own initiative about all questions of housing, physical planning and environmental policy.

7 VROM-Raad 2008, p. 37 *et seq*. This report refers to Sadeleer, Roller & Dross 2005.

citizens in these procedures is not very effective as the principal decisions have been taken at a political level and the authorities are no longer open minded and do not want to consider substantial alternatives. As well as these political factors, the *Elverding* Committee also identified delaying factors in the official decision-making procedure and in judicial review, both labelled as 'judicial factors'.[8] However, these judicial factors were, in relation to the 'political factors', considered to be of minor importance. As will be seen, the measures taken in reaction to the *Elverding* Report mainly concerned the judicial factors and not the political factors.

The latter reports were published in spring 2008, a few months after the financial crisis had hit. As an effect of the financial crisis and the economic crisis which followed, the topic of speed in decision-making, mainly with regard to all kinds of housing and infrastructural projects, was given a very high priority. In April 2009, the Prime Minister decided that a temporary 'Crisis and Recovery Act', or CRA (*Crisis- en herstelwet*, Chw)[9] was needed to cut down the duration of (planning) procedures and to speed up decision-making. The draft act was delivered to Parliament just three months later. The CRA entered into force on 30 March 2010 and should have lasted until 2014. The First Chamber of the Parliament adopted the act only after the government promised a thorough evaluation of its effects.[10] However, in November 2011, before the first evaluation of the CRA was available, the government launched a draft act to make the CRA permanent. This finally happened during 2013 and 2014. After about three years, some of the provisions of the CRA became part of the GALA, hence governing general administrative law.

The discussion about speeding up decision-making procedures did not end there. For many years there has been a discussion to simplify environmental law in the broadest sense (law on physical planning, environment, water, nature conservation) by streamlining or integrating the procedural rules and also substantial requirements. As a result, the General Act on Environmental Law (*Wet algemene bepalingen omgevingsrecht*, or Wabo) came into force in October 2010. This Act mainly integrated the procedures of permits which may be required on the basis of 25 different acts, like the Water Act (*Waterwet*), the Environmental Act (*Wet milieubeheer*) or the Planning Act (*Wet op de Ruimtelijke Ordening*). The idea is that someone who wants to run a certain project should only need to apply for one single permit at one single (front) office (one-stop-shop). At the back office, however, competences remain unchanged and widespread. The Wabo permit can therefore only be granted with the agreement of all the authorities that have the competence to decide on a certain aspect of the application. As all allowances are bundled in one procedure and one decision which only can be challenged once, decision-making is fastened compared with the former situation with several permits and several judicial review procedures which often had to be run through one after the other.

In future the scope and content of the (future) *Omgevingswet*, which will enter into force after 2018, will be much broader than the Wabo. It is hard to translate

8 Commissie Versnelling Besluitvorming 2008, p. 6 *et seq.*

9 Crisis- en herstelwet, *Stb.* 2010, 135.

10 *Handelingen I* 2009/10, 32 127, n. 22, p. 949.

Omgevingswet into English. The result would probably again be 'Environmental Act'. The idea of the *Omgevingswet,* however, is to integrate all laws which concern the physical surroundings in the same way as the Water Act, Environmental Act, Planning Act, Nature Conservation Act (*Natuurbeschermingswet*), and many others. As the term 'Environmental Act' suggests a much too limited scope we will use the original Dutch term: *Omgevingswet*. The preparations for this enormous and fundamental legislative operation started in 2009 or 2010. In 2010 the Ministry of Infrastructure and Environment published 15 essays on the future of planning and environmental law.[11] The ministry installed a new directorate called 'Directorate Simply Better' (*eenvoudig beter*) to manage this major legislative operation. In June 2014, the government submitted the draft *Omgevingswet* to Parliament, which agreed upon the draft on 1 July 2015 (Second Chamber) and on 22 March 2016 (First Chamber). The *Omgevingswet* requires huge integration of secondary law (some 120 ordinances (orders in council, *algemene maatregel van bestuur*) will be integrated into 4 decrees) and will not enter into force before 2018. The *Omgevingswet* will not only integrate existing laws, but should bring about substantial deregulation, decentralization and simplification of the existing law on the environment in the broadest sense. It should also increase flexibility and, of course, decrease the time needed to get projects started.

Parallel to these developments which mainly concerned physical planning and environmental law, very substantial changes took place in general administrative law, especially in the rules and practice of judicial review, which were mainly a consequence of a shift from a (partly) *recours objectif to a recours subjectif* in administrative court procedures. Up until the 80s the system of Dutch judicial review was mainly inspired by French law. The main task of the judge was to control the legality of decisions of the administration. If a decision infringed written provisions or general principles of administrative law, it was quashed and the case was referred back to the authorities. The authority had to decide again and if the outcome was not what the appellant wanted, he or she would have to bring another claim against the new decision. From the viewpoint of a balance of power within the *trias politica,* this is coherent.

However, judicial review might not have been very efficient as it did not bring litigation to an end in due time. When the (first parts of the) GALA came into force in 1994, the legislator made clear that Dutch law should 'more clearly' follow the idea of *recours subjectif.* However, some elements of *recours objectif* remained. This may have been the cause of a fundamental change in the practice of administrative litigation. The legislator mainly followed this trend of the practice of judicial review, partly also triggered by the discussions in environmental law (mentioned above). On 1 January 2013, an Act on changes in administrative litigation rules entered into force.[12] An important programmatic provision introduced by this act is Article 8:41a GALA which reads as follows: 'The administrative judge should conclude the lawsuit brought before him in a way which is as final as possible'. This basically means that the task of the judge is not to control whether a certain decision was legal or not but to reach a final solution for the case and if possible the underlying

11 Ministerie van Infrastructuur en Milieu 2011.

12 Wet aanpassing bestuursprocesrecht, *Stb*. 2012, 682.

conflict which was brought before him. This provision condenses the changes which had already developed in practice.

2. Acceleration Initiatives Concerning the Administrative Decision-Making Process

2.1. *Measures Taken to Speed Up Decision-Making*

The general decision-making procedure in title 4.1 GALA (Arts. 4:1 *et seq*. GALA) has not changed since the coming into force of the GALA (1994). Generally, single-case decisions (*beschikkingen*) should be taken within six weeks from when an application has been submitted (Art. 4:13 GALA).[13] However, during the last two decades a whole range of changes has appeared in environmental and planning law to speed up decision-making on all kinds of building and infrastructural projects.

2.1.1. EIA Procedure

Originally Dutch law provided an extensive and effective EIA procedure with the requirement of advice from an independent 'Committee on the EIA'[14] on both the scope of the EIA (before an EIA report is drafted) and on the EIA report itself. Gradually, the EIA procedure has been scaled down. In most cases the advice is no longer obligatory and its costs have to be paid by the authority who is asking for it.[15] The authority often asks the initiator of a plan or project to reimburse these costs. The most recent 'simplification' has been brought about by Article 1(11) CRA.[16] According to this Article, for all projects within the scope of the CRA - even for major infrastructural projects - it is not necessary to assess alternatives and nor is the EIA Committee's advice needed. One may argue that this implies an attack on the quality of decision-making as the need to assess the environmental effects of reasonable alternatives of the proposed project touches the 'heart of the EIA requirement'.[17]

2.1.2. Integration of Approvals and One-Stop-Shop

The most intensively discussed topic with regard to decision-making in the area of building and infrastructural projects of the last decades concerns the integration of legal regimes and approval requirements. This process had already started in the 80s. An important milestone was the integration of different environmental permit requirements for specific environmental sectors (in a narrow sense: noise, air-quality, waste) into the 'integrated' environmental permit on the basis of the Environmental Management Act (*Wet milieubeheer*, or Wmb)[18] in 1993. However,

13 Art. 4:1-4:2 and Art. 4:3 GALA.
14 Commissie voor de milieueffectrapportage, available at: <www.commissiemer.nl>.
15 Art. 2.23a Wmb.
16 Art. 1.11 Chw.
17 Verschuuren 2010, p. 8 *et seq*.
18 Wet milieubeheer, *Stb*. 2005, 282.

permits for discharge of substances into the water, nature protection, the building licence and many others remained separate. The next important step was the procedural integration of all these permit procedures into one permit on the basis of the aforementioned Wabo in 2010. This Act introduced the one-stop-shop approach. As a consequence, an initiator of a proposed project may apply for one single permit only. This permit integrates most environmental requirements in the areas just mentioned. As there is only one single permit, objection and judicial review is also possible only once. The one-stop-shop approach makes life much easier for applicants and accelerates decision-making significantly: at least it is supposed to. Moreover, a Wabo permit can contribute to better coordination of different environmental aspects. However, this approach does not lead to a real, substantial integration of the permit requirements. The single permit only concerns an integration of the front offices of the administrative authorities. At the back office the authorities keep their limited competences, for example to decide on the discharge to water or on nature protection aspects. They have to coordinate and finally procedurally integrate their decisions into one permit.

The evaluation of the Wabo has demonstrated that the aims of the integration of permit requirements were only partly achieved. According to the 'users' the Wabo did not always speed up and simplify decision-making.[19] The *Omgevingswet*, passed by Parliament in 2016, but which will not come into force before 2018, is supposed to integrate the procedures of the various permit requirements but also their content. However, it is yet to be seen whether and how this will be possible as many of the criteria for decisions on environmental effects of projects are based on EU law and cannot be integrated.[20]

2.1.3. *Lex Silentio Positivo*, Penalty Payments and Direct Appeal

Over the last decade three further instruments aimed at speeding up decision-making have been introduced: the so-called *lex silentio positivo*, penalty payments, and direct appeal.

Introduction of the *lex silentio positivo* was partly required by the EU Services Directive.[21] There were also autonomous reasons to use this instrument to increase pressure to keep within the time limits for decision-making. The general rule of Article 6:2(b) GALA is that if the time limit to take a decision on a request has expired the administrative inactivity is challengeable. As stated, if no time limit to issue a requested decision is determined by law, the general time limit (Art. 4:13 GALA) is six weeks. If on the basis of Article 6:2(b) GALA an application receives no response by the due time the applicant may file a suit at the administrative court. The court can then find the appeal well-founded and order the administrative authority to decide within a certain time (a few weeks), probably completed with an order to pay a fine if the authority does not comply.[22] This all takes some time. To

19 Borgers *et al*. 2012, p. 14.

20 Critical: Tolsma 2014, p. 81 *et seq.*; Backes 2013, p. 99-112.

21 Directive 2006/123/EC of the European Parliament and of the Council of 12 December 2006 on services in the internal market [2006] OJ L 376/36.

22 Art. 6:2(b) and Art. 4:13 GALA.

speed up decision-making and investments, in 2011 the *lex silentio positivo* was introduced (Arts. 4(20)(a) *et seq.* GALA), which is applicable to some cases. Unlike the general rule, exceeding a time limit for decisions on an application leads to a (fictive) positive decision on the application.[23]

In 2009, the Act on penalty payments and judicial review in a case of delay in decision-making[24] was introduced. According to Article 4:17 GALA, an applicant can send a reminder to the administrative authority after the time limit to decide on the application has passed. Two weeks after having received the reminder, the authority has to pay a daily fine of 20 EUR to the applicant. After 14 days the fine increases to 40 EUR. In total, a maximum fine of 1,260 EUR can be charged. A further consequence of having sent the reminder is that the applicant can directly bring a claim to the administrative court without first having to object to the decision (Art. 6:12 GALA).[25]

Article 4:17 GALA is often used and misused. An easy way to misuse it is to lodge quite general requests to provide information or disclose documents. Often applicants try to hide these requests, such as in job application letters. As applicants do not have to prove a special interest, these requests cannot easily be rejected. In past years, authorities have paid approximately 8 to 14 million EUR on penalty payments alone, relating to requests for the disclosure of information. In 2016, a bill was pending which aimed to prevent this misuse. According to this bill the rules on penalty payment will no longer apply to requests to disclose information.[26]

In 2014, an evaluation of three instruments to speed up decision-making was published. The researchers evaluated the *lex silentio positivo*, the penalty payment (which they called *astreinte*) and the possibility of direct appeal if a decision was not made on time.[27] It is illustrative to quote some parts of the English summary of this report:[28]

> 'The existence of the acceleration-instruments contributes to the awareness within the administration. Attention for the timeliness of decision-making has increased as a result of it. This increase of attention corresponds to the increase of attention as far as the quality of service of the administration in general (apart from the three acceleration-instruments) is concerned. The preventive effect of the *'astreinte'*-instrument has been the result mainly of the fact that those *'astreintes'* identify and quantify in a clear way the exceedance of time limits for decision- making. This results in fear for damage of reputation on both a personal and an organizational level, which increases the awareness for timeliness.
>
> The preventive effect of the instrument 'appeal in case of not deciding in time' turns out to be very limited, mainly because citizens and companies only rarely choose to use this instrument and, if they do, the administrative authority will be able to take the decision belatedly. [...]

23 Knook 2010, p. 147 *et seq.*
24 Wet dwangsom en beroep bij niet tijdig beslissen, *Stb.* 2009, 383.
25 Arts. 4:17 and 6:12 GALA.
26 *Kamerstukken II* 2014/15, 34 106.
27 Schueler *et al.* 2014.
28 Schueler *et al.* 2014, p. 54 *et seq.*

The *lex silencio positivo* applies to a wide diversity of decision-types. Those types concern licences within the scope of the Services Act (*Dienstenwet*), licences without that scope (or licences with regard to which it might be doubtful whether they are within that scope), like licences according to the General Act on Environmental Law (*Wet algemene bepalingen omgevingsrecht, Wabo*). As far as licences under the Services Act are concerned, it turns out that only very few positive fictitious decisions have been 'issued'. This is a bit different as far as non-services licences are concerned. Environmental licences have been issued 'automatically' more often, which might be explained by the numerous applications for such a licence. If the *lex silencio positivo* applies, the preventive effect is quite strong. This can be explained by the fact that administrative authorities (and officials) do not want to be responsible for the damaging effects that a fictitious licence might have on the interests of third parties and the general interest as such. The effectiveness of this acceleration-instrument in individual cases turns out to be problematic though. An applicant who has obtained a fictitious licence might legally assume to be in the possession of a licence, but this licence is surrounded with many more uncertainties compared to a genuine licence. [...]

It is remarkable that both citizens and companies quite rarely choose to deploy one of the acceleration instruments. The main explanation seems to be that the familiarity with those instruments is limited. But even if citizens and companies are aware of these instruments, they often decline to use them. Reason for this turns out to be the desire to maintain a constructive relationship with the authorities. As far as the instrument of appeal is concerned, sometimes fear for litigation costs plays a role.

Because of their nature, the unwanted side-effects of the acceleration-instruments do not justify the abolition of those instruments. [...]

Also quality of decision-making is under pressure because of time limits. And authorities more often make use of the possibilities for suspending time limits for decision-making in an improper way. The *lex silencio positivo* leads to the damaging of the general interest and interests of third parties because of licences that are issued automatically. Also legal certainty for citizens and companies is not very well served by the fictitious license, because of the uncertainties that go along with this instrument. A further improvement of timeliness of decision-making should primarily be sought for through organizational improvements (monitoring time limits, questions relating to the agenda, monitoring in general)'.

2.2. *Shortening Time Limits of Decision-Making?*

The general time limit for decisions in individual cases on application has been unchanged from six weeks even by the CRA (Art. 4:13 GALA), unless a specific legal provision determines otherwise. The same applies to the time limit (six months) for decisions taken on the basis of the more elaborated 'uniform public decision-making procedure' on the basis of Section 3.4 GALA, which will be dealt with below.[29]

Shortening of the decision-making phase has been achieved also by other means. The most important one is a provision on how long results of preparatory research may be used to substantiate a decision. In practice appellants often questioned about how up to date fact findings which were carried out to prepare

[29] Art. 4:13 and Section 3.4 GALA.

decisions on building or infrastructure projects were, like investigations of flora and fauna. If, for example, such an investigation was undertaken a year before the final decision and this decision was quashed because of a procedural fault, the administrative authority often went over the investigation again, just to be able to prove that nothing had changed and that it fulfilled the requirement that decisions must be based on the facts known at the moment the decision is taken. The CRA introduced legal provisions in most of the acts governing environmental decision-making which require that decisions may in any case be based on the results of research and investigations which are not older than two years at the moment the decision is taken (see Art. 13.5 Environmental Management Act).[30] Being allowed to rely on research which was carried out earlier and not being obliged to repeat this research means that the decision-making process has become faster and shorter. The reason the CRA does not prescribe this in general relates to Article 6 Habitats Directive.[31] According to the government, a provision on how up-to-date surveys are would not be in accordance with Article 6(3) Habitats Directive, according to which the decision must be based on 'the best scientific knowledge in the field'.[32] Hence the Dutch Nature Protection Act (*Natuurbeschermingswet* 1998)[33] does not contain a provision on the durability of research results.

2.3. *Participation Rights*

An attempt was made to restrict participation rights in the so-called 'uniform public decision-making procedure' (para. 3.4, Arts. 3:10 *et seq*. GALA).[34] Unlike the way decisions are generally taken, in this procedure a draft decision has to be published. Anyone can lodge his or her view and opinion on this draft, without having to demonstrate any special interest. According to the draft of the CRA, the possibility to do so would have been limited to 'interested parties', hence requiring one to demonstrate a special interest. However, during discussions in Parliament this proposal was withdrawn as the government did not want to risk a conflict with Article 6 Aarhus Convention, which urges the parties to let 'the public' participate in decisions falling under the scope of this article.[35] This is one of the examples which demonstrates that international environmental law and transposing EU environmental law have worked as a sort of final barrier for cutting down participation rights.

One of the most important conclusions of the report of the *Elverding* Committee (described in para. 1) was that public participation procedures were

30 Art. 13.5 Wmb.

31 Council Directive 92/43/EEC of 21 May 1992 on the conservation of natural habitats and of wild fauna and flora [1992] 206/7.

32 Case C-127/02, *Landelijke Vereniging tot Behoud van de Waddenzee and Nederlandse Vereniging tot Bescherming van Vogels* v. *Staatssecretaris van Landbouw, Natuurbeheer en Visserij*, EU:C:2004:482, para. 54.

33 Wet van 25 mei 1998, houdende nieuwe regelen ter bescherming van natuur en landschap (Natuurbeschermingswet 1998), *Stb.* 1998, 403.

34 Arts. 3:10 *et seq*. GALA.

35 Convention on Access to Information, Public Participation in Decision-Making and Access to Justice in Environmental Matters, 2161 UNTS 447; 38 ILM 517 (1999), Art. 6.

neither very effective, nor efficient. The main reason is the lateness of the participation within the decision-making process. When a draft decision is published, this is often the outcome of long-lasting negotiations within and between the administrative authorities. If citizens at that stage of the decision-making process come up with alternative suggestions, the authorities are not very keen to revise the choices they have already made. They will not openly discuss all alternatives, but defend their choices. Often public participation is perceived as a procedural duty only, not as a chance to reach better solutions. To let public participation be more meaningful and work more effectively, it should, according to the commission,[36] take place earlier.

The *Elverding* Committee therefore suggested an early, broad public discussion before the authorities make up their mind (so-called frontloading). The outcome of this discussion should be a narrowing of the alternatives on the table and finally a general decision about which option(s) should be worked out further. It should not be possible to challenge this general decision in court.[37] As a result, such a broad and early participation procedure was introduced in Articles 2-7 of the Act on Planning of Main Roads (*Tracéwet*).[38] The draft *Omgevingswet* will introduce such a procedure for all kinds of projects of public interest. It remains to be seen whether such an approach to make participation more meaningful by prescribing (early) 'frontloading' will be successful. In the 80s the Dutch General Act on Pollution Control (*Wet algemene bepalingen milieuhygiëne*) already provided for a public participation procedure in an early stage - before the authorities had made up their mind and before a draft decision was taken: the so-called 'extended public decision-making procedure' (which later was transformed into the GALA, former para. 3.5 GALA). This early stage participation was abandoned because it was not effective and lengthened the procedure.

2.4. *Deregulation and a Greater Role for Private Parties as a Way to Reduce Administrative Burdens*

2.4.1. General

Deregulation has been some sort of constant hype over the last three decades. It concerns many areas of public law (social security, road safety, taxes, public labour law and environmental and planning law). In all these areas, substantial requirements have been diminished or abandoned and private parties and 'the market' have been given more room for manoeuvre. Reducing costs of administrative burdens has been a major topic for many governments over the last twenty years. In 2000, an advisory council on the burden of public regulation (*Adviescollege toetsing regeldruk,* Actal) was officially installed for a period of four years. Its mandate has been kept alive ever since.[39]

36 Commissie Versnelling Besluitvorming 2008, p. 13.
37 Commissie Versnelling Besluitvorming 2008, p. 14.
38 Gierveld 2016, p. 48 *et seq.*; Arts. 2-7 Tracewet.
39 16 June 2011, *Stcrt.* 2011, 12119.

Deregulation did not lead to significant changes in the GALA. An example of such a change, however, is the deletion of the former 'extended public decision-making procedure' in 2001. This procedure tried to assure effective public participation in an early stage of the decision-making process before the administrative authorities would have made up their mind. This procedure has been abandoned because it was said not to have been effective and efficient.

In the area of environmental and planning law, the *Omgevingswet* aims at a further substantial deregulation of procedural and substantial requirements. Amongst others, the requirement to have an environmental permit will be skipped for many thousands of installations. Deregulation is one of the main aims of the government for the large-scale legislative action of the *Omgevingswet*.

2.4.2. General Rules Instead of Tailor-Made Permits

Since the 80s an ongoing process of deregulation has led to a very significant reduction of the number of installations which need an environmental permit - from more than 400,000 to around 14,000.[40] The *Omgevingswet* ought to reduce this figure further to about 4,000. Many or even most installations do not need an individual permit anymore and are regulated only by the requirements laid down in general rules. The need to apply for a building permit was also minimized. Smaller constructions for which a permit used to be required may now be built after having announced the intention to do so to the authorities or even without any possibility of control *ex ante*. These deregulation operations obviously have sped up investments and will have led to substantial savings for undertakings. It is not clear whether this process has had negative effects on the quality of the enforcement of public law requirements. When the process of deregulation started, it was argued that authorities could spend the spare time they had on allowing intensification of the enforcement of general rules. It seems that this did not happen. One of the main reasons is that monitoring and enforcement of general rules is more difficult, complicated and time consuming than monitoring and enforcement of permits.[41]

3. Legal Protection and Court Related Measures

3.1. *Introduction*

The organization of the Dutch judiciary is rather complicated. The majority[42] of administrative law disputes are dealt with by administrative courts. In general, after

[40] See the explanatory memorandum (MvT) of the *Omgevingswet* and the Wabo for figures about how many installations will, according to the *Omgevingswet*, still need a permit in future.

[41] On this see, for example, De Gier *et al.* 2011, p. 576-586.

[42] A decisive criterion in general is to be found in Art. 8:1 GALA: only administrative decisions as described in Art. 1:3(1) GALA are challengeable. Some administrative decisions are excluded and there is a list of exemptions in chapter 8 of the GALA and Art. 8:88 GALA still provides for a role of ordinary courts in administrative litigation in case of actions for damages.

preliminary administrative proceedings, being either paragraph 3.4 ('uniform public decision-making procedure', Arts. 3:10 *et seq.*) or Article 7:1 GALA (objection proceedings), district courts (in particular, their administrative divisions) are competent. These district courts function as courts of first instance in the majority of the cases. If the dispute continues, however, several different administrative courts of higher appeal come into scope, each with its specific expertise and competence, depending on the area of administrative law the dispute relates to.[43] For disputes regarding planning and building law, environmental law and infrastructure projects, the Judicial Division of the Council of State is the competent court in the second and final instance.[44]

In order to identify the huge significance of court-related measures, it makes sense to first briefly explain what the relationship is between court procedures and the administrative decision-making process. The traditional mechanism is as follows: if the administrative court is of the opinion that the appeal of the applicant is well-founded and hence the contested administrative decision contains one or more irregularities, the court quashes the decision.[45] Traditionally, after this annulment the administrative authority is under the obligation to make its next move by issuing a new decision, replacing the former and annulled one, which due to the annulment disappears from the legal order. This process takes time, sometimes a lot of time. Moreover, it is uncertain whether the new administrative decision is lawful and even if so, interested natural and legal persons can challenge the new decision again. If the court then annuls the decision again, the public authority has to issue a new decision and the entire process repeats itself.

In the past, administrative courts felt restricted in ruling on what was wrong with the administrative decision instead of stating how to arrive at a sound decision. They were very reluctant to interfere with administrative decision-making, and even to give the public authority instructions on how to come to lawful decision-making. In the majority of cases they restricted their judgments on well-founded appeals to annulment. The main reason for this is that courts want to fully respect the '*trias*' notion. In this respect sometimes reference is also made to the lack of court expertise of the underlying policy and the subject matter (for instance, technical expertise) and the lack of knowledge of all possibly involved interests and interested parties.[46] However, the disadvantages of this mechanism are obvious. It brings about legal uncertainty and has a negative societal impact. It is a hindrance for final and fast decision-making. Due to this mechanism, it sometimes takes a long time before important large economical and societal infrastructure projects can actually start. Besides, 'stakeholders', that is, interested (legal) persons who are

43 Currently, five main courts of higher appeal exist, and four of them are a court of last instance. In the near future (presumably 2018) the legislator will simplify the system and reduce the number of different administrative courts of higher appeal. At the top of the future pyramidal model, presumably two peaks will remain in existence: the Supreme Court and the Judicial Division of the Council of State.

44 In some (although not that many) cases this Judicial Division is competent at first and final instance. Legal protection with only one court available is not in conflict with international law such as the ECHR.

45 Arts. 8:70 and 8:72 GALA.

46 See comment by A.M.L. Jansen on: CRvB 3 November 2010, *AB* 2011/243.

opposed to the project, can (mis)use the aforementioned mechanism to bar or at least delay the decision-making and hence the actual implementation of the project. As a consequence, an urge was felt to create more efficiency and speed in administrative litigation.[47]

Now that the relationship between court procedures, judgments and administrative decision-making has been described, this contribution will examine in more details the developments and measures which took place in this context.

3.2. *Acceleration Measures in General*

Many developments and measures concern administrative procedural law in general, including areas such as spatial planning law and the law applicable to large infrastructure projects. Some of the measures have been introduced by the legislator, others have been developed by the courts in their case law. The questions of whether a measure aims at speeding up court procedures or at speedier (final) subsequent administrative decision-making cannot be separated because they are very much intertwined, as is described above.

Administrative judges received new tools from the legislator. And tools they already had at their disposal have been used differently and with less strict application conditions, and are therefore easier to use.

3.2.1. Developments in Case Law

From 2008 onwards, the Dutch case law shows that administrative judges are less cautious in their attempts to achieve final dispute settlement. Courts of the highest instance really made a 'U-turn' by stating that an obligation for administrative judges exists to seek possibilities for final dispute settlement.[48] Alongside this, the case law of the highest administrative courts expressly broadened the scope of certain remedies and accessory tools, combined with annulment, to finalize procedures.[49] As a consequence of this, existing instruments are used more frequently to avoid the aforementioned mechanism of annulment and renewed decision-making in the same case.

The first instrument we need to discuss in this respect is the power (which has existed since 1994) of the court to annul the decision but to direct the legal effects of the annulled decision to be left in place.[50] To understand what this instrument means, one should keep in mind that after an annulment the legal consequences of the contested decision are also usually annulled. The main conditions for the use of this power are: whether the administrative authority that took the decision still supports it, whether the irregularity is sufficiently repaired, whether other parties had the opportunity to have their say, and last but not least, whether the outcome

47 Backes *et al.* 2014, p. 21.

48 CRvB 3 November 2010, *AB* 2010/341 and *AB* 2011/243, with extended comments of A.T. Marseille and A.M.L. Jansen.

49 ABRS 10 December 2008, *JB* 2009/39; ABRS 12 August 2009, *AB* 2009/368.

50 Art. 8:72(3)a GALA.

after restoration is lawful.[51] It is applied, for example, in case the administrative authority did not weigh up all involved interests or in the case of poor motivation.[52]

Furthermore, administrative judges are (and have been, also since 1994) entitled to rule that their judgment replaces the annulled decision of the administration.[53] The conditions for application, again all developed in case law, are quite similar to those for the allowance to let the legal effects of an annulled decision stand in full or in part. The main, if not only, difference is the outcome: contrary to the aforementioned instrument, the administrative decision is not lawful and must be replaced (which is then done by the judge).[54] A rule of thumb for (non) application is that the court does not interfere with the discretion and policy-making freedoms of the administration.[55]

It is obvious that both instruments that can come together with annulment put an end to the proceedings. No follow-up administrative decision-making proceedings are necessary any longer, and neither are any subsequent or continuing court procedures.

3.2.2. Legislative Developments

Since 2010, legislative measures have also been passed, often expanding the toolbox of the court. One of the instruments is to be found in Article 6:22 GALA. This article was already in existence but was amended a couple of years ago. According to the current Article 6:22 GALA an administrative court (and an administrative authority, for that matter) may uphold an administrative decision despite an infringement of an (un)written rule or principle if it is plausible that this does not harm interested parties.[56] In the past, this was only possible in the case of procedural errors. The scope of Article 6:22 has now been widened, since it no longer concerns necessarily a *procedural* irregularity.[57] Against the background of the main theme of this book, one could ascertain that as a result of this instrument to bypass legal flaws, imperfect administrative decisions remain valid and can be executed. In conclusion, it can contribute to quicker final decision-making but also leaves unlawful decisions intact, which makes it an example of the tension between speed and quality. However, as will be seen below, Article 6:22 GALA is not used often.

A completely new instrument created by the legislator is the so-called administrative loop (*bestuurlijke lus*).[58] The rationale of this novel instrument was, once more, to promote faster and easier dispute settlement.[59] To a certain extent it resembles Article 6:22 GALA: it enables the administrative judge to circumvent annulment as well. By interim judgment the judge may request the administrative

51 Sometimes phrased differently (with more brief conditions): ABRS 21 December 2011, 201105686/1/H1; CRvB 16 October 2012, *AB* 2013/56.
52 ABRS 21 October 2009, *AB* 2010/29.
53 Art. 8:72(3)b GALA.
54 ABRS 21 March 2012, *AB* 2012/233.
55 See, for example, Schueler 2012, p. 110.
56 Art. 6:22 GALA.
57 The predecessor was Art. 1.5 Chw.
58 Art. 8:51a to Art. 8:51d, Art. 8:80a and Art. 8:80b GALA.
59 *Kamerstukken II* 2007/08, 31 352, n. 3.

authority to correct the unlawfulness in the decision-making. Such a reparation can consist of the adaptation of a new decision or an elaboration on parts of the decision. Thus, the loop can result in a new decision or in submitting, for instance, an extended motivation or an advice of an expert (committee). Unlike Article 6:22 GALA, this loop does not bypass the violation of the law but within a time-limit fixed by the court the judge invites[60] or obliges[61] the administrative authority to repair the decision. And the judge provides the administrative authority with guidelines or concrete directions on how to restore the decision.

Courts seem to fully respect the notion of the *trias politica* and the position of the administration and do not interfere in the contents of the administrative decision-making process of repair.[62] Since initially the administrative loop was intended (and invented...) to fight the viscous decision-making in large infrastructural projects, it is remarkable to note that in procedures about such projects, the loop has been applied only by exception. And if it was applied in such cases, it was not often successful.[63] The main criterion to decide whether the administrative loop is suitable to launch is the question of whether the remaining dispute and the required remedy is measurable. In case of uncertainty about what ought to happen after the loop, or in complex situations, courts do not apply the loop.[64] And disputes in which third parties may possibly be disproportionately harmed by the loop tend to fall outside the scope of application.[65]

This was not all the legislator and the government did in this respect. As mentioned above (in the introduction), a symbolic but important provision introduced in 2013 is Article 8:41a GALA which states that the administrative judge should conclude the claim brought before him in as final a manner as possible.[66] It underlines that the task of the judge has changed from primarily controlling whether a decision was lawful to reaching a final solution for the claim which was brought before him. Along with this, parliamentary memoranda emphasized the importance of final dispute settlement and explicitly gave a hierarchical order of all available instruments, which is now partly confirmed in Article 8:72 GALA.[67]

3.2.3. How Do the Novel Instruments Work Out?

It is clear the aforementioned adaptations aiming at final dispute resolution are not just black letter law, since administrative courts themselves took the lead. What is the actual effect then? The use of Article 6:22 GALA (which according to the list of order, is the fastest, simplest and hence in this regard favourite instrument of the

60 If applied by a district court of first instance.

61 If applied by an appellate court.

62 See Backes *et al.* 2014; Jansen 2014, p. 521 *et seq.*

63 Backes *et al.* 2014, p. 63.

64 For restorations that are easily conducted, judges prefer the so-called informal loop instead of using the formal administrative loop of Art. 8:51a GALA. Contrary to the formal loop of Art. 8:51a GALA, this informal loop is applied without a binding interim judgment or order.

65 Backes *et al.* 2014, p. 55-68.

66 Art. 8:41a GALA.

67 Wetsvoorstel Aanpassing bestuursprocesrecht, Nota van Wijziging, *Kamerstukken II* 2010/11, 32 450, n. 8H, p. 59; Art. 8:72 GALA.

government) is very difficult to determine.[68] The general feeling amongst administrative lawyers is that this is not the most frequently used instrument of the toolbox administrative judges have at their disposal nowadays. This is confirmed by evaluation research concerning Article 1.5 CRA,[69] the predecessor of Article 6:22 GALA. Courts used Article 1.5 CRA only for smaller irregularities.[70]

Regarding the frequency of application of the other three instruments, research has been conducted and data are available.[71] The administrative loop has been restrictively applied compared to other instruments for final dispute resolution. The loop has been applied in less than 7 percent of all cases in which the judge found an irregularity in the administrative decision. In comparison, in 15 percent of these cases, courts decided that the legal effects of the annulled decision were allowed to stand in full or in part and in 19 percent of the annulments the courts ruled that their judgments replaced the annulled decision. Note that significant differences exist between the courts in the frequency of application. In particular, as regards the administrative loop, the question arises whether this instrument resulted in more rapid final dispute settlement. With some cautiousness, the conclusion can be drawn that the disputes in which the administrative loop has been applied successfully (meaning it led to the correction of the decision), have led to quicker final settlement compared to the disputes in which the loop was not applied. Nevertheless, sometimes the application of the loop does not result in acceleration but in delay.[72]

The extended powers of Article 6:22, Article 8:72(3) under (a) and Article 8:51a GALA contribute to more final dispute resolution and consequently to faster final decision-making.[73] True, the risk can exist that the absence of potential negative consequences for the administration after legal norms have been infringed by its decision-making brings about a less responsible and a sloppier attitude of public authorities when preparing and issuing decisions. Research, however, shows that there is little to no indication for the assumption that the introduction and application of these instruments resulted in laziness of administrative authorities or sloppy decision-making procedures.[74]

A relevant measure of another nature, the relativity principle, is codified in the GALA as well, but originates from the CRA and is for that reason discussed below (3.3).

3.2.4. Further Legislative Developments

A development of another nature at legislative level, is the draft code recently accepted by Parliament which aims at a simplification and digitalization of the rules

68 Art. 6:22 GALA.
69 For an analysis of the CRA, see below, para. 3.1.2.
70 Marseille *et al.* 2012, p. 61-65, 91.
71 Backes *et al.* 2014.
72 Backes *et al.* 2014, paras. 4.4, 4.6, 4.8, and 4.9.
73 Art. 6:22, Arts. 8:72(3)(a) and 8:51a GALA.
74 Backes *et al.* 2014; Marseille *et al.* 2012; Marseille *et al.* 2014, p. 53-67, 81.

of legal procedure (which regards civil litigation as well).[75] It contains rules which make it possible to lodge an appeal electronically. If the act would come into force, for professional parties it will even be compulsory to communicate by means of a web portal. With this digitalization, the legislator hopes to make litigation faster, easier and cheaper.

Finally, a recent development in litigation that took place specifically at district court level is quite interesting. This is the so-called *Nieuwe Zaaksbehandeling* (NZB, New Case-Management).[76] The first interaction between the parties and the judge is earlier in this case. During this first contact between parties and the judge, the real conflict is supposed to become clear. Also, that first early session in front of the judge can function to clarify what he wants both parties to prove, to find out and to submit. NZB can contribute to quicker court proceedings and dispute resolution. With this NZB the applicant (namely the citizen) and the public authority receive a sort of court assistance and the opportunity to submit further evidence or arguments. The citizen will get the impression of a genuine balance between him and the respondent, i.e. the administrative authority.

Lastly, we mention the attempts to give mediation a function in administrative law. The idea is that mandatory meditation (attempts) before court proceedings commence can be a filter enabling the avoidance of litigation. A bill proposal for this made by a former member of Parliament (the current Minister of Justice) which would have meant that public authorities were obliged to first try to achieve a friendly settlement if confronted with a challenge to a decision, has been withdrawn.[77] This withdrawal was not because it was considered such a bad idea but because the government intends to put forward its own proposals at short notice.[78]

3.3. *Measures for a Specific Area*

A major legislative development in this regard is the aforementioned Crisis and Recovery Act (CRA). The main purpose of this Act was to accelerate administrative decision-making and the execution of (large) infrastructure and housing projects. With a number of instruments in the decision-making domain, the CRA contained a number of court-related measures affecting legal protection and access to administrative courts.

3.3.1. Relativity Principle

Some of the measures that the CRA introduced also functioned as a trial run prior to the implementation a few years later of the same measures in the GALA, widening the scope of the provisions.[79] An example of the latter category is the relativity (or

75 *Kamerstukken II* 2014/15, 34059, n. 1-3; *Kamerstukken II* 2014/15, 34 059 (No. A is currently pending at the Eerste Kamer).

76 Verburg & Schueler 2014, p. 56-72; Nihot 2012, p. 27-34.

77 *Kamerstukken II* 2012/13, 33 727, n. 2-3.

78 *Kamerstukken II* 2012/13, 33 727, n. 12, 24.

79 Art. 1.5 Chw. See above, where Art. 6:22 GALA is analysed.

connectivity) principle (comparable to the concept of the German *Schutznorm*).[80] The CRA introduced this requirement in 2010 in Dutch administrative litigation.[81] The relativity principle states that the administrative judge will not annul an administrative decision if the decision infringes an (un)written rule or principle if this rule or principle evidently does not aim to protect the interest of those who rely on it. Before the relativity principle came into force, judgments were criticized when the court quashed an administrative decision because it violated a rule, although this rule was not at all aimed at the protection of the interest of the applicant. This approach merely reflected the *recours objectif* concept of administrative procedural law and legal protection.

The legislator decided to let the newly created rule aim at affecting (or one could say preventing) the possible annulment instead of the admissibility. Thus, the relativity principle has no influence on the admissibility and hence on access to court but does have an impact on the review (which the relativity principle partly precludes), on the merits of the case and on the outcome: can the breach of law of the administrative decision result in annulment? For an affirmative answer, the infringed rule needs to intend to protect the interest of the claimant. The introduction of this relativity principle allows the court to leave unlawful administrative decisions intact. Therefore, it does not seem to contribute to the overall quality of administrative decisions in general.

Until 2013, this relativity principle was only applicable in disputes governed by the CRA. Although heavily criticized,[82] the legislator decided to widen the scope of this requirement by its transition to the GALA, and so it became generally applicable in all administrative court procedures.[83] Despite the disadvantages, one could argue that a relativity principle fits in a *recours subjectif* approach which is according to the GALA legislator, the pivotal goal of current procedural administrative law. For example, case law shows that as a result of the relativity principle, it became much more difficult for entrepreneurs to thwart the establishment of competitors by challenging spatial planning decisions.[84]

3.3.2. Article 1.6(2) and Article 1.6a CRA

Another restriction of access to court in cases falling within the scope of the CRA is the impossibility to submit grounds for review after the time limit for bringing a case to court (which is six weeks) has elapsed, as is stipulated in Article 1.6(a) CRA. In line with this restriction is the limitation laid down in Article 1.6(2) CRA. According to Article 1.6(2) CRA grounds of appeal must be submitted before the time limit for appeal exceeds.[85] *Pro-forma* appeals to avoid exceeding the time limit and grounds that follow later on are no longer available. The two provisions taken

80 Also referred to as the requirement of connection.
81 Art. 1.9 Chw.
82 See amongst many, Backes 2008, p. 297-308; Schueler 2011, p. 265-271; Verburg 2011, p. 10-17; De Poorter & Van Ettekoven 2013, p. 109 *et seq.*; Nijmeijer 2014; Van der Veen 2015, p. 160-179.
83 Art. 8:69a GALA (same wording as 1.9 Chw).
84 ABRS 20 May 2015, *BR* 2015/71.
85 Art. 1.6.a and 1.6.2 Chw.

together form a combination which is a fundamental limitation compared to the possibilities in general. The articles deviate from the regime in the GALA which offers claimants the opportunity to submit additional grounds after having submitted their claim.[86] Relevant case law of the respective courts dealing with GALA provisions at the highest instance is divergent. Whereas the Judicial Division of the Council of State ruled that both CRA provisions are in conformity with the law, EU law and the Aarhus Convention included,[87] two of the other highest courts accepted the six week time limit to commence proceedings, but more or less conditionally. They expressly took into account the existing possibility for applicants to file an objection *pro-forma* and to submit grounds at a later date, after a further time limit has been provided by the competent public authority.[88] It is exactly this possibility of the postponement of submitting grounds that has been abolished in CRA cases.

3.3.3. Shortening Time Limits

Several provisions in the CRA either introduced time limits for the court to act or shortened the existing time limits.

Due to Article 1.6(1) CRA, the appeal is dealt with by the fast-track regime of the GALA.[89] The essence of the applicability of this regime is that the time limits for procedural activities (paying court fees, submitting a written defence, response to reports of experts) of the parties involved are shorter. Of more importance is Article 1.6(4) CRA which prescribes that the court issues its judgment within 6 months.[90] The effect of this obligation is somewhat limited but significant.[91] It is 'limited' because in 61 percent of the cases courts do not hand down a judgment within six months. Having said that, often it is close and going over the prescribed six months is limited. The duration of CRA cases is 7.5 months on average. This is faster compared to the average duration of court procedures, which is 11 months. So, the good news is: Article 1.6(4) CRA has a positive, accelerating effect on court procedures in CRA disputes. More good news: the fear that Article 6(4) CRA was likely to negatively affect the duration of other court procedures has not been confirmed by the conducted CRA research.[92] The bad news: the speed of delivering judgments only has (very) limited effect on the time consumed before the project actually starts and is established.[93] There is no obvious causal link. And proceedings have become more complicated for parties.

To complete the picture of court-related time limit provisions we refer to Article 1.6(3) CRA. This provision states that in case the 'StAB', an advisory board for the Judicial Division of the Council of State, is asked to give advice in CRA

86 Arts. 6:5 and 6:6 GALA.
87 ABRS 17 November 2010, *AB* 2011/42.
88 HR 18 February 2005, *AB* 2005/119 and CRvB 23 December 2002, *AB* 2003/209.
89 Section 8.2.3 GALA, Arts. 8:52 and 8:53 GALA.
90 Art. 1.6.4 Chw.
91 Marseille *et al.* 2012, p. 56, 111, 128, 129, 134; Marseille *et al.* 2014, p. 53-67, 81.
92 *Ibid.* From the same authors see the summary of their research in Marseille *et al.* 2015, p. 6-15. The title, to be translated as 'Great expectations/ambitions, hardly any effect' is illustrative.
93 Marseille *et al.* 2014, p. 83, 87.

litigation, it should do so within two months. Although this is considered to be quite fast, it delays the judgment and makes it very hard to give judgment within the prescribed six months. As a consequence of this (imminent) delay, the Judicial Division of the Council of State asks for advice in CRA cases less and less frequently.[94] It could be argued that this is detrimental to the quality of the control by the judge and hence negative for the quality of the administrative decisions.

3.4. *Access to Court*

3.4.1. Court Fees and Costs

Article 8:41 GALA prescribes that court fees must be paid for a claim to be admissible in court. This obligation applies to all court procedures, irrespective of what administrative court is involved. The fees, however, differ in relation to the kind of dispute.[95] If the claim is successful, the administration has to reimburse the court fees of the applicant (but not the other way around, 'one way cost shifting').[96] A few years ago the government had plans to increase the court fees. A draft bill which proposed full cost recovery was criticized.[97] In the end, the government abandoned it.[98] The wish of the government to increase court fees still exists.[99] The most recent draft bill contains a serious increase of court fees at higher appeal levels and a more limited increase for litigation at the first instance.

To finalize the discussion, we make a brief remark about costs. Although in the Netherlands litigation can be expensive for the parties involved, in general the costs of procedures do not constitute a huge obstacle for legal protection in administrative law. Administrative courts are entitled to make cost orders.[100] If the court does so, the administration is usually ordered to pay the costs of the opposite party. Only in the very rare occasion of an abuse of procedural law can natural persons be subject to a cost order. Hence, applicants face very low costs risks when bringing a case to court.

3.4.2. Interested Person

The *actio popularis* which until about a decade ago was applicable in a limited category of cases has been abolished. Nowadays standing in the Netherlands is required to commence litigation. According to Article 8:1 in conjunction with 1:2 GALA the claimant needs to be an interested (sometimes referred to as 'concerned') person or party.[101] If this requirement is not met, the claimant's objection and the

[94] *Ibid.*; Marseille *et al.* 2014.

[95] The fees differ from EUR 45 (for social security cases), to EUR 165 and for legal persons EUR 328.

[96] Art. 8:74 GALA.

[97] *Kamerstukken II* 2011/12, 33 071, n. 2.

[98] *Kamerstukken II* 2012/13, 33 071, n. 11.

[99] *Kamerstukken II* 2013/14, 33 757.

[100] Art. 8:75 GALA.

[101] Art. 8:1 GALA contains the conditions for a claim before a court, 'interested person' being one of them whilst Art. 1:2 GALA gives the definition of interested person.

claim for judicial review will be declared inadmissible.[102] Subsection 1 of Article 1:2 GALA defines 'interested persons'. Case law has further clarified those who qualify as an interested person. Along with subsection 1, subsection 3 of the same provision is of relevance, from which it follows that the interests of legal persons are considered to include general and collective interests, under the twofold condition that (i) this legal person particularly promotes this general or collective interest by virtue of its objectives; and (ii) it is shown by its actual activities that it promotes or protects this general interest. In practice, this means that legal persons which stipulate in their statutes that they deal with certain general or public interests such as, for instance, the (local) environment, may challenge administrative decisions with regard to this general interest.

As stated, an additional condition to be complied with is that the legal person conducts actual activities as well. As far as the component of 'legal' person is concerned, courts are not too strict. NGOs and other interest groups can be granted standing and challenge administrative decisions. This avenue to administrative courts and access to court for NGOs have undergone some changes over the last decade. In particular, the legal regime applicable in environmental matters has become more restricted.[103] The narrowing may have started before, but a main turning point in this regard was the abolition of the *actio popularis* in the GALA in 2005. Another important development took place in case law. In 2008, the Judicial Division of the Council of State narrowed access to court for legal persons in the sense of Article 1:2(3) GALA. The Council of State ruled that the objectives enumerated in the statute of the association were too broad and not specific enough. Moreover, the Council of State decided that the actual activities of the association were not sufficient to qualify as an interested person, as intended in Article 1:2(3) GALA. The activities - giving opinions on decisions and bringing claims - apparently did not suffice, according to the Council of State.[104] So from 2008 onwards, to qualify as a '1:2(3) legal person' became more difficult, which can be considered to be a development influencing the possibilities for NGOs to challenge administrative decisions.

A third development, this time a legislative one, is the amendment of Article 6:13 GALA of 2005. This provision contained the prerequisite that interested parties were under the obligation to participate in earlier stages of the proceedings, otherwise their subsequent appeal would be inadmissible (unless their non-participation was justified). This is still the case, but in 2005 the legislator added to this provision that not only is participation in the earlier stages required, but also a challenge to the *subparts* of the administrative decision.[105] If the appellant failed to raise the unlawfulness of certain subparts of an administrative decision in the administrative (preliminary) proceedings, the appeal would be partly (meaning for those subparts)

102 The very same requirement and consequence of inadmissibility apply to prior-out-of-court proceedings such as objection proceedings.

103 Compare for more detailed developments in the last 20 years: Tolsma, De Graaf & Jans 2009, p. 309-321; Backes 2002, p. 379 *et seq.*

104 ABRS 1 October 2008, *AB* 2008/348. This ruling was followed and confirmed by other judgments.

105 Subparts of the decision must be distinguished from grounds, arguments and facts to prove, explain and underline why the decision is unlawful.

inadmissible. In other words, in case an applicant wants to challenge new subparts of the administrative decision, Article 6:13 GALA excludes such a submission.[106] In practice, this further limitation of access to court does not actually seem to bring about very severe consequences.[107]

3.4.3. Restriction of Access for the Administration

With Article 1.4 CRA, the legislator restricted the possibilities of access to court, albeit only to a specific area and although it was quite limited in its application.[108] Decentralized administrative authorities are prohibited from challenging a decision of the Dutch central government falling within the scope of the CRA.[109] With this bar to appeal, the CRA deviates from the general rule in Article 1:2(2) GALA. The legislator did not elaborately state reasons of this provision. The official rationale was only briefly mentioned: to prevent the delay of the establishment of urgent CRA-governed projects. But the reason behind Article 1.4 CRA is (also) the idea that conflicts between governmental bodies should not be solved by the (administrative) courts.[110] Research justifies the conclusion that Article 1.4 CRA led to only a very modest acceleration, if any at all.[111]

In conclusion, with all the cumulative measures for speedier and more efficient administrative dispute resolution and decision-making, the question is whether administrative procedural law has not in fact become (even) more complicated. This observation can be linked to the issue of access[112] since the possibilities to commence administrative court proceedings and to obtain a court ruling on the merits seem to become more and more difficult.

3.5. *Elimination of a Court Instance*

Administrative procedures can sometimes drag on for years. The more instances are addressed; the longer proceedings go on. Although it is not a requirement that follows from international law, the legal protection very often consists of two court levels. Legal protection starts with an appeal to the (district) court of first instance after which appeal at a higher level is available. As we saw above, this is often the Judicial Division of the Council of State. In the Netherlands, in general the legislator

106 Without going into the details of the rather complicated system of Dutch administrative legal procedure, one needs to distinguish between subparts and grounds and arguments. It is emphasized that Art. 6:13 GALA does not govern the question of whether the applicant can submit new grounds and arguments. Art. 6:13 GALA does not preclude this.

107 Only a minority of the administrative decisions consist of different subparts.

108 Art. 1.4 Chw.

109 Unless addressed to that public legal person or public authority.

110 Compare *Kamerstukken II* 2009/10, 32 127, n. 3, p. 11, 44, 45: these conflicts can still be the subject of *civil* litigation, with all the disadvantages that come along with it, see Marseille *et al.* 2012, p. 48-49.

111 Marseille *et al.* 2012, p. 89; Marseille *et al.* 2014, p. 43-44, 81. In only 1% of the cases of this research, an administrative authority was kept away from the administrative court due to Article 1.4 Chw.

112 Three important measures concerning access have been discussed under section 3.2.

did not seek solutions for overly slow and lengthy proceedings in the removal of one of the (usually two) courts, leaving just one competent court for first and last resort. In fact, sometimes the opposite scenario occurred. In those rare situations in which there is only one administrative court, this is not a district court but the highest court, often the Judicial Division of the Council of State. However, over the last decade the Dutch legislator has decided on a few occasions not to retrench in existing layers of legal protection but to provide for only one instance in newly created legislation for specific fields of administrative law. Examples can be found in the *Tracéwet* and, again, in the CRA.[113] If these acts apply, the Judicial Division of the Council of State is the only available court.

4. The Role of International and European Law

In the last 10 to 15 years, the Europeanization of Dutch administrative law has increased. This European influence can be twofold. It can either work as a catalyst (sometimes of a rather compelling nature) for faster and improved decision-making, or as a restriction or barrier of domestic measures that are too far-reaching to establish faster and more efficient decision-making because they violate EU law.

One of the paramount and perhaps most influential roles in the debate on access to court is for the Aarhus Convention. This Treaty applies to environmental matters and in that respect has a limited scope.[114] However, as regards access to court in this field, much attention was paid to the possible impact of the Aarhus Convention in the academic discourse. Article 9 obliges contracting parties to provide wide access to courts in environmental matters. Article 1.4 CRA was held not to be in conflict with the Aarhus Convention because the Convention stipulates that domestic rules of legal procedure may limit access to court.[115] And, again according to the Dutch Council of State, Article 1.4 CRA does not violate EU law because decentralized administrative bodies may not come under the scope of the Convention and furthermore have alternative access to a civil court.[116] In the *Impact* case the CJEU ruled that the necessity for an interested person to start two different court procedures for compliance with an EU Directive violated EU law.[117] Although the Council of State did not refer to the *Impact* case, it does not go without saying that the situation caused by Article 1.4 CRA with one interested party challenging a decision in administrative court and the other one, the administration, in civil court, complies with EU law.[118]

Some other limitations to access to court have been questioned from a European law point of view. Articles 1.6a and 1.6(2) CRA have been scrutinized in

113 What court is competent, in case a court other than the district court (of first instance), can be found in an appendix of the GALA, the *bevoegdheidsregeling bestuursrechtspraak*. Other examples of the Judicial Division of the Council of State functioning as the court of first and last resort, are the *Flora-en faunawet, Mijnbouwwet, Kernenergiewet and the Ontgrondingenwet.*

114 Convention on Access to Information, Public Participation in Decision-Making and Access to Justice in Environmental Matters, 2161 UNTS 447; 38 ILM 517 (1999).

115 ABRS 1 April 2011, *AB* 2011/108.

116 ABRS 29 July 2011, *AB* 2011/281.

117 Case C-268/06, *Impact* v. *Minister for Agriculture and Food and Others*, EU:C:2008:223.

118 Widdershoven 2012, p. 195-213.

court. The Judicial Division of the Council of State was of the opinion that those CRA provisions were not in violation of Article 6 ECHR (right to a fair trial), EU law or the Aarhus Convention.[119] The main purpose of the provision is to avoid delay and facilitate the court to hand down a judgment within six months (see Art. 1.6(4) CRA). This is a justifiable restriction of access to court, whilst the right of access is not impaired in its essence, according to the Council of State. We now know Dutch courts conclude that the CRA is in conformity with EU law in this respect. It is, however, not yet certain whether EU courts and the ECtHR share this Dutch point of view. In paragraph 3.3 above, different case law was referred to in this regard. The different considerations of the Council of State and the other highest administrative courts also mean it might have been better if the Council of State had asked the CJEU for a preliminary ruling.[120]

In Parliament a firm debate also took place about the conformity of the relativity principle with EU law and the Aarhus Convention.[121] To establish whether a legal rule or principle intends to protect specific interests, sometimes the broad scope of protection of rules of EU law needs to be respected. Therefore, to prevent an overload of requests for preliminary rulings, with all the delay and legal uncertainty they come with them, the word 'evidently' was added to Article 1.9 CRA and its successor Article 8:69a GALA. Only if a violated rule 'evidently' did not protect the interest of the claimant should the unlawful decision be upheld. According to the Judicial Division of the Council of State the relativity principle is not in violation of Article 6 ECHR.[122] The Council of State also ruled that the relativity principle of Article 8:69a GALA complies with EU law in a case about the protection of a 'Natura 2000' area. The line of reasoning of the Council of State was that if the general interest is at stake in the context of an environmentally protected 'Natura 2000' area, legal persons, such as environmental organizations, qualify as interested person (see Art. 1:2(3) GALA) and therefore can promote and protect the interest at stake. Consequently, they can go to court without raising Article 8:69a GALA.[123]

The rule on the preclusion of Article 8:69a GALA constitutes a hurdle for environmental organizations when bringing claims before courts. In *Commission* v. *Germany*,[124] the CJEU ruled that although the national legislature is entitled to confine to individual public law rights to the rights that can be relied on by an *individual* in legal proceedings against a decision which falls within the scope of Article 9(2) of the Aarhus Convention, such a limitation cannot be applied as such to *environmental protection organizations* without disregarding the objectives of that provision.[125] Consequently, those organizations must necessarily be able to rely on

119 ABRS 17 November 2010, *AB* 2011/42.

120 Compare Widdershoven's comment in *AB* 2005/119 and Backes 2009, p. 266.

121 Compare *Kamerstukken II* 2009/10, 32 450, n. 3, p. 21-22.

122 ABRS 21 January 2015, *NJB* 2015/423.

123 ABRS 25 March 2014, *JB* 2014/107. Compare with Ch.W. Backes in *AB* 2011/213 (critical comment on the *Trianel* case (Case C-115/09, *Bund für Umwelt und Naturschutz Deutschland, Landesverband Nordrhein-Westfalen eV* v. *Bezirksregierung Arnsberg*, EU:C:2011:289).

124 Case C-137/14 *European Commission* v. *Federal Republic of Germany*, EU:C:2015:683.

125 Case C-115/09, *Bund für Umwelt und Naturschutz Deutschland, Landesverband Nordrhein-Westfalen*, EU:C:2011:289.

the rules of national law implementing EU environmental law and the rules of EU environmental law that have direct effect. This CJEU judgment possibly affects Dutch administrative law as it renders questionable whether Article 8:69a GALA can still be applied to environmental organizations challenging administrative decisions in their capacity as legal persons according to Article 1:2(3) GALA.[126]

Furthermore, the current predominance in Dutch administrative law of final dispute resolution needs to be highlighted. An example of the influence of EU law on these efforts is the decision in the *Altrip* case,[127] which is bound to influence the application of Article 6:22 GALA. As a consequence of this CJEU ruling, it seems that the assumption that a court can apply Article 6:22 GALA to EIA flaws only if the court is convinced that without the flaw the disputed decision would not have been different substantively is justified.[128]

As regards the administrative loop of Article 8:51a GALA, two main objections can be detected. The first objection relates to the right to an oral hearing of Article 6 ECHR. In case the loop results in a novel decision or an improved motivation, there is no guarantee that parties involved will be given the opportunity to comment orally on the decision before the judge. The other fundamental deficit of the loop concerns access to court. Problems could arise in case third parties are deprived of access to court in so far as they feel aggrieved for the first time by a substantively similar decision for which, however, the administrative authority stated other reasons.[129]

Lastly, a brief remark on the impact of international law on court fees in relation to access to court is worthwhile: administrative courts are willing to reduce court fees as prescribed in the GALA in the (rare) case of the impossibility for an interested person to pay them. This approach, in which the right of access prevails over the strict application of the system of legally fixed court fees, is based on Article 6 ECHR and Article 47 EU Charter.[130]

To conclude, EU law, the ECHR and the Aarhus Convention merely function as a kind of safety net. These European and international influences have not led to a required widening of participation and access to courts. Nevertheless, they work as a kind of ultimate boundary that cannot be passed, and seem to be especially of relevance concerning the measures and attempts of the legislator in the framework of the CRA to speed up decision-making by means of the reduction of participatory rights. EU and international law to some extent prevented narrowing down (citizen) participation in administrative decision-making proceedings - and the (further) narrowing access to court.

126 See comment by Ch.W. Backes on Case C-137/14, *European Commission* v. *Federal Republic of Germany*, EU:C:2015:683, in: *AB* 2015/447.

127 Case C-72/12, *Gemeinde Altrip and Others* v. *Land Rheinland-Pfalz*, EU:C:2013:712.

128 See comment by Ch.W. Backes on the *Altrip* case (Case C-72/12, *Gemeinde Altrip and Others* v. *Land Rheinland-Pfalz*, EU:C:2013:712), *AB* 2014/55; Widdershoven 2015, p. 141.

129 See comment by Ch.W. Backes & A.M.L. Jansen in *AB* 2014/417, p. 2572-2577.

130 ABRS 4 July 2011, *JB* 2011/188; CRvB 13 February 2015.

5. Overall Closing Remarks: What's the Demos Got to Do With It?

In this 'demos' context we refer again to Article 1:2(3) GALA: the question of whether NGOs aiming at protecting environmental and other general or public interests can challenge administrative decisions and how easy or difficult it is for them to bring an admissible claim to court. Due to case law stemming from 2008, it became somewhat more difficult for such NGOs to challenge administrative decisions successfully in case these general interests are at stake. By introducing this less liberal *locus standi* approach, the access to court is narrowed. This negatively affects, to a certain extent, the means that NGOs can use to defend certain general interests.[131] Considering the more restricted possibilities of access to court as brought about by Article 1.4 CRA, Article 1.6(a) CRA, the increase of court fees and the fact that less interested persons can get an unlawful decision annulled (Article 6:22, Article 8:69a, and Article 8:72(3) GALA) one has to conclude that the judicial control of the administration has diminished.

131 In contrast to this line of reasoning, one could argue that it is up to the legislator and administration to safeguard and protect general interests, this is not a task for 'citizens' and therefore this stricter access for NGOs from 2008 onwards is not that big a problem.

BIBLIOGRAPHY

Backes 2002
Backes, Ch.W, 'The Netherlands', in: J. Ebbesson (ed.), *Access to Justice in Environmental Matters in the EU*, Alphen aan de Rijn: Wolters Kluwer 2002, p. 379-397.

Backes 2008
Backes, Ch.W., 'Europeesrechtelijke implicaties van het relativiteitsvereiste', in: G.H. Addink, G.T.J.M. Jurgens, Ph.M. Langbroek & R.J.G.M. Widdershoven (red.), *Grensverleggend bestuursrecht*, Deventer: Wolters Kluwer 2008, p. 297-308.

Backes 2009
Backes, Ch.W., 'Crisistijden voor de waarborgfunctie van het bestuursrecht? De algemeen bestuursrechtelijke aspecten van de Crisis- en hertselwet', *Milieu en Recht*, 2009, p. 622-627.

Backes 2013
Backes, Ch.W., 'Het voorstel voor een omgevingswet - goed voor natuur en milieu?', *Tijdschrift voor omgevingsrecht en omgevingsbeleid*, 2013, p. 99-112.

Backes, Van Nieuwerburgh & Koelemeijer 2005
Backes, Ch.W., Van Nieuwerburgh, T. & Koelemeijer, R.B.A., 'Transformation of the First Daughter Directive on Air Quality in Several EU Member States and its Application in Practice', *European Environmental Law Review*, 2005, p. 157-164.

Backes et al. 2014
Backes, Ch.W., Hardy, E.M.J., Jansen, A.M.L., Polleunis, S., Timmers, R., Poortinga, M.A. & Versluis, E., *Evaluatie bestuurlijke lus Awb en internationale rechtsvergelijking*, Den Haag: WODC, 2014, available at: <www.wodc.nl/images/2331-volledige-tekst_tcm44-574236.pdf>.

Borgers et al. 2012
Borgers, H.C., Van der Heijden, G.M.A., Rengers, J.L. & Vredeveld, S., *Wabo, Een evaluatie van gebruikers-ervaringen met de Wabo en het Omgevingsloket online*, Baarn: AT Osborne 2012, available at: <www.rijksoverheid.nl/binaries/rijksoverheid/documenten/rapporten/2012/12/28/w-abo-een-evaluatie-van-gebruikerservaringen-met-de-wabo-en-het-omgevingsloket-online/lp-i-m-0000002916.pdf>.

Commissie Versnelling Besluitvorming 2008
Commissie Versnelling Besluitvorming Infrastructurele Projecten, *Sneller en beter*, available at: <www.rijksoverheid.nl/binaries/rijksoverheid/documenten/rapporten/2008/04/21/het-advies-van-de-commissie-versnelling-besluitvorming-infrastructurele-projecten/advies-commissie-vbip2.pdf>.

De Gier et al. 2011
De Gier, A.A.J., Van Rijswick, H.F.M.W., Duijkersloot, A.P.W., Groothuijse, F.A.G. & Uylenburg, R., 'Algemeen geregeld, goed geregeld? Een analyse van onderzoeken naar de werking van algemene regels in het licht van de doelstellingen voor de vernieuwing van het omgevingsrecht', *Milieu en Recht*, 2011, p. 576-586.

De Poorter & Van Ettekoven
De Poorter, J.C.A. & Van Ettekoven, B.J., 'Het relativiteitsvereiste in het bestuursrecht: de ene relativiteitseis is de andere niet', *Nederlands Tijdschrift voor Bestuursrecht*, 2013, p. 109-120.

De Waard 1998
De Waard, B.W.N., 'Knellend bestuursrecht. Reactie op het rapport 'Bestuur in geding', van de werkgroep Van Kemenade', *Nederlands Tijdschrift voor Bestuursrecht*, 1998, p. 60-66.

Gierveld 2016
Gierveld, H.A.J., 'De juridificering van de voornemenprocedure onder de Omgevingswet', *Tijdschrift voor bouwrecht en onroerend goed*, 2016, p. 307-324.

Jansen 2014
Jansen, A.M.L., 'Het dilemma van de verantwoordelijke bestuursrechter', *Tijdschrift voor Ambtenarenrecht*, 2014, p. 521-526.

Knook 2010
Knook, A., 'De van rechtswege verleende vergunning in de praktijk', *Nederlands Tijdschrift voor Bestuursrecht*, 2010, p. 147-153.

Marseille et al. 2012
Marseille, A.T., De Waard, B.W.N, Jansen, F.J., De Graaf, K.J. & De Vos, N.A., *Crisis- en herstelwet. Evaluatie procesrechtelijke bepalingen*, Den Haag: WODC 2012, available at: <www.rijksoverheid.nl/binaries/rijksoverheid/documenten/rapporten/2012/05/15/evaluatieonderzoek-procesrechtelijke-bepalingen-crisis-en-herstelwet/lp-i-m-0000002073.pdf>.

Marseille et al. 2014
Marseille, A.T., De Waard, B.W.N, De Graaf, K.J., Van Ling, P.C.E., Tolsma, H.D. & Verheul, E.F., *Crisis- en herstelwet: tweede evaluatie procesrechtelijke bepalingen*, Den Haag: WODC 2014, available at: <www.rijksoverheid.nl/binaries/rijksoverheid/documenten/rapporten/2014/07/10/crisis-en-herstelwet-tweede-evaluatie-procesrechtelijke-bepalingen/lp-v-j-0000006028.pdf>.

Marseille et al. 2015
Marseille, A.T., De Waard, B.W.N, De Graaf, K.J., Van Ling, P.C.E., Tolsma, H.D. & Verheul, E.F., 'De Crisis- en herstelwet. Veel ambitie, nauwelijks effect', *Nederlands Juristenblad*, 2015, p. 6-15.

Ministerie van Infrastructuur en Milieu 2011
Ministerie van Infrastructuur en Milieu, *Bezinning op het omgevingsrecht*, 2010, available at: <www.rijksoverheid.nl/binaries/rijksoverheid/documenten/brochures/2011/02/25/bezinning-op-het-omgevingsrecht/bezinning-op-het-omgevingsrecht.pdf>.

Neerhof, Schlössels & De Werd 1997
Neerhof, R., Schlössels, R. & De Werd, M.,'Enige tegenstrijdige opmerkingen naar aanleiding van het rapport Van Kemenade', *Jurisprudentie Bestuursrecht*, 1997, p. 1254-1266.

Nihot 2012
Nihot, P., 'De nieuwe zaaksbehandeling', *Nederlandse Vereniging voor Procesrecht*, 2012, p. 27-34.

Nijmeijer 2014
Nijmeijer, A.G.A., 'Dynamiek in relativiteit', *Trema*, 2014, p. 226-233.

Sadeleer, Roller & Dross 2005
Sadeleer, N., Roller G. & Dross, M., *Access to Justice in Environmental Matters and the Role of NGOs*, Groningen: Europa Law Publishing 2005.

Schueler 2011
Schueler, B.J., 'Een relativiteitsleer in wording', *Nederlands Tijdschrift voor Bestuursrecht*, 2011, p. 265-271.

Schueler 2012
Schueler, B.J., 'De grote verandering. Finaliteit in een nieuw bestuursprocesrecht', *JBplus*, 2012, p. 101-116.

Schueler et al. 2014
Schueler, B.J., Blekemolen, M., Duijkersloot, A.P.W., Modderman, C.B., Ortlep, R. & Scholtes, H.H.M., *Evaluatie van een drietal versnellingsinstrumenten uit de Awb*, Den Haag: WODC 2014, available at: <www.wodc.nl/images/2172-volledige-tekst_tcm44-520750.pdf>.

Tolsma 2014
Tolsma, H., 'Improving Environmental Permitting Systems: Integrated Permits in the Netherlands', *International Public Administration Review*, 2014, p. 81/95.

Tolsma, De Graaf & Jans 2009
Tolsma, H., De Graaf, K.J. & Jans, J.H., 'The Rise and Fall of Access to Justice in the Netherlands', *Journal of Environmental Law*, 2009, p. 309-321.

Van der Veen 2015
Van der Veen, G.A., 'Het relativiteitsvereiste van Art. 8:69a Awb: de stand van zaken', *Juristenblad*, 2015, p. 160-179.

Verburg 2011
Verburg, D.A., 'Relativiteit in de Crisis- en herstelwet en in het voorstel Wet aanpassing bestuursprocesrecht of: hoe moet het nou met het zeggekorfslakje', *Nederlands Tijdschrift voor Bestuursrecht*, 2011, p. 10-17.

Verburg & Schueler 2012
Verburg, D.A. & Schueler, B.J., 'Procedural Justice in Dutch Administrative Law Proceedings', *Utrecht Law Review*, 2014, p. 56-72.

Verschuuren 2010
Verschuuren, J.M., 'The Dutch Crisis and Recovery Act: Economic Recovery and Legal Crisis?', *Potchefstroom Electronic Law Journal*, 2010, p. 5-25.

VROM-Raad 2008
VROM-Raad, *Brussels lof. Handreikingen voor ontwikkeling en implementatie van Europees recht en beleid*, Den Haag 2008, available at: <www.rli.nl/sites/default/files/40065brusselslof_0.pdf>.

Werkgroep Van Kemenade 1997
Werkgroep Van Kemenade, *Bestuur in geding; rapport van de Werkgroep inzake terugdringing van de juridisering van het openbaar bestuur*, Provincie Noord-Holland: Servicepunt Facilitair Bedrijf, Haarlem 1997.

Widdershoven 2012
Widdershoven, R.J.G.M., 'Back to the Future: de Europese Unie en het algemeen bestuursrecht', *JBplus*, 2012, p. 195-213.

Widdershoven 2015
Widdershoven, R., 'Europese grondslagen van het bestuursprocesrecht', in: A.T. Marseille, A.C.M. Meuwese, F.C.A.M. Michiels & J.C.A. de Poorter (eds.), *Behoorlijk bestuursprocesrecht*, The Hague: Boom Juridische uitgevers 2015, p. 121-143.

Chris Backes
Mariolina Eliantonio
Sander Jansen

CONCLUSIONS

1. Quality and Speed of Decision-Making - Some Introductory Remarks

For many EU and non-EU countries, speeding up administrative decision-making has been a prominent topic over the last decade. In Germany, mainly due to the needs of the reunification, this was already topical at the beginning of the 1990s. This book takes a closer look into the developments in some selected EU countries (Germany, France, UK, Sweden, Italy, and the Netherlands). It is striking that we could not identify a more fundamental discussion about the relationship between speeding up decision-making and the quality of decision-making in any of these countries. Or, otherwise put, the proposals (from politicians and governments) for speeding up decision-making do not really reflect the general discussions about quality of decision-making (in administrative science). As a result, it seems desirable to provide a few general remarks on what is needed for quality decision-making and on how quality and speed relate to each other before comparing any developments in these countries.

1.1. *A Definition of Quality?*

There is no common ground identifying a set of criteria for the quality of administrative decision-making. Whilst many scholars focus quality on the 'right' or legally correct outcome of decisions,[1] others concentrate on the shift from a governmental authority to an efficient service unit, comparable to a commercial private enterprise.[2] Focussing on the latter, quality management systems like ISO 9000 provide lists of criteria. However, these perceptions mainly concern the effective execution of decisions already taken and not the decision-making process itself. In other words, it concerns the operationalization of what was decided and not the way of determining what the administrative authorities should do. Besides legally correct decisions and efficient services, the democratic legitimacy of

1 Thomas 2015.
2 Schütz 2002.

administrative decision-making is a third element of quality of administrative decisions. Accountability, transparency and participation of those affected are the key features to be dealt with concerning this third element.[3]

The question of what constitutes quality of administrative decision-making and how it could be measured is also addressed in some of the contributions. Dubos points out that speed is relatively easy to measure, but that quality is not. Caranta suggests that a main element of quality of decision-making is effectiveness. After a certain policy aim has been identified and priorities between different aims have been made, the quality of decision-making could mainly be measured by determining the efficiency of the policy delivery. Within which time and with which costs have the policy aims been realized? This approach mainly focuses on output legitimacy ('government for the people'). As seen above, this is an important element of quality of decision-making, but not the only one. Even if one focuses mainly or only on effectiveness and output legitimacy, several difficulties have to be addressed. As Caranta points out, sometimes it is not easily measurable whether and to what extent the policy aims have been realized. That may be easy with regard to infrastructural works for example, but is more difficult in other areas. Besides that, Caranta concludes that at least legal science in Italy still mainly concentrates on input legitimacy. If citizens are sufficiently involved in decision-making and policy choices and applicable procedural rules are followed, the outcome is legitimate ('government by the people'). Reforms concerning decision-making processes have not explicitly reflected on these two sides of quality of decision-making.

1.2. *Quality and Speed – Friends or Enemies?*

As already seen above, the speed of decision-making may be regarded as one of the elements of the quality of decision-making. In some countries, efficient decision-making without unnecessary delay is even (an aspect of) a fundamental right. Article 41 of the Charter of Fundamental Rights of the European Union (CFR) also requires the administration to make decisions in due time. As the German contribution demonstrates, undue delay can cause governmental liability. With regard to court procedures, Article 6 ECHR and Article 47 CFR provide similar rights.

Looking at output legitimacy and efficiency, the time needed to come to a decision which can be brought into practice is an important (and relatively easy to measure) criterion for its quality. This means that speeding up decision-making can enhance the quality of decision-making processes. However, as nearly all the authors point out, there is a second, different side to the same coin. Speeding up decision-making can pressurize input legitimacy. If people do not have enough time to take part in the various stages of decision-making, or if they are not involved at all, input legitimacy is reduced or is no longer sufficiently guaranteed. Furthermore, (too) much pressure on the speed of decision-making may lead to poorly balanced or even unlawful decisions. Especially in complex cases, taking into account all

[3] Walter, Gärditz & Pünder 2013; with regard to American agencies see: Bull 2014, p. 611 *et seq.*

interests and weighing them properly takes time. On the other hand, as Dubos points out, freedom of access to documents and participative democracy also take time. There can be a strong tension between the need for speed, input legitimacy and the quality of the content of a decision. Quality and speed are thus friends and enemies at the same time, or, as Dubos describes it, there is an ambiguous relationship between the two.

Looking at the developments in the different countries researched, one can identify two interesting phenomena.

First, the discussion in all these countries is mainly focussed on speeding up decision-making. Whether the quality of decision-making could or should be improved or whether quicker decisions would mean better decisions and better decision-making was not paid much attention. In another way it can be said that the incentive to propose measures for quicker decision-making seems to have been mainly an economical one. Decisions should be taken faster because that makes investments easier. This is true, for example, for Germany. However, after about 2011, the direction of the discussion in Germany changed. Due to massive public resistance against a few big infrastructural projects, mainly the so-called 'Stuttgart 21' project, the discussion and reforms aimed at improving the legal instruments that enable participation of citizens and making it more effective and efficient - not to speed up decisions, but to improve the quality of decision-making and of the decisions themselves.

Second, in nearly all of the countries, measures to speed up decision-making processes mainly concentrate on increasing effectiveness by reducing participation rights: output legitimacy is enhanced whilst input legitimacy may be reduced. The Dutch reforms may be taken as an example. Whilst the report of the *Elverding*-Commission had identified a whole range of factors which are responsible for the long lasting processes of decisions on infrastructural works and whilst, within this whole range, public participation and judicial review were only of minor importance, the means to speed up decision-making focussed to the largest extent on exactly these public participation and judicial protection elements. Other factors, like budgetary issues and weak-minded and inconsistent authorities were hardly addressed. Similar trends can be observed in Germany. Empirical findings show that the time needed for public participation is rather limited, especially when compared with the time needed for the participation of other administrative authorities. Nevertheless, as Roller points out, all German initiatives to deregulate and to speed up decision-making were based on the assumption that the long duration of procedures would hinder investment decisions and that cutting out public participation would solve this problem. Empirical evidence does not support such an assumption. Gipperth also points out that factors other than the time needed for decisions by authorities and courts, namely the poor quality of the applications, substantially influence the total length of the permitting process.

In some countries reforms seem not only to have been driven by the wish to really shorten decision-making periods, but to some extent more by the need for the government to demonstrate that it takes some kind of action to speed up decision-making. An example of this kind of symbolic legislation is the Dutch provision (Art. 1.4 Crisis and Recovery Act) which forbids decentralized administrative bodies, like municipalities, from instituting proceedings at an administrative court against decisions of higher administrative bodies. When this provision was proposed, legal scholars indicated that it was more likely to prolong procedures than to shorten them. Administrative bodies which cannot start proceedings at the administrative court may do so at the civil court. These procedures probably take longer than a procedure at the administrative court. Similar examples can be found in Germany where §71b *et seq.* of the German Administrative Procedure Act set up several kinds of requirements which for most practitioners and authorities were more or less self-evident, such as to conclude the procedure in an 'appropriate time', to provide advice to the applicant or to send the relevant application documents delivered by the applicant simultaneously to the other administrative bodies involved in the decision. In the meantime, most of these provisions have been repealed.

If the discussion about speed of decision-making had been embedded in a more thorough reflection on (enhancing of) the quality of decision-making, the outcome would probably have been somewhat different and governments would perhaps have prioritized measures which serve both the output and the input legitimacy. Recently, the German discussion about participation rights, mainly triggered by the 'Stuttgart 21' project, have developed in this direction.[4] To a lesser degree, one can also identify some elements of this in the deliberations on the drafts of the Dutch Environmental Act (Omgevingswet). In these discussions, it is not the amount of public participation and input that is discussed, but its effectiveness. Does participation come at the right time within the decision-making process and does it have a positive effect on what follows? The main recipe put forward to enhance the quality (and speed) of decision-making seems to be at a very early stage and broad participation with a reduction of participation rights in the later stages.

Little can be said about the effects of reforms aimed at speeding up decision-making on the quality of the decisions taken. There is no or only very little research on that. Sometimes, as the deregulation of the permit requirements for windmills in Sweden shows, reforms intended to speed up decision-making in fact have the opposite effect and have made procedures last even longer. One reason for the poor information about effectiveness of reforms surely is that the quality, other than the duration of the decision-making process, is difficult to measure. Some scholars, especially in Germany, argue that the cumulative effect of all measures to deregulate and to speed up has had or must have had a negative effect on the quality of the decisions.[5] Speeding up decision-making, especially by cutting down time limits, may not only have an effect on the quality of the decision-making and the decisions concerned, but also on the service of the authority as a whole. Short decision-making terms may require an authority to give priority to decision-making processes whilst other tasks like compliance control may be ranked lower.

4 Schuster 2013, p. 337 *et seq.*; Groß 2011, p. 510 *et seq.*
5 Cf. in this book, the chapter by G. Roller, quoting Erbguth 2009, p. 921 *et seq.*

2. National Acceleration Trends, International Acceleration Pressures and Democratic Limitations

2.1. *The Need for Speed: Not a New Issue?*

The contributors to this book have answered in various ways the question of whether the need to increase speed, and above all, efficiency, in administrative decision-making is a recent or long-standing issue, or a generally discussed topic or one which is uniquely linked to times of crisis and the need to relaunch economic growth.

Caranta indicates, for example, that a number of very diverse reforms have been undertaken in Italy over the past 25 years to speed up the decision-making process, ranging

> 'from organisational measures - such as single contact points, collegiate decision making processes, and terms for taking decisions, to measures aimed at simplification through provisions variously reducing not just the red tape but the competencies and powers of public authorities, and of lately the use of IT instruments [...] and the dissemination of best practices'.

Roller also states that measures have been taken to accelerate decision-making procedures in Germany since the beginning of the 1990s. He identifies the rationale underlying these reforms in the need, on the one hand, to rapidly improve the infrastructure of the new German federal states after reunification, and, on the other hand, to reduce overly bureaucratic procedures, seen as a hurdle to economic growth.

In the Netherlands, the need for speedier decision-making is a more recent concern and it is linked to the economic crisis. A specific Act of Parliament (the Crisis and Recovery Act) was developed with the rationale of speeding up decision-making for certain projects, mainly facilitating developers to commence large infrastructure projects (quicker). Administrative courts also made a U-turn. In just a few years, in case of grounded claims, the courts' attitude changed from delivering judgments mainly stating what the administration did wrong (with renewed administrative decision-making as a result) into an attitude which concentrates on achieving final dispute-settlement by stating what is, or at least how to come to a lawful and proper administrative decision within a restricted time-period. The Swedish contribution also only discusses rather recent developments concerning the need to speed up environmental permitting procedures, indicating that the concern for a speedier decision-making process belongs to the newer reform agenda items.

While in Italy, the Netherlands and Germany speed seems to have been at the top of the reform agenda (although with mixed outcomes), Dubos indicates quite clearly that speed has not traditionally been an aim in itself for the French administration. However, because of the development of the Welfare State, it has become increasingly important for citizens to receive administrative services without any undue delay and this is why Dubos' qualifies speed as a 'latent requirement'.

While therefore the section above concluded that efficiency and quality are difficult concepts to define and to measure, this section goes to show that these definitions and evaluations are made even more complicated by the entrenchment of these concepts in the diverse legal cultures and economic backgrounds of the different legal systems. What might be a great result for increased efficiency for the Italian public administration may already have been in existence in Sweden for decades: as Caranta notes, it was not before 1990 that Italy got to enact a basic principle such as the duty of public bodies to bring administrative procedures to an outcome with an explicit decision. Until that point, Italian administration just tended to drag administrative procedures on until the point where ultimately no decision was taken. Similarly to this, Dubos points out that until the 1970s one could have had the impression that the administration worked in favour of the state or even of itself rather than in favour of the citizens. This has dramatically changed over the last decades. In this sense, even a clear statement such as 'the time limit for bringing a claim were halved', may have very different meanings in the different legal systems in light of the very diverse traditions and starting points.

2.2. *The Role of International and European Law: Importantly Unequal and Unequally Important*

The question of the influence of European and international law on the debate concerning the tensions and the balance between speed and quality has been discussed at different levels of depth and intensity by the contributors to this book.

The Aarhus Convention has played a minimal role in Italy, and, apart from strengthening participatory rights, was not a trigger in the debate on quality and speed in administrative action in France.[6]

Other legal systems report very different experiences. Roller emphatically calls European law (and especially the Aarhus Convention as part of the EU legal system) a 'safety net' for participation and access to court rights in the German legal system. Interestingly, according to Roller and the evidence he provides, increased participation and possibilities for access to court increase the quality of decision-making, as claims launched by NGOs tend to be relatively successful. One could, however, see the other side of the coin in that broader chances for NGOs to access courts may also end up in a slower achievement of legal certainty. In the Netherlands too, the Aarhus Convention seems to function as a 'safety net'. However, unlike Germany, this international treaty did not lead to the consequence that participation and access to courts had to be widened, but worked as a sort of last barrier which must not be passed in the attempts made by the Dutch Crisis and Recovery Act of speeding up decision-making by reducing participatory rights and limiting access to justice. We can therefore see an assimilation of both legal orders due to the influence of the Aarhus Convention.

The Aarhus Convention also plays a prominent role in Jenkins' contribution, without, however, delivering the positive news which the German contribution

6 Convention on Access to Information, Public Participation in Decision-Making and Access to Justice in Environmental Matters, 2161 UNTS 447; 38 ILM 517 (1999).

brings to the fore. In particular, a critical point is identified in the UK system of the pre-application consultation by the developer: this system is used in the case of nationally significant infrastructure and essentially entails that the consultation of relevant (governmental as well as non-governmental) stakeholders is 'front-loaded' to a moment before the environmental statement for the purposes of the EIA Directive[7] is finalized. This system seems to be at odds with the Aarhus Convention's requirement to afford the public concerned an 'early and effective' opportunity to participate in environmental decision-making processes. Of course, 'front-loading' implements early participation. Whether it implements effective participation may be questioned, given that the public receives in this way a narrow category of only limited information on the outline of a project and is perhaps not able to substantially influence the actual decision of the authorities. While 'front-loading' is suitable to ensure an 'early' opportunity to participate in the decision-making process, the UK contribution shows some doubts as to whether the 'effectiveness' requirement is equally met if there are no further participation possibilities apart from the 'front-loaded' one. At the same time, the Aarhus Convention and European law did bring about positive changes in the UK legal systems with regard to the costs of judicial proceedings in environmental matters. This issue, which has been contentious in the UK for a long time, has been tackled by the UK legislator, following explicit condemnations by the Aarhus Compliance Committee and the CJEU.

Interestingly, only two contributions mention the ECHR. The Dutch contribution questions whether the so-called 'administrative loop' complies with the requirements imposed by Article 6 ECHR, while the German contribution points to the fact that Germany has repeatedly been condemned by the ECtHR for excessively lengthy court procedures. This conspicuous absence in the other contributions may be explained by the different importance (including from a cultural point of view) attached to the ECHR in the legal systems covered in this book.

What can be concluded from this section is that the debate and the legal regime on speed and quality in administrative decision-making have been influenced by European and international law at various intensities. As such this is not surprising: where national provisions were already in compliance at the outset with the requirements mandated by the European and domestic level, it is rather self-evident that not much debate has arisen concerning their existence, scope of application and obligations. At the same time it is to be noted that even where instances of non-compliance have been identified, they seem to be related to different issues, and even more importantly, to have led to different outcomes. While in the German legal systems the instances of non-compliance have been brought to the attention of the CJEU and have been subsequently repaired at the national level, in the UK the violation of the Aarhus Convention and European law (in as far as the requirement of 'early and effective participation') still seems to be in place.

7 Directive 2014/52/EU of the European Parliament and of the Council of 16 April 2014 amending Directive 2011/92/EU on the assessment of the effects of certain public and private projects on the environment [2014] OJ L 124/1.

2.3. *What Does the Demos Have to Do With It?*

In the debate on quality and speed in administrative decision-making, all the legal systems covered in this comparative analysis need to comply not only with international and European requirements, but also with national overarching constitutional requirements such as the respect for democracy and the separation of powers. Indeed, several contributors stress how striking a balance between different conflicting values in this thorny debate entails, at the same time, attempting to strike a balance between different constitutional values.

Dubos, for example, emphasizes that transparency in administrative affairs, a well-known prong of democracy, stands somewhat in contrast with efficiency. Evidently, the more the administration needs to show and justify, the slower it will reach its decisions. The French example of the duty to state reasons for unfavourable individual decisions stands as a good example of this tension. The open question remains as to how much a legal system may or should sacrifice transparency to achieve speedier decisions. Similar considerations resonate with regard to transparency 'twin brother', participation: while European law and the Aarhus Convention have strengthened individuals' participatory positions in France, it cannot be denied that more participation entails a decrease in speed in the decision-making process. Jenkins' contribution highlights an opposite tendency: in the UK the traditional system of the public enquiry, a forum where local interests can be represented and defended in environmental decision-making, has been seen by many governments in a negative light because of the costs and delays involved. The newly introduced system of public examination is subject to several limitations (such as strict time limits and the adoption of an inquisitorial approach) aimed precisely at balancing participation with efficiency.

Efficiency, on the other hand, can also be seen as a constitutional value itself. Roller, for example, notes that under German law, the competent authority is obliged to execute the procedure efficiently. This is firstly because the administration generally has to perform its activities in the most effective way and, secondly, in cases where fundamental rights of citizens are involved, the right to receive a response from the authority in due time is part of these fundamental rights. He further specifies that undue delays in the decision-making process may even entail governmental liability. Also with regard to court procedures, some *Länder* constitutions have explicitly laid down a right to an efficient court procedure. Efficiency, however, needs to be balanced with a thorough and qualitatively satisfactory examination of the factual situation at stake: in the case of complex infrastructures, this is not an easy task. To a certain extent the current Dutch regime resembles the German regime. First, undue delay in the decision-making process can lead to financial consequences for the administration. Second, a quite recently introduced provision 'obliges' administrative courts to try to finalize disputes as soon as possible.

Compliance with the rule of law is another conflicting value when it comes to achieving a higher level of efficiency in administrative decision-making: the Italian example of 'emergency legislation' provides an interesting example of how far a legal system may go in derogating to the ordinary legal regime for speedier decision-making. The Italian legal system has faced various types of 'emergency' situations by acting outside the applicable rules, including EU environmental and public procurement requirements. The case study illustrated by Caranta shows that the desire for increased speed can legitimately lead, in emergency situations, to the establishment of special legal regimes, but cannot trump respect for EU law provisions.

Finally, if by *demos* one understands the 'public' and the 'public interest', the concerns expressed in the Dutch contribution cannot be overlooked: curtailing access to court for environmental NGOs entails, in essence, curtailing the protection of the environment, something which belongs to nobody and everybody at the same time.

3. Acceleration Initiatives Concerning the Administrative Decision-Making Process

3.1. *Measures Taken to Speed Up Decision-Making*

Looking at the different national contributions, often the same kind of measure is taken to speed up decision-making. However, as a result of different historical (political) frameworks of administrative law and practice, a different focus can be identified.

One Stop Shop

There is a group of measures trying to harmonize, coordinate and simplify different decision-making procedures which apply to a certain activity. Whilst in former times applicants had to consult several different authorities, now there often is only a 'one stop shop'. The need and burden to procedurally coordinate different permits or aspects of permission no longer therefore lies on the applicants, but on the government. The application of the 'one stop shop' principle is a widely known development, which is mentioned in the UK, Dutch, German, French and Italian contributions. However, in some countries, like Sweden, this is hardly applied. In Italy it was introduced quite early on. It is said to reduce complexity and increase transparency and accessibility. Moreover, it helps to speed up the decision-making process. As long as it is only a procedural instrument, as is the case in Italy, one may conclude that it serves both speed and quality. A variety is the *conferenze di servizi*, a system which tries to bring together all the authorities involved in a certain decision-making process. The German *Planfeststellungsverfahren* and the licensing procedure under the Federal Emission Control Act use similar means. This ensures, to a certain extent, that different decisions on one activity are not only procedurally harmonized, but also coordinated content-wise. Although applied in Italy very often during the last decades, Caranta reports that this instrument still does not always work smoothly.

Integration of Decision-Making Procedures

A more far-reaching step is to actually integrate different decision-making procedures. That often requires a shift of decision-making power. If the 'one stop shop' is combined with a shift and concentration of powers to one single authority, things may become different. This seems, at least to a certain extent, to be the case in the UK and Germany and is also planned in the Netherlands. This may lead to a certain devaluation of interests and policy fields which originally were administered by a separate, specialized administrative body. If the competence of these specialized bodies to decide is transferred to a single, general administrative body, certain 'weak' aspects like nature conservation or environmental protection, or local interests may be set aside more easily. There are some fears that this may lead to less quality in decision-making in the countries which do not stop at procedural integration, but have shifted competences or are planning to do so. As mentioned in the German, Dutch and UK contributions, decisions which are taken as a result of integrated permitting procedures sometimes have, to a greater or lesser extent, what the Germans call concentration effect (*Konzentrationswirkung*). The applicant can be sure that all public law requirements are met and that no other consent is needed.

A somewhat different approach seems to have been taken in France. Creating separate, specialized agencies, which operate aside from the hierarchically structured ministries, was a mean to increase the quality and speed of decision-making.

Fictive Decisions and Lex Silentio Positivo

Another instrument, used in more than one of the researched countries, is the fictive permission. If the authorities do not take any decision in time and do not react on a request, the so-called *lex silentio positivo* is applied and the request is deemed to be decided positively. To a certain extent, European law urges the Member States to introduce this instrument, mainly in the area covered by the Services Directive.[8] However, some contributions point out that the *lex silentio positivo* is not used when third parties may suffer disadvantages from such a decision. Other countries (Italy, France and the Netherlands) seem to apply the *lex silentio positivo* even if the fictive positive decision can be detrimental for third parties. The concrete provisions and legal arrangements seem to differ. In France, third parties that cannot know that a fictive decision has been taken, are not bound to any time period if they want to object to such a decision. In France and in the Netherlands, the administrative authority loses the competence to decide after a fictive decision has come into force. In Italy, the opposite is the case. In Italy, this instrument seems to be the most important and a very widely applied means to speed up decision-making. Linked to this discussion, it should be noted that periods granted to authorities to take a decision seem to vary widely. In France, until 2000, four months was the most usual time limit. Reducing this limit to two months was perceived to be a means of speeding up decisions. In other countries, shorter periods such as six weeks, are

8 Directive 2006/123/EC of the European Parliament and of the Council of 12 December 2006 on services in the internal market [2006] OJ L 376/36.

(recently in the UK) common and in even short terms of four or (sometimes in Germany) two (+ four) weeks are known.

Penalty Payments

Some countries, like the Netherlands and France, have introduced penalty payments for administrative authorities which do not meet their deadlines. However, it is not (yet) known whether this instrument has been effective and has reduced undue delays.

Emergency Clauses

A last instrument, which was already discussed in paragraph 2.3, but has also to be mentioned here, concerns the possibility to set aside legal obligations in case of urgency. In France, this instrument is known at least in theory, in Italy it is also applied in practice very regularly. If urgency demands it, certain Italian administrative authorities may deviate from almost all procedural and material rules to manage a 'crisis' or 'state of emergency'. Caranta recognizes that this instrument has a widespread area of application throughout all levels of Italian administrative bodies. Administrative authorities even use these powers to deviate from EU law requirements. This may speed up decision-making. However, it will not often contribute to their quality.

All in all, this overview of measures to speed up administrative decision-making is significant. Some of the very diverse instruments can also improve quality (besides the aspect of speed), like one stop shop-structures, which may improve coordination of different decisions. Others, like penalty payments, are purely meant to speed up decision-making. Their effect on quality is, in most cases, unknown.

3.2. *Shortening Decision-Making Time Limits*

Although, 'the real potential of speeding up administrative decision-making processes lies much more in sound administrative management'[9] (as the German contribution states), legal provisions which provide for strict time limits may to be expected to be one of the most favoured attempts to achieve the goal of quicker administrative decision-making. If the time involved in the decision-making process is felt to be (far) too long, one of the *prima facie* measures to shorten the duration of this decision-making is to reduce the amount of time the administration has to issue an administrative decision.[10] In France for instance, the current regime (which dates from April 2000) has halved the time given to act from four to two months. In this (limited) context, French administrative law made use of the instrument of shorter time-limits to force the administrative authorities to act with the aim of less time consuming administrative decision-making. In the Netherlands, time limits for

9 Cf. in this book, the chapter by G. Roller.

10 This is probably a measure for the legislator to take. Also note that sometimes fixed time-limits are not to be found in legislation as they are prescribed by administrative courts, as for instance in France.

certain steps in the decision-making process have been reduced for certain kind of projects.

Quite often decision-making requires certain steps or conditions to be complied with before the decision can be issued, for example the competent authority has to ask for advice from an advisory board or another administrative authority. As a species of the genus of fixed time limits to take an administrative decision, time limits therefore exist for the required contributions of other authorities or advisory bodies. Some of the legal systems covered in this comparative analysis have indeed enacted measures aimed at reducing the period allocated to advisory boards (such as Italy and the Netherlands). The shortening of such time limits brings about greater speed (as was the case in Germany and Italy). On the other hand, to impose ambitious time limits seems to illustrate the tension between speed and quality, since a priority shift of the administration to meet short time limits could bring about effects to the detriment of other tasks of the administration - such as surveillance and compliance control. This, for instance, happened in Germany.

In case the legislature sets shortened time limits, this sometimes proved to be of only limited relevance, as is illustrated in French law: in cases where the legislature has set time limits for the government to pass implementing decrees for laws, the Council of State considered such deadlines as guidelines instead of strictly obligatory provisions.

The contributions contained in this edited collection show that sometimes legislative measures taken with regard to time limits often concentrate on the *consequences* of exceeding the prescribed time limits to take decisions rather than on the introduction of legal provisions which prescribed shorter time-limits.

One further means to foster quicker administrative decision-making is the concept of the implicit decision of refusal. Fixed time-limits for the conclusion of the decision-making process can be set as a default period in case another act does not provide for a maximum duration of the administrative proceedings (such as in the Netherlands and Italy). If the administration exceeds the fixed time-limit, this can not only result in an implicit refusal which can be challenged in court or, in the opposite case, in a fictive positive decision (as discussed in para. 3.1), but also in an action for damages (for example in Italy).

3.3. *Participation Rights*

As already mentioned, several of the countries looked at (Germany, the Netherlands, England) tried to save time in the decision-making process by cutting down participation rights, mainly in the area of environmental and physical planning law. Especially in the Netherlands and Germany, but also in the UK, a whole range of measures have been taken over the years which make it more difficult for neighbours or environmental NGOs to participate in the decision-making process and to object against (draft) decisions on infrastructural and other projects. Whilst most of these measures concern objection and judicial review procedures, which will be discussed below, restrictions have also been applied in the decision-making phase. This development mainly concerns shorter time periods to take part in the debate before a (draft) decision is taken, often combined with preclusion clauses which hinder claimants from bringing forward grounds in the phase of objection and judicial review which have not been brought forward in the early phase of decision-making. With regard to cases falling within the scope of application of the Aarhus Convention, the CJEU has declared that such preclusion clauses are in violation of EU law.[11] Besides that, some scholars in Germany argue that the combination of these measures in the decision-making and judicial review phases has as a consequence that the requirements of effective judicial protection are no longer met.

However, in the same countries it is discussed whether the 'traditional' way of public participation is an effective one and whether it should, at least in some cases, be replaced by new forms of broad participation at a very early stage. In the UK, this is called 'front-loading'. In Germany and the Netherlands traditionally the public is consulted only on a draft decision of the authorities. Nowadays, or until recently, public consultation took place after the authorities had almost entirely made up their minds. A broad participation at an early phase, when solutions for a certain problem are not yet clear and the authorities are more open-minded, could be more effective and could broaden the democratic legitimacy and so foster the quality of such decisions.[12] The hope is that the extra time needed for such an early phase consultation could (at least) be saved in later phases because those who were sufficiently consulted earlier are less likely to object once decisions are adopted. The new German laws which should foster the enlargement of the grid (*Energiewende*) introduced a very early public participation moment in the general planning of the energy network on the Federal level (*Bundesnetzplan*). The law does not provide for access to court as far as this plan is concerned. Access to court is only granted against the final planning permit, and in this procedure the previous general plan can be examined implicitly by the judge. It is too early to decide what effects this approach has on speed and on quality of decision-making. Also in the UK and the Netherlands, front-loading is combined with restrictions in the phase of judicial review. It seems that the UK is currently the most experienced with this kind of 'front loading' procedure. Jenkins concludes in her contribution that 'front-loading' participation has been significant in increasing efficiency and is 'theoretically' important to create an effective process of participation. However, as already mentioned in paragraph 2.2, the 'quite unsatisfactory' experience when trying to find new locations for nuclear power plants demonstrates some of the difficulties which can be faced when such kind of 'massive' early stage public participation procedures are applied, and which seem to limit the effectiveness of this approach.[13]

3.4. *Deregulation and a Greater Role for Private Parties as a Way to Reduce Administrative Burdens*

Another set of acceleration initiatives is aimed at deregulating administrative decision-making and increasing the role of private parties to unburden the

11 Case C-137/14 *European Commission* v. *Federal Republic of Germany*, EU:C:2015:683.
12 Groβ 2011, p. 510 *et seq*.
13 Cf. in this book, the chapter by V. Jenkins.

administration. The contributions included in this book seem to indicate that many legal systems have opted for this solution. One could legitimately wonder where to strike the balance between deregulation and increasing the role of private parties, and the need to preserve the quality of administrative decisions.

For example Caranta indicates that Italy has long had a system whereby sworn declarations may take the place of certificates as evidence of status and personal conditions (such as place of birth, personal income) in order to alleviate the workload of the administration. Furthermore, specifically in planning matters, the main act in administrative decision-making provides that when an activity is conditioned upon the granting of a licence, authorization, permission, or any other decision by the public administration, the interested party may submit a sworn declaration that he meets all legal requirements for the activity. Different standstill periods were provided in previous versions of the provision, but they were progressively reduced and finally eliminated.

Similarly to the Italian situation, the German legal system has experienced a wave of deregulation initiatives. Roller indicates that in recent years the legislator released industrial plants from the licensing obligation under the applicable legislation in a number of cases. A similar observation is shared by Gipperth with regard to the Swedish situation, where since 2009 many types of installations no longer need a permit or even to send a notification to the local authority.

Another element of deregulation noted by Roller in the German context is the increasing importance of the notification compared to the permit. In cases of simple modification of the installation that does not have a negative impact on the environment, the operator of the plant is not obliged to run through a permitting procedure: he simply has to notify the authority which enables the operator to implement the modification after one month from the notification, even if the authority has not replied.

Deregulation is also an important topic in the Netherlands. In fact, the Dutch contribution calls it a 'constant hype over the last three decades'. As in other legal systems, in many areas of law, substantial requirements have been diminished or abandoned, and private parties and 'the market' have been given more room for manoeuvre. Furthermore, in the area of environmental and planning law, future legislation aims at a further substantial deregulation of procedural and substantial requirements. Amongst others, the requirement to have an environmental permit will become redundant for many thousands of installations.

Also in the UK a greater role for private parties, especially the developer, can be identified in the system of pre-application consultation, whereby it is for the developer (rather the public authorities) to organize the consultation process on a certain project and to incorporate its outcome into the environmental statement to be submitted to the authorities.

3.5. *Special Regime of Major Infrastructure: in Search of More Speed*

Several of the contributions contained in this book highlight how, for largely similar efficiency reasons, major infrastructures have been made subject to a special regime.

In Italy, the applicable legislation provides a specific procedure for major infrastructures, whose approval is given at the central level by the Council of Ministers and it takes the place of any other decision necessary for environmental protection, urban planning, or expropriation which may be required by the law to start the implementation of the project. Clearly, the rationale here is to do away with the complexity caused by different administrative procedures needing co-ordination at different governmental levels.

Similarly, in the UK, the applicable legislation created a special form of authorization for nationally significant infrastructure projects: the main feature of this system is the greater role assumed by the SS at the central level (as opposed to local authorities in the 'normal' regime) who acts upon the advice of the Major Infrastructure Environment Unit of the Planning Inspectorate. A second feature of the authorization system of major infrastructure projects is the presence of the so-called 'NPPS', which are aimed at setting the framework for future planning initiatives by identifying the amount, size or type of development that is appropriate nationally - and even suitable locations. To ensure they have a democratic mandate the NPPS must be formally passed by Parliament and, despite what the term 'statement' might indicate, the NPPS are, once enacted, binding upon the competent authorities unless it is shown that the adverse impacts of the proposed development on the local community would outweigh its benefits.

The need to speed up the approval of major infrastructure has been at the forefront of the discussion about quicker and better decision-making also in the Netherlands. The 'Crisis and Recovery Act' discussed in the Dutch contribution in fact contained several provisions which deviated from the general system of decision-making and legal protection against administrative decisions which were aimed at achieving faster decision-making procedures for major infrastructure. The means to realize this goal were very diverse: shortening time limits, tightening the EIA procedure, reducing judicial review to only one instance, limiting the grounds of review and many more. Interestingly, to quite an extent, changes which were first and foremost introduced in the law concerning the approval of major infrastructure have later been transferred to the General Administrative Law Act and hence now apply in all areas of administrative law.

4. Legal Protection and Court-Related Measures

Next to changes in the context of the decision-making process and administrative managerial and organizational adaptations, courts and court proceedings are involved in the issue of quality and speed of administrative decision-making. Amongst other things, this is because, if challenged, often only after all court procedures have been exhausted does the administrative decision become final. Courts (and their judgments) can contribute to the quality of the decisions, but they (or rather the availability of legal protection against the administrative action) can delay as well, because legal protection and court procedures usually prolong the period before a decision becomes final. Sometimes, the reorganization of the court system can (be intended to) contribute to shorter proceedings. In this context, the reforms which took place in Sweden can be mentioned. The tension between quality and speed is not unique for administrative-decision-making process but is felt within judicial court proceedings as well. The application of specific tools of administrative judges can, however, also result in speedier final resolution of the legal dispute at stake.

The most important acceleration measures related to courts and court procedures can be subdivided into three main categories. The first category consists of measures with the intention to shorten the length of court procedures. The second category in this respect is the limitation of the right of access to court. Third, the removal of one or more levels of legal protection can be considered a factor.

4.1. *Measures to Speed Up Court Procedures*

Additional instruments for courts

In the Netherlands, the legislator provided the administrative courts with additional instruments, in particular new kinds of rulings. Some of these instruments can be regarded as a means to speed up court procedures since they contribute to final dispute settlement and hence final decision-making within a shorter time period, for example by avoiding the continuation or the duration of the court procedures. Dutch courts, for example, currently have an enlarged toolbox at their disposal if compared to about five years ago.

In the last two decades, administrative law has been subject to significant developments likely to influence the speed of administrative judicial procedures in France too, such as the power of the court to issue injunctions to ensure the effectiveness of annulment decisions and the finding that annulments on grounds of ultra vires 'lost ground against full remedy proceedings'.[14]

One of the tools, used in more than one country, that could contribute to stop the continuation of court procedures, is the provision according to which errors of a procedural, but sometimes also of a substantive, nature in the decision-making process no longer necessarily result in the annulment of the decision. For instance, if the decision is correct on the substance, or no other decision could have been taken and the irregularity therefore has no effect on the outcome of the procedure, and interested parties do not suffer any harm, annulment can be omitted (such as in the case of Germany, the Netherlands and Italy).[15] In some systems this instrument is more frequently used in practice (in Germany and the Netherlands) than in others (such as Italy). That is because according to Caranta, in contrast to Germany, Italian courts are reluctant to go into the merits of an administrative decision.

Another instrument for courts is to replace the annulled administrative decision by their own decision. This means that the unlawful decision is annulled, and therefore the administration does not have to issue a renewed decision to replace the annulled one, as the court will take a decision on the matter. By avoiding

14 Cf. in this book, the chapter by O. Dubos.

15 Concerning the Netherlands, such an instrument was introduced in 1994 but the scope was widened in 2013 by setting aside the limitation of applicability only in case of *procedural* irregularities. In Germany, such an instrument, which can also be found in the legislation on general administrative law decision-making and court procedure, is not part of a novel approach and a new toolbox.

the mechanism of renewed decision-making, this 'replacing power' can be considered a sort of measure to speed up court procedures (in total) as well. In the countries where courts have such a power at their disposal, the prerequisites differ. A clear example of this far-reaching court power can be found in the Netherlands. In Germany, a court instrument similar to this one is that in infrastructure planning procedures where the plan is not in compliance with substantive law, instead of annulling the plan, the administrative court determines a supplementary measure to repair the plan. In France, it seems as if the power of administrative courts to award an injunction in case of non-discretionary powers of the administration resembles the power to replace the decision by the court's own decision (French administrative courts can adopt an enforcement measure and order this measure).

Of a different nature and in the field of stating reasons is the power given to the administrative courts to hand down a judgment with very brief reasoning (as is the case for Italy).

Time limits for court procedures

Sometimes the legislator prescribes fixed time limits for administrative courts to hand down a ruling (for example, in the Netherlands). This Dutch obligation to deliver judgment within a certain time (such as within 6 months) only applies to specific disputes, covered by a few specific Codes (such as the Crisis and Recovery Act and some planning law litigation).

In the same context, the strict possibility to challenge a planning decision by way of judicial review within six weeks in the UK and the introduction of a time limit for some actions against regulatory acts in France must be mentioned.

Also in the area of planning law and other infrastructure projects, Caranta reports that the Italian legislator created a fast track procedure by halving most of the deadlines for judicial review.

In complex infrastructure and planning law cases these short time limits can be considered problematic, which makes the tension between speed and (means to guarantee) quality manifest.

4.2. *Access to Court*

Since the use of court proceedings by natural and legal persons (including NGOs and interested third parties) can delay decision-making, one potential measure to speed up decision-making is to restrict their right of access to court.

Firstly, standing can be lost if a participation or objection right was not exercised. The German *materielle Präklusion* comes down to such a restriction of access to court. This limitation applied to all infrastructure planning procedures. Due to the *Commission* v. *Germany* case,[16] however, this *materielle Präklusion* will no longer be applied in any environmental law case. This development also illustrates the tension between 'efficiency' of proceedings and access to court and it emphasizes the significance of European and international law.

16 Case C-137/14, *European Commission* v. *Federal Republic of Germany*, EU:C:2015:683.

To a certain extent the German *materielle Präklusion* resembles the general approach in the Dutch GALA (Art. 6:13 GALA): an objection or appeal is inadmissible if the interested party did not participate or challenge the act in earlier administrative or court stages, without good reason. In light of the *Commission* v. *Germany* case,[17] it is questionable whether Article 6:13 GALA may be applied in environmental cases in the future, at least with regard to cases falling within the scope of Article 9(2) Aarhus Convention.[18]

Another option to limit access to court is the so-called 'connectivity principle' (*Schutznorm*). In both Germany and (recently) the Netherlands the connectivity principle restricts legal protection as it requires that the infringed rule aims at the protection of the interest of the person who relies on it. Whereas in the Netherlands this requirement does not bar the admissibility (but the possibility to get the decision annulled), in Germany it is a hurdle to access to court. In environmental matters EU law and the Aarhus Convention, however, forced Germany not to unduly restrict avenues to legal protection for associations. Hence, in Germany the *Schutznorm* requirement for NGOs has been abolished in cases in which Article 9(2) of the Aarhus Convention is applicable. As already mentioned in paragraph 2.2, there are indications that the latter development affects the quality of the decisions in a positive way. Moreover, the German situation illustrates the tension and possible conflicts between restriction of access to court and procedural safeguards and the boundaries of access-related restrictions set in EU law and international law.

A bar for third parties to challenge the administrative action is also possible by alternative means to a *Schutznorm* mechanism, for instance in a specific area of law. In the UK planning system, for example, sometimes, there is no right of access to court for third parties affected by a decision.

Access to court can also be restricted due to the (risk of) high *costs* of bringing an action. In the UK this is or at least was quite a barrier, and was considered unlawful by the Aarhus Committee.[19] The CJEU similarly (as regards Art. 10a of EIA Directive)[20] found that the use of so-called protective cost orders failed to meet the requirements of the Directive, as Jenkins points out.[21] Such European judgements can – and did in the UK - result in legislative action and led to measures restricting claimants' liability to pay the defendants' costs.[22]

17 *Ibid.*

18 Convention on Access to Information, Public Participation in Decision-Making and Access to Justice in Environmental Matters, 2161 UNTS 447; 38 ILM 517 (1999).

19 'Aarhus Convention Implementation Report', DEFRA, 2008.

20 Directive 2014/52/EU of the European Parliament and of the Council of 16 April 2014 amending Directive 2011/92/EU on the assessment of the effects of certain public and private projects on the environment [2014] OJ L 124/1.

21 Case C-427/07, *Commission of the European Communities* v. *Ireland*, EU:C:2009:457; Case C-530/11, *European Commission* v. *United Kingdom of Great Britain and Northern Ireland*, EU:C:2014:67.

22 (Overly) high costs for procedures and hence for getting legal court protection are not unique to the UK. In Italy the costs for commencing judicial review proceedings have risen considerably, according to Caranta, p. 42.

Finally, with regard to restriction of access to court, it must be mentioned that in France, particularly in the sphere of urban planning law, access to court has been seriously restricted, especially since 2013, to bar frivolous litigation that slows down decision-making processes. This has happened firstly by means of a more restrictive approach towards *locus standi* and secondly by letting applicants bear the risk of paying damages for the undertaker.

4.3. *Elimination of the Compulsory Objection Procedure or of a Court Instance*

The accumulation of available court instances (two or three) as well as preliminary objection proceedings is sometimes a delaying factor. Therefore, some legislators decided to eliminate one or even two courts levels, or the objection procedure.

It is not really a novel development in French administrative law, but in France the legal protection for major infrastructural projects is limited to a single instance (the Council of State). This restriction has been introduced in Germany too, as well as abandonment of the objection proceedings in some cases. In Germany, limiting judicial protection to only one instance was even regarded as one of the most important measures to accelerate the decision-making process. For certain infrastructure and large industrial plant projects, in 1985 the German legislator eliminated the administrative court of first instance. The (overly) long court proceedings hindered planning security and came in conflict with the large investments involved, according to the legislator. Not only the court of first instance but even the administrative court of appeal was removed in the law on the acceleration of traffic infrastructure. Nowadays, the *Bundesverwaltungsgericht* is the one and only court competent in a large number of railway, road and waterway cases, which are explicitly listed in the relevant laws.

On the one hand, the availability of only one court contributes to a shorter duration of court procedures; on the other hand the subsequent question arises whether it may disturb the balance between quality, including judicial safeguards, and speed.

5. Administrative Decision-Making and Court Procedure: Substantially Quicker, but Qualitatively Better?

Speeding up decision-making processes is an issue in all of the countries covered in this book. Although speed and quality of decision-making may be regarded as two sides of the same coin and hence cannot be considered separately, this is exactly what happened in many examples discussed in the contributions to this book. *Accelerating* decision-making and review by courts often was approached as a single issue as part of the fight against the economic crisis. Although, as especially the development in Swedish environmental law shows, not all reforms have led to the expected gains in tempo, and some of the measures taken emerged to be window dressing rather than having substantial effects, it is also true that in all the countries examined the speeding up of decision-making was at least partly successful.

We can be less sure whether the *quality* of decision-making was raised or, on the contrary, even declined. It is much more difficult to measure the quality of decision-making than its duration. Even a good and comprehensive definition of quality of decision-making is missing. A more comprehensive conceptualization of quality of decision-making seems, therefore, to be needed. For a long time, the quality of decision-making has not been the focus of administrative law reforms. In some countries touched upon this is still true today. Attempts to assess or estimate effects of reforms on quality usually are missing. There is a lot to gain in this respect, within the national context and of course also in a comparative context. However, times may have changed. In some countries like the UK, the Netherlands and Germany, the quality of administrative decision-making has become an important issue. Interestingly, in all three countries, this led to try-outs with concepts of very early and broad public participation ('front-loading'). Although the first results of the use of this concept in the UK seem not to have been very promising, a thorough evaluation of the application in the UK and other countries is needed. The results should be compared and discussed not only within a national, but also in a comparative context.

Although measures to speed up decision-making cannot be understood well without their different national legal context and history and the very different economical context and administrative cultures, the overview in this book may provide food for thought for those seeking inspiration for measures aimed to speed up decision-making. Some instruments and concepts applied in one or more countries may inspire discussions in other countries. We hope all the more so that this book will contribute to a discussion about the need to further enhance and better assess the quality of decision-making. Speeding up decision-making has received a lot of attention in the past decades and should not be forgotten in the future, but, we submit, the focus of the discussion should move somewhat forward. Speed should become one element of a more general discussion about enhancing the quality of decision-making. The recent discussions in Germany and the UK raise our hope that quality is moved into the spotlight of the discussion in the future after decades of speed driven reforms. The comparative exchange of ideas makes a lot of sense in that respect.

Bibliography

Bull 2014
Bull, R.T., 'Making the Administrative State "Safe for Democracy". A Theoretical and Practical Analysis of Citizen Participation in Agency Decisionmaking', *Administrative Law Review*, 2014, p. 611-664.

Erbguth 2009
Erbguth, W., 'Abbau des Verwaltungsrechtsschutzes', *Die Öffentliche Verwaltung*, 2009, p. 921-931.

Groß 2011
Groß, T., 'Frankfurt (Main), Stuttgart 21: Folgerungen für Demokratie und Verwaltungsverfahren', *Die Öffentliche Verwaltung*, 2011, p. 510-514.

Schuster 2013
Schuster, W., 'Politikgestaltung als lernender Prozess: "Stuttgart 21" aus einer politischen Sicht', in: F. Brettschneider & W. Schuster (eds.), *Stuttgart 21*, Berlin: Springer-Verlag 2013, p. 329-343.

Schütz 2002
Schütz, G., *Qualität und Qualitätsmanagement in der öffentlichen Verwaltung*, 2002, available at: <http://library.fes.de/pdf-files/stabsabteilung/01187.pdf>.

Thomas 2015
Thomas, R., 'Administrative Justice, Better Decisions, and Organisational Learning', *Public Law*, 2015, available at: <http://papers.ssrn.com/sol3/papers.cfm?abstract_id=2477969>.

Walter, Gärditz & Pünder 2013
Walter, C., Gärditz, K.F. & Pünder, H., *Repräsentative Demokratie in der Krise?*, Berlin: Walter de Gruyter 2013.

IUS COMMUNE EUROPAEUM

A peer-reviewed book series in which the common foundations of the legal systems of the Member States of the European Union are the central focus.

The *Ius Commune Europaeum* series includes horizontal comparative legal studies as well as studies on the effect of treaties within the national legal systems. All the classic fields of law are covered. The books are published in various European languages under the auspices of METRO, the Institute for Transnational Legal Research at the Maastricht University.

Recently published:

Volume 142: *The Application of the Theory of Efficient Breach in Contract Law. A Comparative Law and Economics Perspective*, W. LIAO
Volume 143: *A European Legal Framework for Nuclear Liability. Rethinking Current Approaches*, T. HELDT
Volume 144: *The Development of European Private Law in a Multilevel Legal Order*, E.A.G. VAN SCHAGEN
Volume 145: *Property Law Perspectives IV*, D. GRUYAERT, E. RAMAEKERS and L. ROSTILL (eds.)
Volume 146: *The Citizen in European Private Law: Norm-setting, Enforcement and Choice*, C. CAUFFMAN and J. SMITS (eds.)
Volume 147: *Legal Certainty in Real Estate Transactions: A Comparison of England and France*, B. DU MARAIS and D. MARRANI (eds.)
Volume 148: *Scarcity and the State I. The Allocation of Limited Rights by the Administration*, P. ADRIAANSE, F. VAN OMMEREN, W. DEN OUDEN and J. WOLSWINKEL (eds.)
Volume 149: *Optional Instruments of the European Union. A Definitional, Normative and Explanatory Study*, W.A. BULL
Volume 150: *The European Union and National Civil Procedure. A Smooth Process or a Rocky Road for Member States?*, A. NYLUND and B.H. KRANS (eds.)
Volume 151: *Different Paths Towards Sustainable Biofuels? A Comparative Study of the International, EU, and Chinese Regulation of the Sustainability of Biofuels*, T. YUE
Volume 152: *Regulation of Cross-Border Establishment in China and the EU. A Comparative Law and Economics Approach*, G. SHEN
Volume 153: *The French Contract Law Reform: a Source of Inspiration?*, S. STIJNS and S. JANSEN (eds.)
Volume 154: *Convergence in European Consumer Sales Law. A Comparative and Numerical Approach*, C. GOANȚĂ

www.ingramcontent.com/pod-product-compliance
Ingram Content Group UK Ltd.
Pitfield, Milton Keynes, MK11 3LW, UK
UKHW051927100926
8556IPUK00022B/1422

9 781780 684451